WAYS OF MEDIEVAL LIFE AND THOUGHT

WAYS OF MEDIEVAL
LIFE AND THOUGHT

ESSAYS AND ADDRESSES

by

F. M. POWICKE

Boston · THE BEACON PRESS · 1951

CONTENTS

		PAGE
	PREFACE	5
I	AILRED OF RIEVAULX	7
II	THE DISAPPEARANCE OF ARTHUR OF BRITTANY	27
III	THE MURDER OF HENRY CLEMENT AND THE PIRATES OF LUNDY ISLAND	38
IV	GUY DE MONTFORT (1265-71)	69
V	THE ORIGINS OF FRANCE	89
VI	ENGLAND AND EUROPE IN THE THIRTEENTH CENTURY	115
VII	REFLECTIONS ON THE MEDIEVAL STATE	130
VIII	BOLOGNA, PARIS, OXFORD : THREE *STUDIA GENERALIA*	149
IX	SOME PROBLEMS IN THE HISTORY OF THE MEDIEVAL UNIVERSITY	180
X	THE MEDIEVAL UNIVERSITY IN CHURCH AND SOCIETY	198
XI	OXFORD	213
XII	MASTER SIMON OF FAVERSHAM	230
XIII	DANTE'S ROMEO	239
XIV	AN AMERICAN SCHOLAR : GEORGE LINCOLN BURR	249

PREFACE

The fourteen essays and addresses in this little book fall into three divisions. The first four have a personal interest. If Ailred of Rievaulx may be described, in the words which are the title of his first piece of writing, as a mirror of charity, the murderers of Arthur of Brittany, Henry Clement and Henry of Almaine may be called vessels of wrath. The second group comprises three papers on the interplay of experience and ideas in the formation of medieval political societies, the third five papers on various aspects of the history of the medieval universities. The two short papers which conclude the volume are different in character and intention from the rest.

Only two papers are here printed for the first time. Three or four of the others are reprinted with little change, the rest have been more or less heavily revised. I have stated in each case where the original versions may be found, for the curious may wish to trace my blunders or first thoughts and the student may feel the need of critical and other references which I have deliberately omitted in these reprints. The volume is intended for the general reader. Some kind friends have encouraged me to believe that there is a public glad to read a compilation of this kind; one in particular generously insisted on taking the initiative in the arrangements for its appearance.

I am indebted, for permission to make use of twelve of the essays and addresses, to Messrs. Nelson and Sons, publishers of the work on Ailred which will appear in their series of medieval classics, to the editors and publishers of the *English Historical Review* and *History*, to the Delegates and Secretary of the Clarendon Press, the Council of the Royal Historical Society, the Harvard University Press, the Association of Foreign University Professors and Lecturers in Great Britain, the publishers and editors of the *Mélanges d'histoire* presented to M. Ferdinand Lot, and the editor of *Medium Aevum*.

F. M. P.

Oxford, 1949.

I

AILRED OF RIEVAULX

Ailred was born in 1110. In 1147 he was elected the third abbot of Rievaulx, the first Cistercian abbey founded in the north of England (1131-2). He ruled the abbey till his death in January, 1167. His family was well-known in Northumberland, where his ancestors had been hereditary priests of the church of Hexham which, in 1114, gave place to an archiepiscopal foundation of Augustinian canons. He got the rudiments of a sound education in Hexham and, probably, in the monastic school at Durham. As a boy he seems to have attracted the attention of David, the son and successor of Saint Margaret, Queen of Scotland, and had as a companion David's son Henry. For a short time he held a high and responsible office at King David's court as dispenser or steward. He entered Rievaulx about the year 1134.

Ailred's biographer, Walter Daniel, entered Rievaulx in 1150 and knew the abbot with increasing intimacy for seventeen years. Although he is never so described, Walter probably became the fermerer or head of the monastic infirmary. The first part of the following paper is a translation of Walter's account of Ailred's change of life, how he heard about the new foundation, what he was told about it, and under what circumstances he entered it. In the second part I try to give a picture of Ailred at Rievaulx.[1]

[1]The second part is a section, with a few omissions and additions, from the introduction to an edition of the greater part of Walter's work which appeared in the *Bulletin* of the John Rylands Library in 1921-2. A complete edition with a translation and revised introduction will be found in a volume of the series of Medieval Classics edited by V. H. Galbraith and Roger Mynors (Edinburgh, Nelson, in the press).

1. *Walter Daniel on Ailred's introduction to Rievaulx.*

God now willed that for the welfare and comfort of many, Ailred should give himself more strictly to the way of quiet and holiness and, so to speak, enter into his chamber where the floods of the evil world do not flow and the tempest of the sea is not roused, where there is no rushing of storms and whirlwinds and the burning winds do not scatter the branches of the vines, where dust is not stirred to afflict the eyes nor the deep mire drag back the steps of those who walk, but where the voice of the turtle dove is heard, the voice of rejoicing and salvation[1], where a new song is sung, the song of Sion, and a continual Alleluia, where the heart of man is rejoiced by the wine of gladness and is drunken with the sweet wine of a pure conscience; God willing, I say, by his grace to call his servant to this laudable and happy state, inspired him to despise the vainglory of this wicked life and to make profession of the religious life of an accepted kind, and, making nought of all earthly counsel, ties and duty, to put the King of Glory before a prince of flesh and blood. In his cogitation on these things and how he could the more speedily, fully and profitably put them in practice, he realized that the monastic life was the perfect way to receive the heavenly promises; but, fearing to give open expression to his joyful intention, lest he should be disturbed by his fear for his lord and suffer delays, he concealed his determination before the prince and stilled the healthy operation of his sworn intention with the medicine of dissimulation. In the meantime the heat of his desire invades his heart, fills his mind, takes possession of his soul, stays all his senses in the effort not to seem the man that he is, and wishes to be and to become. His bones stiffen as his marrow melts away, his flesh withers, the pulse beats slow, his whole body

---

[1] Psalm cxvii. 15 (V): *vox exultationis et salutis in tabernaculis justorum.*

trembles and his spirit grows faint in the wretchedness of suspense. The hero of the Lord in his plight continually prays his Creator that with the good will of his lord he may escape from the slippery passage of the world and be counted worthy to join the monastic society. And the Lord who delivers him that is bound from prison, and the blind man from his darkness and raises the poor man from his filth and snatches the needy from the hand of the mighty comes to the rescue of his servant. It happened in this way.

Shortly afterwards he was in the neighbourhood of the city of York where he was come on business to the archbishop of the diocese. By a happy chance he heard tell, from a close friend of his, how two years or more before certain monks had come to England from across the sea, wonderful men, famous adepts in the religious life, white monks by name and white also in vesture. For their name arose from the fact that, as the angels might be, they were clothed in undyed wool spun and woven from the pure fleece of the sheep. So named and garbed and gathered together like flocks of seagulls, they shine as they walk with the whiteness of snow. They venerate poverty, not the penury of the idle and negligent, but a poverty directed by a necessity of the will and sustained by the thoroughness of faith, and approved by divine love. They are welded together by such firm bands of charity that their society is as terrible as an armed camp. Trampling the flowers of the world with the foot of forgetfulness, counting riches and honours as dung, beating with the fist of conscience on the faces of mutable things, spurning fleshly desires and vain glory in food, drink, act, affection, alike in the abundance and scarcity of goods, running an even course in the fit use of them between right and left, they observe at all times a discreet uniformity, using only so much and such means of sustaining life as will just maintain the needs of the body and their fervour in the worship of God.

For them everything is fixed by weight, measure and number. A pound of bread, a pint of drink, two dishes of cabbage and beans. If they sup, the remnants of their former meal are dished up again, except that, instead of the two cooked dishes, fresh vegetables, if they are to be had, are served. When they rest on their beds, each of them lies alone and girdled, in habit and tunic in winter and summer. They have no personal property; they do not even talk together; no one takes a step towards anything of his own will. Everything they do is at the motion of the prelate's nod and they are turned aside by a like direction. At table, in procession, at communion and in other liturgical observances, all of them, small and great, young and old, wise and ignorant are subject to one law. Personal standing is merged in the equality of each and all, there is no inequitable mark of exception, except the greater sanctity which is able to put one man above others. The only test of worth is the recognition of the best. The humbler a man is the greater he is among them, the more lowly in his own esteem the more pleasing in the opinion and judgement of the rest. Women, hawks and dogs, except those ready barkers used to drive away thieves from houses, do not enter the gates of their monastery. By their exceeding love they stifle among them the bane of impatience, and every growth of anger and the smoky emanations of pride, and so, in the words of the *Acts of the Apostles*, by the grace and love of the Holy Spirit they are made "of one heart and one soul".[1]

Well, as I have said, these holy men reached England safely from their monastic wrestling ground across the sea. They set up their huts near Helmsley, the central manor of their protector, Walter Espec, a very notable man and one of the leading barons of King Henry I. The spot was by a powerful stream called the Rie in a broad valley stretching on either

[1]Acts, iv. 32.

10

side. The name of their little settlement and of the place where
it lies was derived from the name of the stream and the valley,
Rievaulx. High hills surround the valley, encircling it like a
crown. These are clothed by trees of various sorts and maintain in pleasant retreats the privacy of the vale, providing for
the monks a kind of second paradise of wooded delight. From
the loftiest rocks the waters wind and tumble down to the
valley below, and as they make their hasty way through the
lesser passages and narrower beds and spread themselves in
wider rills, they give out a gentle murmur of soft sound and
join together in the sweet notes of a delicious melody. And
when the branches of lovely trees rustle and sing together and
the leaves flutter gently to the earth, the happy listener is
filled increasingly with a glad jubilee of harmonious sound, as
so many various things conspire together in such a sweet
consent, in music whose every diverse note is equal to the rest.
His ears drink in the feast prepared for them, and are
satisfied.

Such was the story—and a true story—which Ailred was
told by his friend. At this point he exclaimed, "And where,
oh where, is the way to those angelic men, to these heavenly
places?" "Don't be disturbed," said his friend, "they are close
to you, and you know it not. You have only to ask and they
can easily be found". He replied, "O, how greatly do I desire,
how ardently I thirst for the sight of them, and to see for myself what you have told me about that happy place". "Go
thither", returned the other, "but seek first the leave of the
archbishop and receive his blessing, and, if you wish, God
will satisfy your desire before the sun sets". Carried away by
eager desire for the things to come he hurries to the prelate,
obtains his leave and blessing, rushes back to his lodging,
mounts his horse, does not stop to go in, and with the hastiest
of farewells to his hosts, speeds his mount he knows not where.

But his informant makes him follow behind and, spurring their horses to a gallop, they reach before nightfall the castle of Helmsley, two miles from Rievaulx. There the lord, Walter Espec, the founder of the abbey, gives them a triumphant welcome. They spend the night with him very happily, and as he told him still more about the life of the monks Ailred's spirit burned more and more with inexpressible joy.

Next morning the lord Walter, accompanied by a few people of the vicinity, goes with him to the monks. Ailred meets the prior, the guestmaster and the keeper of the gate. They take the young man to prayers, his face washed with tears, his heart consumed in humble confession to his Lord. After prayers, they preach the word of God. The power of their talk of spiritual things is almost too great for him to bear. He gives full vent to the outpourings of his breast; the fountain of his tears gushes forth like a deluge flooding the earth. His heart of flesh[1] was so full of pious affections and moist with the dew of continual mercies, that it was easier to refuse a smile at urbane jests and honest pleasantries than to restrain his tears at words of admonishment and the talk that edifies. Yet it was not on that day that the call of the place made him choose it as his home. He returned with the lord Walter Espec to the castle and spent another night there, like the last. After some talk among the company about a number of things they went to bed until the morning star appeared. Then, aroused from sleep, he called to his servants to bridle, saddle and harness the horses and, when all was ready, he said farewell to the most noble Walter and set out on the journey to his lord the king in Scotland. Now he had to pass along the edge of the hill overlooking the valley, where a road led down to the gate of the monastery, and when he reached

[1] Cf. Ezekiel xi. 19: *et auferam cor lapideum de carne eorum et dabo eis cor carneum.*

the spot, still aflame with the heat of the Holy Spirit, that is
to say, with the love of the Lord Jesus, he asked one of his
companions, who was a friend of his, if he would like to go
down to the abbey and learn something more than he had
seen the day before. Oh, the mercy of our God, ever to be
proclaimed by those who wish to make their home in Christ!
Oh, how faithful is our God in clemency and kindness! For,
as our father would tell us, if he whom he had asked if he
wished to go down to the monastery or not, had said "I have
no mind to go", he himself in that hour would not have gone
down as he did with him. Take note here of the outshining
humility of this gentlest of men, whose own will depended on
the will of his servant. God indeed opened the mouth of that
servant. He said "I am for going down", and what the servant preferred to do the lord decided should be done. So they
went down to the monastery of Rievaulx. Today as yesterday
the prior, with the guestmaster, and the keeper of the gate
and a great company of the brethren hasten to meet him and
do him honour. They have a shrewd suspicion that the will of
the visitor, who has come to them again, has been prompted
by longing for his well-being; and, since he listens to their
words with an eager and unreserved attention, making them
his own with tears as things to be embraced, they are led on
to probe his mind with more searching admonitions. I need
say no more. He agrees at last to become a monk. They all
rejoice and are glad together. There was no more conceal-
ment for him, now that his duty had been made clear. He
divided all his goods, he abandoned everything that he had.
He kept beside him only the one man of his company who
was not unwilling to stay. As he owned to me afterwards, the
four days of waiting where he was were like a thousand years,
so great was his longing and haste to be taken to the novices'
cell. He had no eyes for the light of day; all that time he saw

only the horror of night. All the same, during those four days, though he could find small pleasure in the companionship of the monks, he greatly edified the brethren in the guesthouse by the humility with which he prostrated himself at the feet of all, the fervent charity with which he burned to serve them, the wisdom with which he talked to them so effectually of the divine commands.[1]

When the four days were ended he is borne off to the novice-house; but first he was brought before the whole convent to be examined about his intention, and there, as elsewhere, he moved all to tears by the grace of the replies which proceeded out of his mouth. It is not easy for me to speak of him as he was in the novice-house; for there earth was turned to gold.

2. *A picture of Ailred at Rievaulx.*

Walter Daniel was not much interested in Ailred's public life and political views; he tells us more about his monastic life, of his experiences as novice, monk, novice-master, abbot. His biography does not show us the abbot as an administrator. We get few of those glimpses at the material and domestic life of a Cistercian abbey—the abbot on his journeys, the work of charity, the economy of the demesne farms or granges—which give interest to Jocelin's life of St. Waldef, the abbot of Melrose. We hear nothing of the extensive building operations which, apparently, were undertaken in Ailred's time. Walter is concerned with the inner life of the saint and his personal relations with his monks. His work is a good, though casual, commentary on the observance of the strict Benedictine rule enforced by the Cistercians.

It is, however, much more than this. Walter Daniel's

[1]For the days of waiting in preliminary probation see the Rule of St. Benedict, c. 58 (ed. Butler, pp. 105, 106).

work, if it is studied in the clear light of Ailred's books on the mirror of charity and spiritual friendship, shows us a self-centred but frank and humble-minded friend and disciple reflecting the Cistercian discipline as it appealed to men of independent outlook in a social environment quite different from that of St. Bernard. Its very *naïveté* makes it a psychological study of the greatest value. We see the kind of man who sought Rievaulx whether as a refuge or as a home of entrancing adventures of the spirit, how one would find composure and another be driven mad, how Ailred, as he dealt with a second and third generation of monks who succeeded the grave and happy men who surrounded the first abbot, William, sought to unite them in the invisible bonds of charity and affection. How far Ailred succeeded we cannot say, though some episodes in Walter Daniel's story go to strengthen scraps of evidence that the next abbot, Silvanus, himself a fine man, found it necessary to tighten the reins of discipline.

Ailred is his own best commentator. Walter Daniel is not so easy to understand. The more one studies him, the more one's natural impatience with him gives way to a sort of affectionate delight in him. Even in his most turgid and extravagant moods he is so vivid. He always feels what he says. Life in Rievaulx was so interesting to him that he cannot have had a dull moment. And he could write.

It is important to remember that Walter Daniel was, in his way, a scholar. Some time, perhaps, a competent student of the intense and incoherent world of thought and feeling which he knew, and which his companionship with Ailred refined and enlarged, may be found to trace to their sources all his allusions and casual recollections; but the mental atmosphere of the north of England in the middle of the twelfth century has not yet been recaptured. The sympathetic familiarity which alone would make such a study worth while could come only from many years of leisurely untrammelled observation, and would require a rare mastery, not only of the experiences of mind and spirit in the north-west of Europe, and particularly in Durham and York, since the days of Alcuin, but also of the intangibles in history. Indeed, it would need the sort of insight shown by the late Livingstone Lowes in his *Road to Xanadu*. Walter Daniel, however interesting he may be, can hardly be set beside the great poet who wrote *The Ancient Mariner* and *Kubla Khan;* yet I cannot but feel that it might be profitable to study even Walter Daniel in this way.

In more disciplined days he might have been a fine essayist, a clear sighted observer of nature, and an experimental scientist; but he was anything but disciplined; he was capricious and wild. He was at his best when he let himself go with deep feeling in simple unaffected narrative, though at any point affectation might break in. He liked the sound and implications of sophisticated words. What, for example, made him describe the first strivings of St. Bernard's disciples on the continent as a *palaestra*? His ready use of Biblical phrases, when not unconscious, was not always so apt as it seemed to him to be. He could not resist a dramatic recollection. While he was describing Ailred on monastic business with the cellarers in the orchard, late in the day, and how the abbot was hastily summoned to the deathbed of a sick monk, he could not resist the sudden memory of the phrase in the Gospel of St. John, *erat autem nox*, and he slipped it in, though the little group was certainly not doing business in the orchard in the hours of darkness, and there was no connection between the incident and the dramatic passage of the traitor Judas from the upper room to the outer blackness so befitting the dark deed he was going to do[1]. Walter Daniel's mental processes are not

[1] John, xiii. 30.

16

often so clear as in this case, and we should not overlook the fact that the conflict between exact memory and literary recollection could easily distort the truth of his narrative or impede the course of his argument.

But we must return to Ailred. Ailred's monastic life falls into three periods. For nine years he was at Rievaulx as novice, monk, confidential adviser of Abbot William, and novice-master. For about four years he was abbot of Revesby in Lincolnshire, one of the daughter houses of Rievaulx. From the end of 1147 to his death in January 1167 he was abbot of Rievaulx.

Ailred heard of Rievaulx when he was at York on the business of King David, probably in 1134. He decided to visit the new monastery at once. He stayed with Walter Espec at Helmsley, went to Rievaulx, and next day set out for Scotland. He passed along the road which still traverses the hillside above the valley of the Rie, where the ruins lie, and was decided by the curiosity of one of his companions to pay another visit. He could resist no longer, and after passing the customary four days in the hospice—a modest building, with low-stretched beams—he was received into the house of the novices (*probatorium*). Walter tells us how he showed his coolness during a fire which broke out in the hospice; when the distinguished young man rose with a smile and threw a jugful of English beer upon the flames, the fire miraculously ceased. In the *probatorium* his novice-master was Simon, afterwards abbot of Wardon, or Sartis, in Bedfordshire, who was still living when Walter Daniel wrote.

Ailred himself became novice-master—though only for a year—after his return from Rome in 1142[1]. Walter's account of his work contains a reference of archaeological interest.

[1]Ailred had been selected as one of those sent to express Cistercian and other opposition at the papal court to a recent election to the archbishopric of York.

According to the Benedictine rule the novices lived together —meditated, ate and slept—in a separate room, the *cella novitiorum*, or, as it was frequently called, the *probatorium*. The *probatorium* at Rievaulx was apparently built over a spring, for Ailred, following the example of St. Bernard, used to restrain the heats of his flesh by standing up to the neck in a bath which he had caused to be made in the floor and which was concealed by a stone. A more enduring record of his short tenure of the office of novice-master is his work, the *Speculum Caritatis*. Internal evidence shows that he wrote this analysis of the religious life while he was actually teaching novices.

Ailred was prompted, or rather ordered, to undertake this task by no less a man than the abbot of Clairvaux himself. Indeed, no other man than Bernard, who had sent his former secretary William to England and regarded Rievaulx as one of his favourite creations, could have written as he did, passing over the abbot of Rievaulx with a direct and personal call to Ailred's obedience. During the controversy, not yet over, about the election to the archbishopric of York, Bernard had, of course, learned about Ailred and had doubtless been visited by the young monk on his way to or from the papal court a few months earlier. That Bernard was the writer of the anonymous letter which precedes the text of the *Speculum Caritatis* has, however, only come to light within the last thirty years.

Ailred had tried to excuse himself, in reply to a previous letter. The abbot of Clairvaux brushed his excuses aside. Taking up Ailred's plea that he was almost illiterate and had come from the kitchens, not from the schools, he made characteristic play with it, in a series of phrases culled from the scriptures. That Ailred is no grammarian fans rather than puts out the spark of Bernard's desire, for he is a learner in the school of the Holy Spirit and his treasure is in earthen vessels "that the excellency of power may be of God" and not of himself. He has spoken of his rough and hard retreat, among rocks and hills, where he works with axe and hammer under a rule of silence; but, Bernard replies,

> I find no terror either in the hard mountain steeps, nor in the rough rocks nor in the hollow places of the valleys, for in these days the mountains distill sweetness and the hills flow with milk and honey, the valleys are covered over with corn, honey is sucked out of the rock and oil out of the flinty stone, and among the cliffs and mountains are the flocks of the sheep of Christ. Wherefore I judge that with that hammer of yours you may cut out of those rocks what you would not find by your native sagacity in the libraries of the professors, and that not seldom, in the midday heat, you will be aware, under the shade of the trees, of something that you would never have learned in the schools.

And of Ailred's experience at the court of King David of Scotland, Bernard, with a play upon the word *dispensatio*, says how pleasant it was that, as a presage of things to come, he passed to the hermitage from the kitchen. It may well have been, he writes, "that the dispensing[1] of carnal food was committed to you for a time in the royal household, that, in due course, you might concoct spiritual things with spiritual[2] in the household of our King, and refresh the eaters with the food of the word of God". Bernard concludes with an instruction. To spare Ailred any feelings of shame, his letter was to be prefixed to the work, so that whatever might displease the reader in the *Speculum Caritatis*—for Bernard gave this name to the book—might be imputed to him who had compelled Ailred, against his wish, to write it, not to the author who had obeyed him. And so Ailred set about his task. When all was

---

[1] i Cor. ix. 17: *dispensatio mihi credita est.* Bernard quotes these words in referring to Ailred's duties as *dispensator.*

[2] i Cor. ii. 13.

19

done he added a formal preface addressed to his anonymous superior:

> Scarcely hoping to finish it, but that it might be finished,
> I have wrought to the best of my power on the charity which
> you commanded, with the hammer to which you referred,
> certain of this, that when hope and other things fail, charity
> always remaineth. He who endowed me with no skill, gave
> grace. And, as his face is seen in any mirror only by one who
> is in the light, to no one will the countenance of charity
> show itself in this mirror of charity, unless he abides in
> love.[1]

The *Speculum Caritatis* is Ailred's finest work, and was inspired by St. Bernard; but it also deserves special attention because Ailred tells us how he wrote it. Throughout he seems to have been sustained by the sweet and solemn sense of obligation to two close friendships, one—the greatest friendship of his life—for a monk called Simon, who had recently died, and to whom he devotes in his book a moving chapter, the other to the prior Hugh, who had left Rievaulx. Simon had brought Ailred and Hugh together, and in associating his new and absent friend in the preparation of his book, Ailred was paying a debt of fraternal charity to the dead as well as to the living. As his thoughts crowded his mind in luxuriant disorder he felt the need of some restraint, and he found this by sending his meditations to Hugh—*plus mecum quam ego ipse*—in the form of letters. He then arranged all this material—we must suppose that Hugh returned the meditations with his comments—into three books, and divided each book into chapters. Most of the manuscripts contain a preliminary table of contents.

The first book deals with the excellence of charity, both in

[1] i Cor. xiii. 8, 13; John, xv. 9, 10. The letter of Bernard, the concluding passages of the *Speculum* and Ailred's preface have been edited by the late Dom André Wilmart.

its own right or *dignitas* and by contrast with its opposite, cupidity, the second with inept objections, the third with the way to show charity. Part of the second book is cast in the form of a dialogue between Ailred and a novice. It shows Ailred at work in the *probatorium*. In the preceding chapters he has discussed the fact that the gift of tears comes more easily to men living in the world than to the religious in the cloister. Ailred does not think that this is strange. The experiences of those who live delicately are no matter for boasting; their tears are no certain sign of grace, for humours flow easily to the heads of such people. And if no sense of sweetness follows the profession of a more severe life, this is no reason for depression. Ailred feels that he can best explain his meaning by recalling a conversation which he had had not long before with a novice. The newcomer had been perplexed by the contrast between the spiritual rapture of the past and the aridity of the present. His old life had certainly not been more holy, for had he lived then as he was living now he would have become almost an object of worship. Ailred led him on to analyse his early experiences. They had been very delightful, but they had passed as quickly as they came. He had found equal pleasure in devout tears and in worldly jests, in the love for Christ and the companionships of the table. Now his life was very different: scanty food, rough dress, water from the well, a hard pallet. The bell rang just when sleep was sweetest. He had to toil and sweat for his daily bread; his conversation with his fellows was confined to a few necessary words with three people[1]. He agreed gladly that this was only one side. Discipline meant peace: no wrangling or complaints of injustice, no lawsuits, no respect of persons nor regard for birth, no favouritism in the distribution of the daily tasks. He

[1]The abbot, prior and novice-master seem to be intended.

21

was now a member of a community united by a common interest in the common good, controlled by one man whose will was law for three hundred others[1]. The novice, in spite of the hardships of this new life and his own irresponsiveness, was fain to admit that he preferred it to the old. And then Ailred brought him face to face with the main issue: why in that old life, no longer preferred, had he a livelier sense of his love for Christ? The conclusion was gradually drawn: to love is one thing, to love with full self-surrender is another and a harder thing. Love without service is like the emotion of the playgoer who weeps at the sight of sufferings which in the street he would pass unmoved. At this point, the novice hung his head. He remembered how he, who had been so lightly moved to tears by his love for Christ, had been wont to cry with equal facility over the story of Arthur.

In 1143, William de Roumare, earl of Lincoln, founded the abbey of St. Laurence at Revesby in Lincolnshire. In accordance with the Cistercian rule he would consult the abbot of Rievaulx, by whom he desired his foundation to be settled, about a suitable site and would build a church, refectory, dormitory, hospice, and other necessary buildings. Copies of the Benedictine rule, the Cistercian customs and the service books would be provided, and then the first inmates, twelve monks and an abbot, would take possession. All Cistercian houses were dedicated to St. Mary, and Walter Daniel is careful to state that the name of St. Laurence was preserved because the existing church was dedicated to this saint. Abbot William chose Ailred as first abbot of St. Laurence. With this advancement began the last and most important period of his career. In 1147 he was elected abbot of Rievaulx.

Ailred was abbot of Rievaulx for nearly twenty years. In

[1]This number included the *conversi*, novices, servants in the monastery and granges as well as the monks. It increased greatly under Ailred's rule as abbot.

his time Rievaulx was the real centre of Cistercian influence in England. The once Savigniac, but now Cistercian house of Furness and the Surrey house of Waverley were older, but as Ailred once said of the latter, they were hidden away in a corner (*in angulo*). The source of the new religious life lay in Yorkshire, a few miles off the big road which goes from York to Durham through Northallerton, and within easy reach of the road through Catterick to Carlisle and Clydesdale and Galloway. And the new abbot was fitted to extend the work begun by William and his companions at Rievaulx. His prestige in the province of York was great. He had been the confidant of King David of Scotland, and in course of time he was permitted to advise King Henry II and the powerful earl of Leicester. For some years after his election, the archbishopric of York was ruled by a close friend and ally, Henry Murdac, himself a Cistercian. Ailred was by nature a man of alert mind, sound in judgment, interested in affairs. He excelled as an arbitrator, and adjusted more than one of the perplexing controversies which disturbed the monastic tempers of the north. In spite of constant ill health, he was an indefatigable administrator. Indeed, the first important recognition of his leadership and reliability was the choice of him as arbitrator in the most difficult monastic dispute of his time, the rival claims of the Norman abbey of Savigny and the abbey of Furness to the obedience of the foundation at Byland (1151). He composed disputes between Rievaulx and her neighbours, and ruled his large family with moderation and patience. He found time, between attendances at the General Chapter of his Order at Citeaux and visitations of the Cistercian houses in Scotland, the inspection of the monastic granges and the composition of sermons, dialogues and historical works, to take some share in the ecclesiastical

affairs of the diocese. In short he was one of the most considerable persons north of the Trent.

It is to be feared that Ailred's life was not always a peace-
ful one, even when he was free to forget the distractions of the
world within the walls of Rievaulx. His difficulties would be
increased by his unwillingness to refuse applicants and to keep
the number of the community down. Under his rule he had
140 monks, and the well managed estates provided employment for 500 lay brethren and servants. On great feast days,
says Walter, the church was so packed with the brethren as
to resemble a hive of bees. Ailred could not know all his
monks nor control all the affairs of this large establishment.
He was by conviction a mild disciplinarian. It says much for
his moral influence that life at Rievaulx was as smooth and
happy as it was. He knew well that one of the greatest dangers
which beset the monastic life is restless curiosity about external affairs; a chatterer about war and politics might cause
a wave of disturbance which would change the temper of the
whole monastery. He was a restless man himself, inclined as a
young monk to let his thoughts wander, and one of his most
grateful memories was of his dead friend Simon, whose presence had always sufficed to make him collect himself. He
compared the monastic life to a castle, with its ditch, wall and
keep—just such a castle as that of Lord Walter Espec at
Helmsley. *Intrauit Jesus in quoddam castellum*, and no castle is
strong if ditch or wall has to stand alone, or if the keep is not
higher than the rest; in this castle humility is the ditch,
chastity the wall and charity the keep. But Ailred had to
suffer still more from stupidity and envy within than from the
assaults of curiosity without. One gathers that he was refined,
courteous, gentle in manner and firm almost to obstinacy. He
was, one fancies, just and impartial from principle rather than
by nature; he was inclined to favouritism and the joys of

spiritual friendship with charming young men, like his friend
Simon and the handsome young monk of Durham whom he
had with him in his visit to St. Godric at Finchale. He was a
man of pleasant and easy speech, with a memory stored with
anecdotes; he was distinguished, industrious, and physically
frail—an interesting combination of qualities which tended
to confine him to the society of a few chosen helpers. By
special permission of the General Chapter ten years before his
death the rule was relaxed in his favour, so that he might per-
form his abbatial duties in spite of the very distressing malady
from which he suffered. He lived and slept in a little room
built near the infirmary, took hot baths and—as his end drew
nearer—crouched over a fire. In his cell, which contained a
little oratory, where he kept his glossed psalter, the Confessions of St. Augustine, the text of St. John's Gospel, some relics
of saints and a little cross which had once belonged to
Archbishop Henry Murdac, he would talk with his monks,
sometimes twenty or more together. A man of this kind, who
offers no sharp angles to the outsider and has more to forgive
than to be forgiven, provokes unreasoning exasperation in
envious or unbalanced minds. Ailred found enemies in
monastic circles as he found them at King David's court, and
Walter Daniel's life was written in part as a passionate refuta-
tion of the suggestions that he was ambitious, a wirepuller,
fond of luxurious living, a successful prig who in his time had
been no better than he should have been.

Ailred left behind him "as a heritage of the family", to use
Dom Wilmart's words, the pastoral prayer which he had
composed and used. This survives in a Rievaulx manuscript,
which also contains the catalogue of the monastic library as
well as other items. The prayer reveals Ailred at his best. The
felicitous phrases could only have been written by a man of
sensitive and disciplined mind, quickly responsive to what was

best in the literature available to him and well-grounded in the use of Latin, as traditionally practised in Durham. The easy and almost unconscious reliance on the Scriptures and the reminiscences of the Confessions of St. Augustine and the devotional writings of John of Fécamp, derive from deep, personal meditation nourished by the *lectio* which, as Dom Wilmart reminds us, was part of the Benedictine discipline observed by the Cistercians. And, most of all, the prayer shows us Ailred as the good abbot, brooding in constant solicitude over the welfare of his spiritual sons. I venture to translate one passage:

> Thou hast entrusted them to be ruled by me, a sinner, Thy little slave. Thou knowest, my God, my folly, and my infirmity is not hidden from Thee. Sweet Lord, I do not ask Thee to give me gold or silver or precious stones, but wisdom, that I may know how to rule Thy people. Release it from the seat of Thy greatness, O fount of wisdom, that it may be with me, toil with me, work with me, speak in me; may, according to Thy good pleasure, direct my thoughts, words and all my works and counsels, to the honour of Thy name, their profit and my salvation.

II

THE DISAPPEARANCE OF ARTHUR OF BRITTANY[1]

Within thirty or forty years of his death that great southerner Richard the Lion Heart had become a peculiarly English hero of English romance—romance full of confused reminiscences and picturesque nonsense, which in its amplified anti-French form was used by Shakespeare; and the notorious John suffered by comparison in popular history. Most of the popular version of John's misdeeds may be put on one side; but the more critical narrative of Holinshed is a suggestive starting-point for a study of the medieval tradition about the death of Arthur of Brittany. Holinshed gives his authorities. The story of Arthur's interview with Hubert is based on a contemporary Essex chronicle of Coggeshall. Holinshed repeats the three of four rumours made current by Matthew Paris that Arthur died of grief, or was drowned in trying to escape from the town of Rouen, or was killed by his uncle. The most authentic version of Arthur's death is unknown to Holinshed, and therefore to Shakespeare. Hence in the famous play, the Hubert scene naturally becomes the central theme.

There was a Breton tradition also, which was familiar in the fifteenth century and was worked into the narrative of the Breton historians of the seventeenth century. According to this

[1]This short essay is based upon a longer critical paper which first appeared in the *English Historical Review* for 1909, pp. 659-674. I have omitted the argumentative parts which were subjected to minute criticism by my friend, the late Charles Petit-Dutaillis, in his work *Le déshéritement de Jean Sans Terre et le meurtre d'Arthur de Bretagne* (Paris, 1925). The problem of the alleged condemnation of King John for the murder of Arthur requires further examination in the light of this and later work.

version the barons and bishops of Brittany assembled in great
numbers and charged John with the murder fifteen days after
it was committed. On the strength of this charge King
Philip of France condemned the English king to lose all his
possessions. So far as this story is true, it can be traced, as
M. Bémont pointed out, to the events described by the Essex
chronicler to whom I have referred.

King John captured Arthur at the castle of Mirabeau on
1 August, 1202. Arthur was between fifteen and sixteen years
of age—nearly a man in those days—and had been invested
by King Philip Augustus of France with all the Angevin lands
outside Normandy. At the time of his capture he was be-
sieging his grandmother with some display of insolence. He
was taken to Falaise and imprisoned in the tower. John is said
to have promised that if, with the aid of William des Roches,
the most powerful baron and official in Maine and Anjou, he
succeeded in defeating Arthur, he would act on William's
advice. His trickery after the successful march on Mirabeau
and his cruelty to the prisoners cost him the allegiance of
William and of the barons of the west. They joined with the
Bretons and the rebels of Poitou. Some of the Normans were
won over. The Coggeshall chronicler is the sole authority for
what happened at Falaise. John's counsellors saw that so long
as Arthur was kept in Falaise, away from his followers, yet
safe and well and clamorous, John was in danger. It must be
remembered that the king was already under sentence of
deprivation at the French court, on account of the appeal of
the Poitevin barons. If the alliance was not to be overwhelm-
ing Arthur ought either to be handed over to William des
Roches or to be put out of the way. Some of John's friends
suggested mutilation. In his anger at failure, after one of the
few brilliant military achievements of his life, John agreed,
and sent two servants to Falaise, where, his feet fettered by a

triple chain, the young man was guarded by Hubert de Burgh, the chamberlain. Hubert, moved partly by the agony of Arthur, partly by the folly of the deed, prevented John's agents from accomplishing the royal command. Yet he felt also that the only way to coerce the Bretons was to convince them of Arthur's death. What folly there might be in multilation or murder lay in the fact that John's subjects, especially his knights, would refuse to serve a parricide. Hubert announced that Arthur had died. For fifteen days (we see here the fifteen days of the Breton story) the rumour spread. The place of Arthur's burial was known also. Then the Bretons, fully aroused, swore that they would never cease their attacks on the king of England after this atrocious deed. They believed that Arthur had been murdered. It is not at all unlikely that they held a solemn assembly; the Coggeshall narrative seems to imply common action.

From that time Arthur disappeared. Hubert, when the danger increased rather than diminished, announced that he was alive, but the Bretons could have no proof of this. They would naturally prefer to believe that Arthur was dead, if he was not handed over. Philip and they clamoured for his release and offered hostages in vain. Their scepticism is expressed distinctly in a charter of King Philip in which he refers to Arthur "if he still lives". Till the spring of 1204 this scepticism was maintained; then it became certainty that Arthur was dead; but there was no proof. The semi-official chronicler Rigord of St. Denis, who lived till about 1206, makes no mention of his death. A few chroniclers tell us that Arthur was removed to Rouen; and no doubt, as time went on, this fact became common knowledge. But after that, all was darkness and vague rumour . Only here and there— e.g. by the chronicler of Tours—Arthur was supposed to have been killed. In 1204, Philip refused peace, partly because he was confident of success in war, partly because he had heard that Arthur had been drowned in the Seine. Many years later even Matthew Paris, who was not exactly friendly to John, can only give the various stories of his death and hope doubtfully that the story of murder is not true. Gradually, in popular talk Arthur's fate became subject to the variations of time and place and incident which control all mysteries.

Our chief authority for this summary had been the chronicler of Coggeshall. All historians, except Miss Norgate, are convinced of the value of this writer. His narrative is at bottom annalistic, embroidered by tales of visitors and neighbours. There is no attempt at continuous history, but, mixed with jejune summaries, we find two kinds of story, both of which show the sort of authority upon which they are based. One of them is the religious marvel, the other the striking political incident. We do not need the chronicler's explicit statement to know that a special source—a visitor, a monk who has been on business, a neighbouring baron—has produced these stories. The vivid narrative of Richard's capture was related by the royal chaplain, Anselm. Another eyewitness, Hugh de Nevill, brought back a story of the crusade. The account of the condemnation of John in 1202 has been amply verified by French scholars; nor is there any reason to disbelieve the circumstantial relation of the events at Falaise, though they are not mentioned by any other writer. Now if the widespread tale of Arthur's supposed death at Falaise has only come down in one chronicle, his mysterious fate would be still more likely to pass unchronicled, or would only be revealed accidentally through the gossip of the few people who knew what had happened. It is only when a chance discovery, like that of the biography of the Marshal, brings some unknown authority to light that we can realize faintly what a vast story lies untold. By accident or good fortune a chronicler here and there heard one thing out of a hundred, or a rhyming biographer put down the reminiscences of his hero. Except in rare and definite cases the argument *e silentio* is invalid for the medieval historian. Further, when there is reason for secrecy, the chances of truth are of course less. Arthur *subito evanuit*, said Roger of Wendover; "out of sight out of mind", says the proverb. We must not think of Arthur as a popular hero, except in Brittany. He was just a baron of royal blood, a noble youth, a tool of Philip, an enemy, a nuisance. When John's crime was made a political question by Philip and his son Louis in 1216, the pope did not trouble himself to deny it. He made little of it. The chronicles, he said, tell us of the murder of innocent persons by many princes, the kings of France as well as others, but we do not read that the murderers were ever condemned to death. Arthur was no innocent victim; he was captured at Mirabeau, a traitor to his lord, to whom he had done liege homage (*cui homagium et liganciam fecerat*), and he could rightly be condemned without a formal trial to die the most shameful of deaths.

In this year some English barons had urged Louis of France, King Philip's son, to come over and help them. Philip had twice before been baulked in an attempt to invade England, and he was not prepared to let this third chance slip. Both in France and at Rome the French case was justified—in France before the legate Guala, in Rome before the pope himself. One argument upon which great stress was laid was thus expounded by Louis's proctor a fortnight after Easter at Laon, before king and legate and all the assembled barons and clergy: "My lord king, it is well known (*res notissima*) to all that John, styled king of England, was condemned to death in your court by the judgment of his peers for his treachery to his nephew Arthur, whom he slew with his own hands, and that afterwards, because of his many crimes, he was repudiated by his barons in England". A famous literary controversy has been fought round this text. Was John in fact ever condemned in Philip's court for the death of Arthur? We are not concerned with this controversy but with the truth about Arthur's disappearance.

Our main authority is the annals of Margam, a Cistercian abbey in South Wales. Like the Coggeshall chronicle, the chronicle of Margam is a brief record amplified by narrative passages. It exists in a manuscript of Trinity College, Cambridge. The chronicle ends abruptly and imperfectly in 1232; the manuscript belongs to about 1240. It does not seem to be the original, and there is little evidence as to the dates of the original compositions, but the part with which we are concerned was put together certainly after 1210 and probably ten or more years later. The monks of Margam had heard, circumstantially, how John had killed Arthur in a drunken fury, on a certain day, in a certain place, at a certain time, in the tower of Rouen Castle, after dinner on the fifth day before Easter, that is, 2 April, 1203. He had tied a stone to the body and thrown it into the Seine. It was discovered by a fisherman, recognized, and, for fear of John, buried secretly in Sainte-Marie-de-Pré, one of the priories of Bec. When Philip was convinced that Arthur was dead he summoned him to the French court to answer the charge of murder, for Arthur was a very important man. He never came, and was condemned *per iudicium curie regis et principum Francorum* to lose all the lands held of the French crown. And it was a righteous judgment.[1]

It is easy, but erroneous, to suggest that the abbey of Margam was too obscure to be well informed. Just as Coggeshall was in a land of royal forest and manors, near London,

[1]Petit-Dutaillis argued, not very convincingly, that this account reflects opinion in South Wales as late as 1232. All that we can say is that the annalist confused rumours of the alleged second condemnation with the facts of the condemnation of 1202.

just as St. Albans was on one of the great roads, so Margam
had special advantages for hearing strange information.
Gerald of Wales speaks of its importance, its hospitality, its
connection, when scarcity of corn made connection useful,
with Bristol. When we turn to the Margam records we find no
ignorant and secluded community, but a powerful house,
favoured and harassed alternately by great neighbours who
were some of the greatest barons in England and the Marches,
an abbey which lay on the road from England to Ireland, and
was twice visited by King John himself. At one time it came
under the king's special protection, favoured almost as much
as his peculiar foundation, the Cistercian house of Beaulieu.
The delightful studies of M. Bédier have shown us that the
information and influence of a monastery depended not so
much upon its general position as upon the road on which it
lay, or upon what friends the abbot had. He has demonstrated
that the isolated and obscure house of Saint-Guilhem-du-
Désert could mould the history of a great epic cycle, because
it was visited by pilgrims on their way to Compostella. Con-
versely, special information could make a chronicle of the
most meagre and unpretentious range a very valuable
authority. The monks of Coggeshall knew a great deal more
about Richard's captivity than did many great abbeys,
because Anselm, the king's chaplain, "told us all these things
as he saw and heard them". Now is it possible to suggest the
chief channel of communication open to the monks of
Margam?

In reading the chronicle one or two suggestions occur to
mind which must be put aside. It might be observed that the
compiler seems to have been interested in Bec. He knows that
Saint-Marie-de-Pré is a priory of Bec; he notes that Hugh of
Nonant, bishop of Coventry, died at Bec in 1198. Again, it is
worthy of mention that in November, 1203, Margam had an

agent at Rome, who was engaged in securing lengthy privileges and confirmations from Pope Innocent III. On his journey to and from Rome the person entrusted with the business of the abbey, whether a monk or not, could acquire information which might interest his employers. But it is not very likely that this would be of unique importance. Let us approach the problem from the other direction and ask who was likely to know what happened before and after the murder of Arthur. Ralph of Coggeshall say that Arthur was entrusted to the care of Robert of Vieuxpont at Rouen; but Robert was a north-country magnate, nor does he appear in the story of the murder. He was a busy official who probably did not live constantly at Rouen. Two of John's companions and counsellors, however, were very conspicuous in Glamorgan, and both of them probably knew a good deal more than they cared to say. William the Marshal, Earl of Pembroke, and William of Briouze (*de Braosa*) granted privileges to or attested the charters of Margam more than once. The Marshal kept complete silence. It is difficult to say to what extent he knew how Arthur died. He was certainly acquainted with the course of the negotiations which followed the murder during 1204-1205, since he was one of the embassy. I think that his biographer knew a good deal, and hints at Arthur's fate, but there is not a word of explicit reference to the matter in the poem which tells us so many new things. Nor were the Marshal's lands in South Wales near the abbey of Margam. But William of Briouze was in a very different position. The story of his life would, if it were thoroughly known, be the most important record we could have of the personal history of John and his baronage during the first part of the reign. He was the king's constant companion during the Norman campaigns. The official records reveal the presence of John near Rouen just about the time when, according to the

Margam annals, the murder was committed, and they show that William of Briouze was with him. About 1207, William lost the king's favour, and in 1210 John tried to exterminate him and his family. His wife, Matilda, is said to have refused to hand over her children as hostages to the murderer of Arthur, and John pursued her thereafter with a ferocity unusual even in him. The grisly story of her and her son's death by starvation in Windsor is the most awful of many awful tales. It is impossible to believe that the debts of William of Briouze were, as John said in the official account, the cause of this persecution. The natural supposition is that this chosen companion knew too much to be allowed to live after he and so many others had quarrelled with the king. In 1210, he managed to escape to France; in 1211 he died and was buried at Corbeil on the eve of St. Lawrence. All this we know apart from the evidence of Margam.

Now by far the most conspicuous person in the annals of Margam, and one of the most important figures in its records, is this William of Briouze. He was lord of Brecon, Radnor, and Gower. Between 1202 and 1207 he was responsible for the administration of Glamorgan, in which Margam lay. He attests the charters of local benefactors to the abbey. In the annals we are told how William of Briouze was chiefly responsible for John's accession to the throne in spite of his previous condemnation. Except the great semi-official chronicler, Roger of Howden, the Margam annalist is the only writer to mention this condemnation of John at the court of King Richard. He is interested in William's life and alone tells us that after his death in France he was buried by the exile Stephen Langton, archbishop of Canterbury. Finally, the relations of John and William were a theme of popular tradition in South Wales nearly eighty years after the death of Arthur. On 23 February, 1203, John had granted the land of

Gower to William. In 1279, the earl of Warwick contested the right of William's descendant to this honour, and especially to the castle of Swansea, on several grounds, including the significant plea that William had extorted the original charter from John when the king was in a panic and feared that his companion was going to leave him. In short, the man who was most in John's confidence was William of Briouze, and if any chronicler was likely to hear about the death of Arthur and its consequences it was the chronicler of Margam.

Another significant fact adds an element of certainty to this view. It has often been observed that the Margam story only reappears in one place—and there with some variation—in the epic, *Philippid*, of King Philip's chaplain William the Breton. The variations are not great, and show that the chaplain was giving the same story independently. Now it is very curious that he singles out William of Briouze, who is not mentioned elsewhere in the poem, as the spokesman of those barons who were with John near Rouen at the time of Arthur's death. John brought Arthur to Rouen (I summarize the flowery verses) and aroused the suspicions of the barons. William of Briouze declared that he would be responsible for him no longer, and that he handed him over safe and sound. After a moody seclusion at the royal manor of Moulineux, John did away with his nephew at Rouen by night. This comes in book VI, which with the beginning of book VII has been shown with some probability to have been composed before 1214. As William the Breton wrote his poem in three years, this part could not have been composed much earlier than 1214, in any case after the flight of William of Briouze to France. He was in almost constant attendance upon Philip, and likely to hear what was going on. He would be interested in the famous fugitive who had experienced such a turn of fortune and fled like a beggar from the English coast.

Is it not possible that at last the full story of the murder was known at the French court, and that in the *Philippid* we get the tale—naturally favourable to William of Briouze—which is found elsewhere only in the chronicle of a Welsh abbey? This would partly account for the terror and atrocities of John during these years, for the alliance between Philip and the English barons, and for the projected invasion.

III

THE MURDER OF HENRY CLEMENT
AND THE PIRATES OF LUNDY ISLAND[1]

1. *The Murder of Henry Clement*

All that we know of Henry Clement is that he was a clerk and messenger of the justiciar of Ireland, Maurice fitzGerald, and that he was murdered in the spring of 1235 in Westminster. The crime caused a sensation. Better men of his time have left no memorial; Henry Clement has a certain fame because of the manner of his death.

A royal letter of 16 May 1235 tells the story. King Henry had arrived in Westminster on the previous Sunday, 13 May. On the same night Henry Clement was foully murdered in his lodging "before our gates, to our no small dishonour and the scandal of the realm". Several persons were suspected of the murder. Geoffrey de Marisco, a former justiciar of Ireland, fled to sanctuary in Clerkenwell. One important person, Maurice Comyn, was at once caught and imprisoned in the Tower of London. He lay in the Tower from Pentecost (27 May) till the feast of All Saints (1 November), when he was released after finding pledges for his appearance. He was delivered to Geoffrey de Marisco, in whose company he had apparently come to Westminster. The other persons accused of the murder scattered and fled. Some made their way to the west. The king had heard that their intention was to cross to Lundy Island. They were William de Marisco (or Marsh),

---

[1]Based upon a paper which first appeared in *History*, xxv (1941), 285-310. A revised edition, to which reference should be made for information about authorities, will be found in my work, *Henry III and The Lord Edward*, ii. 740-759.

Geoffrey's son, with his household, William of Pont de l'Arche, Philip of Dinant, Thomas de Erdinton and John Cabus. Three others, Walter Sandcinell, Eustace Comyn and Henry of Colombieres, were believed to have gone east, for the earl Warenne and the sheriff of Norfolk and Suffolk were warned and told to intercept them. Every other sheriff was warned to be on the watch for the malefactors; but, with the exception of William Marsh, they disappear from history. They did not come to stand their trial, and, accordingly, they were outlawed.

The official record of the judicial inquiry which followed the murder has fortunately survived. It was noticed by Maitland nearly half a century ago and edited by him in the *English Historical Review*[1]. It gives the evidence of many witnesses and enables us to reconstruct the details of the crime. Henry Clement was staying in a house opposite the main gate of the royal palace—that is to say, in a street or open place to the east of the abbey church and precincts. The cemetery lay to the left, the way to the town to the right, of the palace gates. The house in which Henry Clement lodged belonged to Master David the surgeon. Since a woman in the house, one of the witnesses, is described as the *hospita* of Master David, I imagine that David leased it from her, leaving her the use of part of it—there are examples of such leases—or that she leased it from him, giving him the right to occupy the main rooms when he was in residence. It was of the usual type—a hall, from which an inside stair led to an upper room (*solarium*), an adjacent lodging in which Alice the *hospita* lived, and a courtyard (*curia*), at the back in which there was a smaller house with a stable, probably a stable with a dwelling-room over it. Some men were sleeping in this stable. Opposite the house, on the other side of the paved street some

---

[1]*Eng. Hist. Rev.* x (1895) 294; F. W. Maitland, *Collected Papers*, III. 11-16.

of the king's servants were in tents set up before the gate of the palace. On the night of Sunday, 13 May 1235, Master David and his guest were sleeping in the solar. Early on the Monday morning—the evidence suggests that it was not long after midnight—a number of men rode up to the house. The men in tents heard the neighing of the horses and the clatter of their hooves in the roadway. One of these men said that he thought there were about sixteen horsemen, some of them armed. Half a dozen went to the house, leaving the rest to watch outside. They broke down the door of the hall, climbed the stair and broke down the door of the solar. One of them carried a blazing torch, which was extinguished when they saw that they had found their quarry. Master David was wounded. Henry Clement tried to escape by jumping out of a window, but, seeing the men outside, he drew back. He was killed. A king's messenger who was sleeping in the hall saw what happened, but was too frightened to do anything. His servant who was also in the hall, said that the house seemed full of men. He was so frightened that he covered up his head. He ventured out afterwards and followed the murderers towards the cemetery, where, so another witness said, they had left their horses. Not one of the numerous witnesses could identify any of the strangers, and Alice the *hospita* who cried out from a window could not awaken the men in the stable. The case against William de Marisco and his companions seems to have depended on what is called circumstantial evidence. The surgeon said, for example, that a boy in buttons[1], a messenger of William de Marisco, had called daily to ask where Henry Clement was and where he would lodge. Master David also reported a threatening demonstration against Henry, on the

---

[1] *Quidam parvus nuntius Willelmi de Marisco (ms.* reads in error *Willelmi Marescalli) cum minutis butonibus.* Maitland asks, "Can this be an early appearance of the boy in buttons?"

bridge at Rochester, by Henry Pont de l'Arche and others. Two knights from Ireland said that, when the king was at Windsor [10–16 April], William de Marisco had accused Henry Clement of putting obstacles in the way of his affairs at court and using his influence to avert the royal favour. Brian, another messenger from the justiciar of Ireland, who had been sleeping in the house in the courtyard, said that some of William's men had threatened Henry for the same reason. Alice testified that on that very Sunday in Westminster, Henry Clement had said, in her hearing, that he feared for his life and wished he were in Ireland rather than in England.

Who were these people, and why did they kill Henry Clement?

2. *Geoffrey de Marisco and Richard the Marshal*

Matthew Paris, the St. Albans chronicler, gives us one reason:

> A certain clerk, Henry Clement, a messenger of the ruling men in Ireland, foolishly boasting that he had been the cause of the death of Earl Richard the Marshal, and calling him a traitor and a cruel enemy of the king and kingdom, was killed in London, while the king was there. Gilbert Marshal, taxed by the king himself and by others with the crime, cleared himself after a long process (*plurimis argumentis*).

I am not sure whether the vague words mean that Earl Gilbert—the brother and successor of Earl Richard the Marshal—was formally indicted before his peers, but that his name and reputation were involved is shown by a solemn promise which he made to the king three weeks after Easter in the following year (1236). He made oath on the gospels to observe his promise, in the presence of the king, the archbishop of Canterbury and the chief men of the kingdom, and he attached his seal to the writing which recorded it. His undertaking comprised many points, and the first was that he would not receive nor allow to be received in any of his lands William de Marisco and the other men, whose names we already know, outlawed for the death of Henry Clement. The assassins had obviously been connected with him in some way, and he had been suspected of harbouring them.

Henry Clement, then, was murdered by men in the Marshal's circle. According to Matthew Paris, he had gloried in Earl Richard's death, and boasted that he had had a hand in getting rid of a man who was a traitor.

The deed was an aftermath of a great political crisis and of a tragic event which had stirred passion and bred a crop of rumours. Its origin, like that of so many crimes of the kind, is to be found in Ireland; not, however, among the native Irish, but in the circle of a great Anglo-Norman lord, Richard Marshal, earl of Pembroke, and lord of Leinster. Earl Richard was the second son of the famous William the Marshal who at one time had governed England as *rector regni* (1216–19). He had been forced into a war against his lord, King Henry. He had carried the war from the Marches of Wales into Ireland, where he had gone in February 1234. He had doubtless heard that, in his absence, his interests in Leinster were threatened by the justiciar and barons and servants of the crown. King Henry, of course, was perfectly justified in striking a blow at the Marshal in Ireland, while the Marshal, with the aid of Llywelyn of Wales, was successfully defying him in the Marches; but, in fact, the circumstances of the Marshal's return to Ireland were not quite so simple as this. At the very time when Earl Richard was trying to recover some of his lost castles in Leinster, the king in England was negotiating for peace with him and Llywelyn. Henry had found that he could not win, and he had been persuaded by the English bishops to accept terms which would give the Marshal just what he had been fighting for—the dismissal of his present advisers, and the renewal of co-operation with his barons on the basis of the Great Charter. The object of the negotiations was peace, not to separate the earl from his allies in Wales, and then to continue the war against him. Hence, one would expect to hear that the justiciar and barons in Ireland had made a truce with him. They did offer to negotiate for a truce, so that they could await instructions from England, but when the parties met on the well-known plain in Kildare county, known as the Curragh, they refused to restore, as a preliminary to a truce, the castles which they still held. Moreover, they proceeded to attack the Marshal in superior force (1 April 1234). The Marshal was badly wounded in the fight, was captured, and died on 16 April. By this time his cause in England was already won.

It is a mysterious story. If the justiciar, as may well have been the case, was ignorant that negotiations were proceeding on the borders of Wales, we cannot blame him for refusing to surrender the castles as a condition of a truce. News sometimes took two or three weeks to pass from England to Ireland, or Ireland to England. King Henry, for example, did not hear of the Marshal's death until the beginning of May. Yet, one feels, the movements of events in the two countries, in a matter of such importance, might have been kept in better step with each other. In any case, the Marshal thought that he had been trapped, and very ugly rumours were spread after his death that the justiciar and barons in Ireland had been instructed to pursue the earl to the death. The Curragh was a field, not of negotiations which broke down, but of black treachery. We need not argue whether the scandal was justified or not, though it was certainly false in some of its careful detail; the important point is that it was believed. Any man who, like Henry Clement, gloried in his own share of responsibility, was asking for trouble.

The new earl, Gilbert the Marshal, kept his thoughts to himself. It was his business to get his inheritance and to join in the general reconciliation which the archbishop of Canterbury and his colleagues brought about in England. As we have seen, he could not avoid suspicion after Henry Clement was killed, but he had far too much at stake to allow himself to be mixed up in affairs of this kind. He was a very great man in baronial society and he had his own life to live. Others were not so happily placed. And here we come back to William de Marisco and his father Geoffrey.

William de Marisco was a prominent member of a very important Anglo-Norman family. His father, Geoffrey, had been active in the service of King John and King Henry and had three times been justiciar of Ireland. Geoffrey, whose appearance in Ireland was probably due to his uncle, the archbishop of Dublin, John Comyn[1], was a native of north Somerset, where his nephew Jordan lived[2]. Geoffrey's success was due, not to birth, but to his own energetic ability to seize the opportunities which a career in Ireland gave. When he came to Ireland, the drive westwards, in Munster and southern Connaught, was beginning, and it continued after he became justiciar in 1215. In addition to lands in Leinster,

[1]This relationship explains the fact that Geoffrey de Marisco had a Maurice Comyn and a Eustace Comyn in his company. When Maurice was released on bail from the Tower, he was handed over to Geoffrey. The relationship of these Irish Comyns to the English and Scottish Comyns is unknown. Just as Archbishop John of Dublin brought Comyns to Ireland, so William Comyn, chancellor of King David, brought them to Scotland, where they became lords of Badenoch (see J. H. Round, "The Origin of the Comyns," in *The Ancestor*, x. 104-19, July 1904). The only indication that Geoffrey de Marisco may have been connected with the Scottish family is Matthew Paris's statement that at one time he was protected by the great Walter Comyn.

[2]The problem of Geoffrey's origins and numerous connections has been cleared up by Eric St. John Brooks in his papers on the family of Marisco, published in *The Journal of the Royal Society of Antiquaries of Ireland* for 1931 and 1932.

he had castles and tenements in Limerick county, in Thomond (co. Clare) and along the upper shore of Dingle Bay in Desmond (co. Kerry), where he fought and bargained and settled, now in partnership, now in rivalry, with the house of fitzGerald. He was connected with many of the families which then and later rose to local greatness in south-western Ireland. Through his second wife, Eva de Bermingham, he got a leading position in Ossory, in northern Leinster, not far from Dublin. As justiciar, he was at one time accused of using his authority to feather his own nest, and to divert revenues which ought to have gone to the royal exchequer. He built castles and founded abbeys. He had a large family of sons and daughters, one or two of whom, notably his son Robert, escaped the misfortunes which beset the rest and became firmly rooted in Ireland. His son, William, with whom we are mainly concerned, seemed destined to an equally prosperous career. In 1224 William was taken into the king's service, as a member of the household. He married Matilda, the niece of the archbishop of Dublin, Henry, who in his way was almost as great a man as Archbishop John Comyn had been before him; and who gave a handsome marriage portion to his niece. The murderers of Henry Clement are obscure enough to us, but they were probably well known in Ireland, as knights or men at arms, who held lands of the ex-justiciar and his son, and who had fought with them in the army of the Marshal. For some reason, Geoffrey and William had come to Westminster in the spring of 1235, on business at the royal court, and these men were with them. A fatal impulse led William to the act which ruined his life: he slew a man who was on a mission from the justiciar of Ireland and under royal protection, and he slew him in a place, within the verge of the palace, where the king's peace was especially sacred.

45

William's loss of self-control was, I am sure, due to feelings more personal than anger against a scurrilous civil servant, and devotion to the memory of Earl Richard the Marshal. Henry Clement—who, we must remember, would not be an insignificant person, and for all we know may have been an influential man, with a fine future before him—was, I fancy, an old and hateful acquaintance, and the last man whom William de Marisco wished to see in England. And I think that the quarrel which led to his death must have been connected in some way with the fact that Geoffrey de Marisco and his family had been singled out for peculiar obloquy in the stories which were circulating about the death of Earl Richard and the treachery at the Curragh. For Geoffrey de Marisco is the scoundrel of the piece, as it is told in the pages of Roger of Wendover. According to the chronicler, he had joined the Marshal with the deliberate intention of leading him on with treacherous advice until he was in the net cast for him by the justiciar, Maurice fitzGerald. All the available evidence goes to show that this was untrue, for nobody suffered more promptly by the Marshal's defeat than Geoffrey and his relatives; but suppose that there had been traffic between the ex-justiciar and the leaders of the king's government and army in Ireland—not necessarily treacherous, but sufficiently close to arouse suspicion in the light of later events? Geoffrey would naturally take a leading part in the negotiations which followed the Marshal's return to Leinster. He was one of the big men in Ireland. Had some assurances been given, some plan been discussed? Had Henry Clement had a part in them? And had Geoffrey been double-crossed and left to bear the full force of the king's wrath for his presence in the earl's forces and his share in the fight? This is all surmise. We do not, and cannot, know. But if something like this happened, it would help to explain what has hitherto been a puzzle—the discrepancy between the action of Geoffrey de Marisco and the scandal which ever after was attached to his name; and it would account for the act of his son William.

Neither Geoffrey nor his son had had a pleasant time since the fight on the Curragh. King Henry was able to make a distinction between the war in England and the war in Ireland. In each case it had been a straight war, not a rebellion, for Earl Richard had been formally repudiated in a legal act of *diffidatio*, or renunciation of the lord's responsibility to him as a vassal, just as some of his supporters in England had renounced their homage, and achieved the same result in another way; but defeat none the less meant the loss of lands and rights, and in Ireland the earl and his followers had been defeated and captured. For a time the king had tried, contrary to the spirit of the negotiations in England, to deprive the Marshal's heir, Earl Gilbert, of some of his lands and rights. He failed in this, but he had no intention of including the other companions of the Marshal in Ireland in the English settlement. The Irish Pipe Roll for 19 Henry III —that is to say, for the year ending at Michaelmas 1235— contains a list of thirty-three names of landholders in the country of Limerick alone who had been fined for being against the king in the war with Richard the Marshal. Geoffrey de Marisco and his son William were each fined 3000 marks or £2000, and three of Geoffrey's nephews, William the son of Jordan de Marisco, John Travers and Richard de Marisco, had to pay, the first two £200, the last £100. These sums were the ransoms of men captured in battle. All five men were still in prison on 23 May 1234. Geoffrey and William were still there on 23 September 1234. Other barons and knights who had fought with the Marshal were free, some even pardoned and released from their fines, but Geoffrey and William were obviously considered to be in a separate category. There is evidence of negotiations which, if we knew more about them, would help us to understand the position.[1]

They seem to have been released in October or November, but they were still suspect, for on 27 November 1234 we learn that two of Geoffrey's castles, Killorglin in Desmond and Holywood (*de Sancto Bosco*), probably Hollywood in co. Dublin, and one of William's castles, Coonagh in co. Limerick, had been retained by the king *in tenanciam* for the faithful service of the said Geoffrey and William. In Shakespeare's words, they were enfranchised with a fetter and set at liberty with a clog. This seems to have been their position at the time of the murder of Henry Clement in the following May, and we may suppose, without over-indulgence in fancy, that their presence at Westminster was due to their desire to come to some permanent understanding with King Henry. If this were so, the evidence given by some of the witnesses in the judicial inquiry is intelligible enough: Henry Clement, William de Marisco was convinced, was doing his best to put difficulties in his way.

Geoffrey de Marisco fled for sanctuary to the Knights of the Hospital of St. John in Clerkenwell. Here I will leave him for a time, while I follow the story of his son William, who was regarded as the chief murderer.

It will be remembered that the king, only three days after the murder, had reason to believe that William de Marisco and his companions were making for Lundy Island. The

[1]Maurice fitzGerald, the justiciar, was personally interested in preventing the release and return to royal favour of Geoffrey de Marisco and his son. He was still afraid of the Marshal's party in England, and so wanted to have a safe-conduct from its leader, Archbishop Edmund. This was in the autumn of 1234, before he came to England. After his return he sent Henry Clement to England on Irish business, and no doubt instructed him to prevent, if he could, the efforts of Geoffrey and William to come to terms with the king.

reason must have been a good one, for the statement is so explicit. Persons who fly from justice might, after much wandering, find their way to a remote place like Lundy Island; but if they go straight for it, like an arrow to its mark, they must have some close association with it. Why was this conspicuous person supposed to be seeking a refuge on a rocky island in the Bristol Channel?

3. *William, Son of Jordan de Marisco and Lundy Island*

Lundy Island is part of Devonshire. Its situation is succinctly described in a charter of King Richard I as "in the sea in the mouth of the river Severn between Tenby and Barnstaple". This is roughly correct, though the island is a good deal nearer to the Devon than to the Pembroke coast. It was granted to the Templars by King Richard, whose charter I have cited. King John confirmed the grant; but when, in February 1227, in one of his first charters, Henry III confirmed the grants of his father to this military order, he omitted the grant of Lundy Island. The chancery and exchequer records enable us to understand what happened; but first let us look at a letter sent soon after Henry Clement's murder:

> Grant to William son of Jordan de Mariscis that he may safely come out of his island of Lunday with his men, come to England and stay there and retire from there; grant to him also that merchants may safely go to and from his said island as they used to do; and mandate accordingly to all bailiffs.

The date is Windsor, 9 June 1235, only three weeks or so after the letters announcing the flight of William de Marisco. On the very same day Geoffrey de Marisco was allowed to leave the Hospital of St. John at Clerkenwell in safety, with his men, except those who were charged with the death of Henry

Clement. William son of Jordan was Geoffrey's nephew, and it is obvious that he and his uncle had been busy clearing themselves of any suspicion of complicity in the murder. And William son of Jordan had been conducting his share in the negotiations from his island of Lundy. Lundy was *his* island. We can now understand why William son of Geoffrey was believed to have made for Lundy Island, and perhaps we can understand why its lord, William son of Jordan, was anxious to be allowed to leave it. He had no wish to be confounded in the royal mind with his cousin and his band of suspects.

Lundy Island had, in fact, been held by the family of Marsh in the later twelfth century. When King John came to the throne, an earlier William de Marisco, who had lands in Huntspill in Somerset, near the Bristol Channel, and other lands in the same shire, had maintained his right to it. He had resisted the new rights of the Templars and held the island against them and the king. He had in short, rebelled and had been outlawed. He was restored to favour in Feburary 1204, and was put in charge of some of the royal galleys. The Templars were compensated for the loss of Lundy. This explains the omission of the island from the charter of 1227. Before he died, sometime after September 1225, William had been in trouble again. He was a naval administrator in King John's service, and he had joined the rebels who had supported Louis of France during the civil war of 1215–17. He had put his wife, sons and daughters on Lundy Island and gone to sea against his king. The island was captured but restored to him, with his family, in November 1217. This William—obviously an important man in his way among the knights of Somerset —was the brother of Geoffrey, the justiciar of Ireland, and the father of Jordan, who was his successor at Huntspill. Jordan had been with his uncle Geoffrey in Ireland before he succeeded to the lands in Somerset and to Lundy Island, and his son William who succeeded him in his turn in 1234 had done the same. When William, son of Jordan, is described as a *nepos* of Geoffrey de Marisco, the word here means grand-nephew. What happened is quite clear. Jordan de Marisco had important holdings in Ireland, where, like his uncle Geoffrey, he was closely connected with Richard the Marshal. When war broke out in England, his sympathies naturally led him to join the Marshal in the Southern Marches of Wales, not very far from Huntspill on the other side of the Bristol Channel. His son William, who was in Ireland, joined his uncle Geoffrey and was with him at the fight on the Curragh. It is not surprising that, when Jordan died, William, who had until recently been a prisoner of war and owed the king a ransom of 300 marks (£200), found much greater difficulty in getting possession of his Irish lands than he had had in England. In fact, his kinship with his great-uncle Geoffrey and his cousin William kept him out of his castles and lands in Ireland until October 1237. His position in Huntspill was more secure, but here also William son of Geoffrey's unwelcome attentions to his island of Lundy brought him under suspicion, and, as we shall see, he was forced in 1243 to surrender the island to the king. For some time, owing to his cousin's use of it as a base for robbery on land and piracy at sea, his rights there had been only nominal. He recovered the island in 1281, three years before he died.

4. *William Son of Geoffrey de Marisco turns Pirate.*

William de Marisco managed, somehow or other, to hold out in Lundy Island and elsewhere until 1242. For seven years he lived desperately, a doomed man, as a pirate. Most outlaws just disappeared from history. They fled abroad, or skulked about in hiding, and were lost to view. William de Marisco was a man of a different kind, quite as respectable in his way as the famous men who swept the seas from the same parts of England in the sixteenth century. He had no Spaniards to prey upon, as Drake and Grenville had, no distant seas to roam. He stayed in home waters, and ranged from the coasts of Galloway and Ireland to the Bristol Channel. His memories were incredibly bitter. He was consumed by a sense, not of wrong inflicted by himself, but of wrongs suffered. He nursed feelings of peculiar hatred against King Henry. To the end he denied that he had killed Henry Clement; but his refusal to stand to justice, his flight and his later deeds of violence made all denials futile.

As an outlaw William lost his Irish lands. His wife Matilda suffered with him. The king kept Matilda's cantred and castle of Coonagh in his hands for a year and a day, according to the law in cases of forfeiture, and then, regarding them as an escheat of the see of Dublin, handed them over to the existing archbishop, Luke. This was in August 1236. Whether his wife joined William or not, we do not know. His depredations began to cause anxiety in the early summer of 1237. Although we may assume that Lundy Island was always one one of his places of refuge, the records are silent about his control of the island until 1241. It is quite possible that William used several bases during the five or six years of his maritime activities. At first, the evidence suggests, he worked from Scotland, probably from Galloway.

. In 1237 William de Marisco was again on the fringe of great events. Until outstanding disputes were settled in a general agreement of peace between the two kings, Alexander II of Scotland seemed in this year to be heading for war against his brother-in-law, King Henry. Why this was so, and what Alexander wanted, are not our concern; but it is clear that he hoped much from his friends and relatives in England, and that some business of a subterranean kind went on between parties in the two countries. William de Marisco played an obscure part in the movement. On 18 June the barons of the various Cinque Ports were ordered to equip the king's galleys and a good ship from Winchelsea and to send them to Portsmouth to await orders. The reason given for this order was that certain evildoers, to wit, William de Marisco, his brother Robert[1], and their accomplices of the land of the King of Scotland had put to sea with galleys and were preying upon the merchants and others crossing from Ireland to England. They had attacked and taken merchants of Bristol, Dublin and Drogheda, killing some, wounding others and holding others to grievous ransom. A few days earlier the bailiffs of Bristol had been authorized to sell the merchandise on board the ships which had been attacked, up to the amount of the ransoms, so that the hostages could be saved. Later letters sent to the bailiffs of Bristol give the names of merchants, including a Norman, who had suffered from the marauders. A prison, in which the captives or their hostages were detained, is mentioned, and one thinks of Lundy Island. When such incidents as these occurred, it was the duty of the bailiffs in the ports to take possession of the ships attacked, and of any merchandise which might be recovered, until the rightful owners could appear and prove their ownership. The pirates wanted ransoms, not ships and goods. Also, ships could be held on suspicion after a robbery at sea. The bailiffs of Bristol, the justiciar of Ireland, the earl of Ulster, the mayors and good men of Dublin and Drogheda had detained ships and merchandise. The authorities in Ireland were ordered to restore ships and goods, "arrested on account of a robbery lately committed at sea by William de Marisco". It is significant that this order was made in letters sent from York

---

[1]Probably an error for Reginald de Marisco. There is no other indication that the reputable Robert was an associate of William.

on 28 September, when the treaty with the king of Scots was announced. In their zeal the king's ministers in Ireland had also seized the lands of another William de Marisco, confounding him perhaps with his kinsman, and the unhappy man had to seek redress from the king. I suppose that in him we may see the son of Jordan.

5. *The Attempt to Murder King Henry at Woodstock, the Assault on Lundy Island and the Execution of William Son of Geoffrey de Marisco.*

William de Marisco came safely out of this adventure. The ransoms of the merchants amounted to £120. William was in funds, for £120 sterling was a large sum in those days. A really good pirate story would tell us how exactly the money was paid over to him and how the hostages were released; but we hear nothing about this, nor about the king's galleys at Portsmouth which ought to have been looking for him. Perhaps the merchants had found the king's bailiffs too attentive, and were glad to get away again with their ships and goods and to say no more about their experience. At any rate, William turned in the following year to a much more dangerous and dreadful crime. He was believed to have contrived a plot to murder the king. Henceforward, he was worse than an outlaw. He was a traitor, *proditor regis*.

The story is told by Matthew Paris in his best manner:

> On the morrow of the nativity of the Blessed Mary [9 Sept. 1238], a certain man at arms, a man of some education (*armiger literatus*) came to the king's court at Woodstock. Pretending to be mad, he said to the king: "Resign to me the kingdom which you have unjustly usurped and long detained." And he added that he had the mark of royalty on his shoulder. When the king's servants ran upon him, intending to beat him and drive him away from the king's presence

the king checked them, saying " Let him alone in his folly."
But in the middle of the night, the madman climbed into
the king's sleeping chamber by the window, a naked knife
in his hand, and came to the king's bed. He did not find him,
and was perplexed. He looked for him in various parts of the
chamber. By the providence of God the king was with the
queen. One of the queen's damsels, Margaret Biset, happened to be on duty. She was reciting her psalter by the light
of a candle, for she was devout. When she saw the madman
searching every corner so that he could kill the king, shout-
ing wildly, she was astounded and began to scream. The
servants were awakened and came running in haste. They
broke down the door which the burglar had barred, over-
bore his resistance, seized him, bound him with chains and
put him to the torture. At length he confessed that he had
been sent by William, son of Geoffrey de Marisco, to slay
the king in the manner of the Assassins. He asserted that
others also were concerned in the crime.[1]

Matthew goes on to describe in gruesome detail the execution
of the would-be assassin at Coventry.

His story, in its main lines, is confirmed by the records.
The king *was* at Woodstock on 9 September 1238, and on 20
September, when he was at Bridgenorth, he sent letters to the
bailiffs of various ports, between Dover and Chester, ordering
them to be on the look-out for William de Marisco and his
accomplices, and if possible to catch them. He told how
William had recently plotted his death, "as we know for
certain through a certain ribald whom he sent to kill us and
our queen". On the same day another letter was sent to the
sheriff of Kent, for the king had learned on the best evidence

[1]*Chronica majora*, iii. 497-8. The phrase *more Assassinorum* is used elsewhere by Matthew Paris in reference to emissaries of murder (*e.g.*, *Historia
Anglorum*, ed. Madden, iii. 21). The reference, of course, is to the Ismailians of
the Lebanon, ruled by the Old Man of the Mountain. The St. Albans chronicler,
Roger Wendover, had incorporated a long account of their alleged customs from
William of Tyre, and this was well known to Matthew Paris (Roger of Wendover, ed. Coxe, ii. 245-7). For the Ismailians see R. Grousset, *Histoire des
croisades*, iii (1936), in the index, pp. 813-4.

that William was in that part of England. William, then, was in England. He was not captured, and somehow or other managed to survive until 1242, when at last a definite and successful attempt was made to dislodge him from Lundy Island. By this time his marauding exploits on sea and land were notorious. Something had to be done about them.[1] According to Matthew Paris, certain nobles who had passed near the island on their way from Ireland and had made inquiries, reported to the king how he could best capture him and his men. They had learned that guile was necessary. Direct assault would be of no use. However this may be, Henry took measures. In December 1241 the sheriff of Devon captured three men of William's "society" and by the king's orders sent them to the sheriff of Hampshire, who put them in the prison at Winchester. Early in January the men of Bristol handed over William's wife to the constable of Gloucester castle. In the meantime the men of Devon were ordered to take counsel how best to guard their coast against incursions from the king's enemies on Lundy Island. If they failed to take effective action, Henry Tracy and three other local landholders had power to devise plans at the cost of the shire. This last order was made on 7 February. Finally, when the spring had come, an assault was made on the island. The operations were under the control of William Bardolf, a Norfolk baron, who was sent down to Devonshire by the government[2]. A certain Richard de Chilham was sent to Bardolf's assistance with two knights and a dozen men-at-

[1] The abbot of Margam in Glamorgan aroused the king's indignation against him, because on one occasion, probably early in 1242, he "received" William and his men.

[2] The king sailed on his Gascon expedition in May 1242, and the council left in England was really responsible for putting an end to William de Marisco. William Bardolf, heir to the honour of Wormegay, was Hubert de Burgh's step-son, being the son of Hubert's second wife, Beatrice de Warenne, by her first husband.

arms in the end of May. They succeeded in capturing the outlaws. In a later copy of his chronicle Matthew Paris added a story that William was betrayed by one of his men, whom he had detained on the island against his will. The rocks protecting the place could only be scaled at one point, and William imprudently set this man to guard the weak spot. It was a misty day, and William was sitting at meat when the king's men came. William and his band were taken to Bristol, where he and his more powerful men were put in the safest and strongest part of the main tower of the castle, and the rest in the town. Burgesses were appointed to join with the constable of the castle in keeping guard over them. A day or two later arrangements were made for the transference of the outlaws to London (16 June 1242). William Bardolf was to hand over William de Marisco and four or five of the more important prisoners whom he had captured to the constable of the Tower. Of the others as many as could be safely guarded there were to be put into Newgate prison, the rest in the Fleet. The constable and wardens of these prisons were straitly ordered to put their dangerous charges in irons and in strong places. The treasurer was asked to provide as many suitable men to guard them as were required to prevent any possible risk of escape.

On 14 July the constable of the Tower, Richard de Bovill, delivered William de Marisco, Aimeri de Beaufeu, Reginald de Marisco, Robert de Montibus and William's chamberlain Richard, for trial. Others were tried with them, for Matthew Paris describes the execution of William with sixteen companions on 25 July. The murderers of Henry Clement, it will be noticed, had disappeared by 1242. These are new companions. They were taken from Westminster to the Tower, and thence dragged by horses to the "penal machine, vulgarly known as the gibbet", on which they were hanged.

The manuscript of the chronicle contains at this point a lively drawing of William being dragged to execution. The unhappy knight lies on the ground. Ropes are attached by one end to his feet, by the other to the horse's collar. A young man sitting on the horse looks back at him with curiosity[1]. Before his execution William made his confession to the famous Dominican, John of St. Giles, a beloved friend of the bishop of Lincoln, Robert Grosseteste.

6. *The Relatives of William de Marisco. The Episode of the Abbess of Shaftesbury.*

The names of two or three relatives of William, who were apparently his companions, are known. Two of them, Richard de Marisco and Geoffrey de Marisco, parson of Bathymegait, were clerks. Their tonsure saved them, and they were taken from the Tower to the castle of Devizes. In 1244 Bishop Grosseteste demanded benefit of clergy on behalf of an Adam de Marisco, a clerk of his diocese, who was in prison at York on a charge of robbing foreign merchants at Stamford and Grantham. Adam was handed over to the bishop on the condition that he entered a religious order and left the kingdom. Unless a family failing, the robbery of merchants, connects them, I have no evidence that Adam and William were related or had worked together. Five men who were captured on the island of Lundy, but presumably were not members of the society, were taken to Exeter. At the end of the year they were allowed bail to await the arrival of the justices.

Matilda, the wife of William de Marisco, must have had friends at court and in Ireland. She was kept at Gloucester until the summer of 1243, when the king, in letters sent from

[1] The drawing is reproduced by M. R. James in "The drawings of Matthew Paris" (*Walpole Society*, xiv. 1926, Plate XVI).

Bordeaux on 20 June, ordered her release. The council executed this order early in July, and a month later gave Matilda letters which authorized the mayor and bailiffs of Bristol to deliver to her the chattels—about four pounds in money, a silver drinking-cup and a kerchief valued at ten shilling—taken from her when she was arrested. Two of her servants were not set free till the end of the following year (November 1244) after judicial inquiry had elicited nothing against them except that they had been with her. These unhappy men had been in gaol at Gloucester for two and a half years. Matilda in the meantime had been trying to get back her castles and lands in Ireland. This was a very slow business, for, as we have seen, her marriage portion, given to her by her uncle Henry, archbishop of Dublin, many years before, had escheated to the archbishopric of Dublin, and Matilda had to show that the reigning archbishop, Luke—Hubert de Burgh's former confessor and friend—had no right to hold it. The case dragged on from June 1244, when she first got an order for the restoration of her lands, until at least August 1247, when Matilda, after she had obeyed a command to come to the king, no doubt to give him proper assurances, was at last put in possession of Coonagh and her other castle at Blathach near Limerick. The legal point at issue had been an interesting one. Inspection of Archbishop Henry's charter revealed the fact that his grant to Matilda was sealed with the seals of his two chapters of St. Trinity and St. Patrick as well as with his own. Her title was a good one. The question then arose, could the outlawry of her husband affect the wife's possession of her *maritagium*? The answer was that forfeiture of the wife's *maritagium* did not follow. Matilda's lands, therefore, should never have been escheated.

King Henry and his council were very thorough in their dealings with the relatives of William de Marisco. Justice was

incredibly slow, suspicious, remorseless, yet in the end justice
was done. There were two kinsmen of William, John and
Richard, who seem to have been detained at Chester, while
inquiries were made in Ireland. The justiciar's investigations showed that they had not "consented with the felony
and deliberate malice" of William. So in June 1244 the justice
of Chester was ordered to deliver them to the justiciar of
Ireland, who, after they had given security that their release
would result in no harm to king and realm, was to set them
free and put them in seisin of their lands. And there was the
nun who was alleged to be a relative of the traitor. This was
Agnes Ferrers, a nun of the abbey of St. Edward at Shaftes-
bury. As its patron and a devotee of its patron saint, King
Henry felt a deep personal interest in the fortunes of this
famous house. Its dignity was a reflection of his own. The
nuns were anxious to make Agnes Ferrers their abbess, but
unfortunately the vacancy occurred in 1242, the year of
William's execution. She was elected, but the king, then in
Gascony, refused to confirm the election, and she had the
good sense to renounce her claim. The execution of her kinsman was too recent. When the new abbess, Agnes Longspée,
a nun of Wherwell, died in 1246, and the nuns got licence to
elect, they again wished to have Agnes Ferrers as their abbess.
The king was still opposed to the idea. He ordered Robert
Passelew, the custodian of the abbey during the vacancy, to
appeal publicly in his name, if the nuns proceeded to elect
Agnes, "whatever spirit might lead them". Agnes, he wrote,
"is sprung of the blood of traitors, and the king has other good
grounds of exception to her, which, when put forward and
proved, would make her utterly ineligible and put her out of
consideration (*repulsa*)". This was strong language; but the
nuns were not frightened by it, and the bishop of Salisbury
was brought upon the scene. The great issue of liberty to elect

was raised, and some compromise had to be reached. Henry and the bishop agreed that, without prejudice to the church of Salisbury, a royal clerk might on this peculiar occasion be sent to take part in the proceedings on the king's behalf and to examine the election in his interests. In October 1246, five months after the trouble had begun, Master William of Powick was sent. The deadlock must have continued, for in November we find that the jurisdiction of Canterbury had been invoked. The nuns had presumably appealed to the provincial court. By this time the king was getting weary; he gave his clerk, Master Roger de Cantilupe, full power to settle the affair with the archbishop's official, and by the end of the year all was well. On 9 January 1247 the royal assent to the election of Agnes Ferrers was given, and a mandate was sent to the dean and chapter of Salisbury to do their part therein. We see how at every turn the murder of Henry Clement, years before, led to difficulties in the lives and fortunes of innocent men and women whom we should never expect to be involved, to high questions of law and politics, to problems in the relations between church and state, to issues affecting the welfare of the kingdom and the dignity of the crown.

We have yet to see what happened to Lundy Island and to the old Geoffrey de Marisco, the traitor's father.

7. *The Fortification of Lundy Island*

King Henry, who was kept informed of events, was determined not to let go of Lundy Island. The exploits of William de Marisco and the difficulty in dislodging him had revealed its importance. At some time during the recent operations against William he had taken the precaution of seizing the lands of William son of Jordan, the nominal tenant of the island, and always, at his home in Huntspill, a possible ally of his cousin. Henry, as the phrase went, wished to speak of certain things against him, in his court. One of these matters, no doubt, was his ransom, not yet fully paid; another, we may be sure, was his responsibility as tenant for the deplorable behaviour of his outlawed relative in Lundy Island. The object in view was, of course, the return of the island to the crown. In June 1243 at Bordeaux the seneschal of Gascony became surety for William's appearance in court, when required, and the king gave orders for the restoration of all William's lands in Somerset and Ireland, "with the exception of the island of Lundy, which the king wishes to retain in his own hands".

The council in England had not awaited the issue of these formalities. William Bardolf, before he left the island, had made arrangements for the erection of a stone tower, and a constable of Lundy had been appointed. Towards the end of June 1243 Henry Tracy, lord of the honour of Barnstaple, and the greatest man in the parts of Devon opposite the island, who had gone to court to report on local affairs, returned with orders from the council. These referred to the distribution of the wages of the men who had taken and were guarding the island—Henry Tracy brought £100 with him for this purpose —but they also contained the information that a very important person indeed might be expected early in August. One of the three chief men in the government, William de Cantilupe, the seneschal of the royal household, was coming down in person to take charge of the island. Nothing could reveal more clearly the serious view taken at court of the activities of William de Marisco. Before the great man arrived, Henry Tracy was instructed to go to Lundy with the sheriff and to decide whether the time was suitable for the construction of the fort which William Bardolf had planned. By time, we should understand weather, for it was no easy matter, even if the stone could be quarried on the spot, to get materials across and to carry on building operations. The castle was begun, as we learn from a letter of the following April. The constable of Lundy—I suppose William de Cantilupe's deputy—had caught 2500 rabbits on the island, and the sheriff of Devon was told to sell the skins "by view and witness of lawful men" and place the proceeds towards the expense of building the new tower. This rocky place contained something more precious than rabbits. There was an eyrie of falcons, which about this time was given by King Henry to one of his favourite clerks. One begins to get a vivid impression of Lundy, with its castle, rabbit-warrens and birds, and, I should add, its shipping, for the constable had a galley at his disposal.

William de Cantilupe was relieved of his responsibility for Lundy Island in May 1244 and was succeeded as constable by Richard Clifford. A change was made, however, in July 1245. A constable sent from outside had not much to do and was expensive; hence the government decided to entrust the island to Henry Tracy, the man who by this time must have known most about it. He and Richard Clifford made an agreement by indenture—that is to say, Henry Tracy received the island with its stock and profit, and the details of the transaction were described in documents identical except for the names of the parties. Henry kept Richard's and Richard kept Henry's. Henry was to hold the island for the king at the royal pleasure, and in return was allowed to keep all profits and make what he could out of it. So the island remained legally in the king's hands, but without any expense to the royal treasury.

The memory of William de Marisco is enshrined in that invaluable work, Samuel Lewis's *A Topographical Dictionary of England* (1840), in the article on Lundy Island:

> It is recorded that one Morisco, having been frustrated in a conspiracy to assassinate Henry III, made this his retreat, became the chief of a band of pirates, and for his crimes was executed here by command of the king; and also that Edward II, at one time during his disturbed reign, proposed retiring hither for safety from his rebellious nobles. Morisco's castle, situated near the south-eastern point, was originally a strong fortification, with considerable outworks: it is encompassed by a moat, but no ordnance are now mounted upon the battery, though a few dismantled guns occupy the ramparts, beneath which is a remarkable cave.

The true story is good, but this is better. That frustrated gentleman, William Marsh, has become Morisco. His name has a fine Barbary flavour. The castle is his; William Bardolf did not plan it, Henry Tracy and the sheriff of Devon and William de Cantilupe took no part in the building of it. Morisco's ghost walks among grass-grown batteries in the garb of Captain Kidd or Long John Silver. Romance has taken William Marsh for its own. He breathes the spice-laden air of the Indies; he brings to the Bristol Channel the spirit of the corsairs of the Mediterranean. His exotic, mysterious figure moves in the company of the sea dogs of Devon. He is hanged on his island, where there is a remarkable cave.

8. *The End of Geoffrey de Marisco*

And now, in the end, we must come back to William's father, Geoffrey de Marisco, lord of Killorglin, once the servant of King John and justiciar of Ireland. We left him in sanctuary in

Clerkenwell, just after the murder of Henry Clement in May 1235. Although he had no share in the crime, he had run to shelter, afraid that he would be involved in the fury which was to break his son. Before long he was released from suspicion. In August 1235 the king took him into his grace and gave him letters of protection while he was in England trying to arrange for the payment of his heavy ransom. He was allowed to pay this on easier terms and could go back to Ireland and receive possession of his lands there. Till 1238 he was trying to regain possession of Kilmallock, which he claimed to hold of the bishop of Limerick, Hubert de Burgh, a nephew of his famous namesake. Geoffrey had subinfeudated Kilmallock to his son the outlaw, and the bishop, in flat contradiction to the rules of feudal law, had seized it as an escheat after William's disgrace. The escheat, after being held a year and a day by the king, should have gone to its immediate lord, William's father. How far Geoffrey was successful in his case against the bishop is not clear. By 1238 he was in trouble because he had not paid the instalments of his ransom, and as he had no lands in England, where the money should have been paid, the justiciar of Ireland was ordered by the king to distrain on his lands in Ireland "to satisfy us for the fine at our exchequer in Dublin".

Matthew Paris, who always had some authority for his stories, however much he distorted them, gives a much more gloomy picture of the old man's last years. One of his scandalous remarks is illuminating. Matthew, in spite of the capture of Geoffrey at the Curragh and the murder of Henry Clement by his son, was firmly convinced that Geoffrey had betrayed Richard the Marshal. He could think no good of him. Naturally enough, therefore, he says that Geoffrey had incited William de Marisco to plot the assassination of the king in 1238. Now we may be sure that what he thought, others thought, and, when we remember how carefully the king and his servants traced out and held in suspicion William's relatives between 1238 and 1242, we cannot assume that Geoffrey, his father, escaped attention. I suggest that after the attempt on the king's life at Woodstock in September 1238, Geoffrey's lands in Ireland were seized, and that this explains his disappearance. The end had come. He was an outlaw for the death of a man.[1]

King Henry, Matthew Paris writes, was informed that, after the execution of his son, Geoffrey had gone to Scotland and had been received by King Alexander II. He had probably gone earlier than 1242. Scotland was, in fact, the only refuge in the British Isles open to him, and his connection with the Comyns may have encouraged him to seek protection there, for the head of the Scottish branch of this widespread family was one of the chief men in Scotland. The reception of Geoffrey de Marisco was one of the grievances which King Henry had against King Alexander and Walter Comyn, when he made a military demonstration against Scotland two years later, in 1244. The ejection of Geoffrey from Scotland may well have been one of the unwritten understandings at the time when peace was made[2]. The unhappy man, in any case, was forced to leave. He died in the following year (1245).

[1]Geoffrey de Marisco is so described in 1244, in a royal letter which also describes him a tenant in Linford (Bucks.) and Crowmarsh (Oxfordshire). These lands were not his but had come to him in right of his third wife, Alice widow of Roger Pipard and daughter of the great Anglo-Irish lord Hugh de Lacy I. Hence in 1238 he could be said to have no lands in England.

[2]The *carta* of King Alexander (August 1244) contained, as its main clause, a promise that he would make no pacts with Henry's enemies (Rymer, *Foedera*, I, i. 257). This would cover the case of Geoffrey de Marisco, although its object was to prevent any understanding between Alexander and the French.

Matthew Paris, pitiless to the end, reports his death in a studied epitaph:

> About this time died Geoffrey de Marisco, a man once noble and not the least among the magnates of Ireland. In exile and misery, a fugitive, he was stained indelibly with the death by treason of Richard earl Marshal. Driven from Scotland, banished from England, disinherited in Ireland, he survived the disgraceful death of his son and the loss of all his friends, to end the tale of death with his own.

9. *Epilogue*

The search after truth plays strange tricks with an historian. He sets out to tell a plain straightforward story, and he finds himself running about in all sorts of places. Insensibly the interest of his story is merged in the excitement of the chase. He cannot bring himself to believe that his readers will not be as interested as he has been in seeing how one point leads to another, how this fact throws light on that, why one clue has to be discarded, and another pursued to the end. As Maitland once wrote: "Out of the thicket may fly a bird worth powder and shot"; but the thicket must be a clue, not any thicket, and the bird must be worth powder and shot, not any bird. If this condition is observed, the story becomes more than a story; it breathes a troubled life of its own as part of a living past. The things which first stirred interest, the picturesque, the amusing, the dramatic, are still there, but are no longer the essential things. Sometimes, as I work at a series of patent and close rolls, I have a queer sensation; the dead entries begin to be alive. It is rather like the experience of sitting down in one's chair and finding that one has sat on the cat. These are real people, this casual official letter is telling something that really happened, it was written on the impulse of a real emotion. To be sure that this William is William son of Geoffrey and not William son of Jordan becomes as important as any problem of identity can be in a court of law to-day. It is necessary to take great care, no longer in the interests of learning, but for their sakes. I fear that the historian is quite incorrigible, when he has once had this experience. He becomes indifferent to insinuations of pedantry; for pedantry is a kind of darkness, and he is trying to let in the light.

All the same, the story of William Marsh is a gift to any good historical novelist.

IV

GUY DE MONTFORT (1265–71)[1]

I invite my reader to follow me along a bypath which gives
access to wide prospects. I do not intend to tell an old story,
but to try to give to it, or rather to draw from it, the significance which it seems to possess. It is a story of Guy de
Montfort, the third son of the great Earl Simon. The most
important documents are accessible in printed books or have
been noted by M. Bémont in his *Simon de Montfort*, and by Dr.
Robert Davidsohn in his great *Geschichte von Florenz*. But
Bémont compresses the story and treats it as an appendix to
the life of Earl Simon, and Davidsohn is concerned with it as
the historian of an Italian city. Both historians seem to me to
have overlooked the importance of some pieces of evidence.
The best-proportioned and most touching narrative is still
that of Reinhold Pauli (1867), and there is much valuable
material in William Henry Blaauw's book on *The Baron's War*
(1844, 1871). Blaauw's book is now unduly neglected. One
might say of it, as one of their successors gracefully said of the
work done by Warburton and Samuel Johnson on Shakespeare, that their errors were sometimes more important than
the corrections of them.

Most of us think of the children of Simon de Montfort, if
we think of them at all, as powerless refugees of whom very
little is known. One of them, Guy, burst into notoriety and

---

[1] A presidential address to the Royal Historical Society, delivered 14
February, 1935. For the original form, here modified, see the Society's *Transactions*, 4th series, xviii. 1–23.

earned a most uncomfortable position in Dante's *Inferno*, when he murdered his cousin, Henry of Almaine, in an Italian church; but how or why he and his victim found themselves together in an Italian church at all has, I imagine, been a mystery or may still be a mystery to most of us. The first points to emphasise, therefore, are that the Montforts were very important people and that a great deal is or can be known about them. Indeed, if the published and unpublished material relating to the family after 1265 were collected together, it would make a large book. The family collected and kept its archives at Montfort l'Amaury, west of Paris, and many *disjecta membra* of these archives survive, partly in a collection formed by Clairembault early in the eighteenth century, partly in other manuscripts in the Bibliothèque Nationale, the French Archives, and the British Museum.[1] Bémont has made us familiar with these, and I would merely add two observations about them. Firstly, the presence of numerous documents relating to the English family at Montfort l'Amaury may remind us that the exiles were always in close touch with the great French house from which they sprang; secondly, internal evidence suggests that one collection of documents may have been made by Earl Simon's clerical son, Amaury. Amaury, who cannot have been more than twenty years of age in 1265, became a very well educated man. As a boy he had attracted the notice of a family friend, Odo Rigaud the famous archbishop of Rouen, who had made

[1]The manuscript compiled by Pierre Clairembault, now *fonds Clairembault*, no. 1188, was one of a great collection formed by Clairembault for the purpose of a history of the Order of the Holy Ghost, and was originally no. 78 in this series. It contains a few originals, which are pasted in, and copies of documents which were in the Montfort archives. These archives came to Clairembault in 1707 and 1708. Bémont printed some of the contents of the Clairembault MS. in the first edition (Paris, 1884) of his book on Simon de Montfort (Appendix, nos. ii, xxviii bis, xxx, xxxi, xxxiii, xxxiv, xxxviii, xxxix, xlviii-liv).

him a canon and given him a prebend in his cathedral.[1] Roger Bacon, writing in 1267, casually refers to his tutor as one of the best mathematicians of the day[2]. This, by the way, looks as though one of our refugees travelled with a tutor. Amaury went about this time to the University of Padua, where he studied with acceptance for at least three years. He was a papal chaplain, *magnae litteraturæ*. He was also a very persistent litigious person with a keen sense of his importance and his rights, a man who never gave up a lawsuit and, under the cloak of deference, liked to write impertinent letters to his cousin, King Edward. Moreover, he was a man of means, for his mother, the Countess Eleanor, seems to have passed to on him the share of *her* mother's inheritance in Angoulême, which she persuaded the French lawcourts to extract for her from her kinsfolk in La Marche. Now several documents in the Montfort archives refer especially to Amaury, and it is not unlikely that he formed a little collection.

The family archives, however, do not carry us very far. The papal registers, the English chancery rolls, the documents preserved in the English exchequer, and the records of the Angevin Kings of Naples tell us more; and the city records of Florence, Pisa, Volterra and other places, so carefully explored by Davidsohn, tell us most of all. In the light of these, some unnoticed passages in the French and Italian chronicles acquire significance.

I propose to consider the following points: (1) the attitude of the royal government in England to the Montfort family; (2) the importance of the connection between the English branch and one of the French branches of the family, the

[1] The archbishop gave Amaury the prebend on 5 July, 1260, while he was in London *pro negotio domini regis Francorum*, and installed him at Rouen on 14 August (*Journal des visites pastorales d'Eude Rigaud*, edit. Th. Bonnin, Rouen, 1852, pp. 369, 370). Amaury obviously accompanied him back to Normandy.

[2] Roger Bacon, *Opus Tertium*, edit. J. S. Brewer (Rolls Series), p. 35.

Montforts of La Ferté-Alais; (3) the rapid rise of Guy de Montfort to wealth and power in Italy; (4) the murder of Henry of Almaine.

I

From one point of view Eleanor and her children were the widow and children of a traitor. Three of the sons were dangerous. Simon, the heir, a young warrior in his twenty-fifth year in 1265, showed fight; Guy showed resource, and Amaury, if the story of the treasure which he carried away is true, cunning, in his flight[1]. But, in the royal correspondence of the years 1265-7, the attitude towards the Montforts is one rather of pain and resentment than of remorseless justice. After the murder of Henry of Almaine in March, 1271, the tone changes. Richard of Cornwall, king of the Romans, the bereaved father, at once described the murderers as the sons of that foul traitor, Simon de Montfort. If the Westminster chronicle reflects current speech, Earl Simon became the traitor Guenelon, the villain of the piece in the *Chanson de Roland*, and the type of treachery in more than one medieval epic. His children were of the race of Guenelon. But this had not been the attitude at first. King Richard had been friendly and had taken Eleanor and the young Simon under his protection[2]. King Henry, angry though he was, never forgot that Eleanor was his sister, and he very soon found that the Montforts had strong backing across the Channel. Until she died in pious seclusion at the family nunnery of Montargis (1275),

[1] Amaury was treasurer of the church of York, and was believed to have taken the treasure with him. Pope Clement IV refused to recognize the validity of the act of deprivation issued by King Henry after Evesham: see the papal letters, dated Viterbo, 19 March, 1267 (*Cal. Pap. Letters*, i. 434). Amaury by this time was apparently in Viterbo.

[2] Although evidence can be found for this statement it should be pointed out that Richard's good offices were promised under duress, when he was in the younger Simon's power at Kenilworth after the battle of Evesham. Some days

72

Eleanor was treated with consideration by Henry and afterwards by Edward. She had a good income, she was allowed, through her proctors, to pursue her interminable litigation in the English courts, and after her death her last will and testament was executed without serious interference. But it has not been sufficiently noticed that at one time the King was prepared to be generous to young Simon. He stipulated that Simon should have no *right* to live in England and must be prepared to sell his lands either to him, Henry, or to one of of his sons, if required; and he imposed a time limit within which Simon must accept the terms offered to him, terms which Simon did not deserve and which would not be renewed. Subject to these conditions, he was prepared to restore to Simon his lands; or, if Simon did not care for this arrangement, to allow him to return to England, under a safe conduct, to stand his trial. He added that the sins of the father would not be visited upon the son. Moreover, in his desire to please King Louis, Henry consented that the French king should act as arbitrator—for example, should fix the price of the lands up to the maximum of ten years purchase, the current price of land in England. Henry also agreed to submit to ecclesiastical discipline if he failed to observe the arrangement. Richard of Cornwall would act as arbitrator during the preliminary survey or "extent" of the Leicester inheritance. Why these terms were not accepted or implemented, it is hard to say. It is possible that Henry's baronial advisers disliked them for they had not originated with them, but in discussion be-

before he was released (he reached his manor of Wallingford on 9 Sept., 1265) he entered into a written obligation, which was sealed with the seals of three pledges, to befriend, aid and counsel Eleanor, her children and household. The instrument, which survives in the French archives (*Trésor des Chartes*, J. 1024, no. 14; cf. Bémont (Eng. ed.), p. xvii), is dated from the friary at Kenilworth, the Sunday before the feast of the Nativity of Our Lady, in the forty-ninth year of King Henry, i.e., 6 Sept., 1265. The inference that Richard was asked to make this promise as a condition of his release is obvious.

tween King Louis's envoys and the *secretarii*, or more intimate counsellors of the English king. In later years—but this was after the murder of Henry of Almaine—King Edward was most punctilious in refusing to treat either with Guy or with Amaury without the consent of parliament, and it is clear from Archbishop Pecham's correspondence that the debates in parliament about this matter could be lively. On the other hand, Simon may have refused to join in the scramble for clemency. He was devoted to the memory of his father.

2

The French envoys with whom, in May, 1267, King Henry and his *secretarii* discussed the future of the young Simon de Montfort, were led by King Louis's butler, John of Acre. The significance of this simple statement has escaped notice. John of Acre was the son of John of Brienne, who had been in his time King of Jerusalem and Emperor of Constantinople. In other words, King Louis, who had recently taken the cross for the second time, sent on behalf of the Montforts the chief dignitary in his court, a man who, in virtue of his ancestry and social position, might be regarded as a symbol of peace and unity. The great earl, for whose son King Louis pleaded, had been a Crusader, and had been formally nominated by the barons of Syria and the Holy Land as guardian of the Latin Kingdom; his father had been the hammer of heretics in the Albigensian Crusade.. Now, the younger Simon and his brothers, exiles though they were, resumed their position as members of a French house which inspired traditional respect. In spite of their follies and misfortunes they never entirely lost their claim to support. The energy with which one pope after another urged the cause of Amaury, the repeated representations by Charles of Salerno on behalf of Guy, the concern felt in England when one or other of them made a

hostile move or a tentative advance, testify to their importance. The way in which the chroniclers of St. Denis discuss
the murder of Henry of Almaine is itself an illustration of this
fact. They treat it as a regrettable incident in a family ven-
detta, not as an unprovoked and brutal crime. Earl Simon, in
their view, had sought to correct the weaknesses of his royal
brother-in-law. His fall had been due to the treachery of
Richard of Cornwall and his son, and his body had been
foully maltreated. The assassination of Henry was the answer
of Earl Simon's sons, an act of retribution which, if it could
not be excused, was quite intelligible. In short, the Montforts
belonged to the Île de France. They were French, not
English. They had Norman, Angevin, Poitevin ancestry, but,
unless we insist upon the exiguous drops which came from
their great-great-grandmother, the Empress Matilda, they
had no English blood in their veins. In particular, they were
French, of the Île de France, and close kinsmen of the greatest families in the land. We are brought up to regard Earl
Simon as the incarnation of the English spirit, as a medieval
Cromwell. It is true that he was not an alien, as the half-
brothers of Henry III, or the relations of Eleanor of Provence
were aliens, for he succeeded to his earldom by hereditary
right. But the fact remains that he was a Frenchman, who
held an English earldom for thirty-four years, and lived in
England for about a quarter of a century.

In the second half of the thirteenth century the main line
of the house of Montfort gradually disappeared. Its lands
were carried by one heiress after another to other French
families. The process had already begun when the sons of
Earl Simon came to France. They might find hospitality and
friendliness, but not opportunity and adventure in these pious
households. Another branch of the Montfort family had much
more to offer. This was descended from Guy, the brother of

the hero of the Albigensian war and the uncle of Earl Simon. Its French home was at La Ferté-Alais, a few miles to the south of Paris, and not far from the Dominican nunnery to which the Countess Eleanor retired. Guy had fought in the south, where he held Castres in the Albigensian county and other lands in the counties of Carcassonne and Narbonne. He had married a lady of the famous crusading family of Ibelin, and his son Philip became one of the leading men in Latin Syria. Philip was, in right of his second wife, lord of Tyre, and of Toron. He had known Earl Simon, for the earl had gone on crusade to Syria early in 1241, and Philip had been one of the barons who had wished to make his cousin guardian of the Latin Kingdom. By his first wife, Eleanor of Courtenay, daughter of the Count of Auxerre, Philip had a son Philip, destined to succeed to La Ferté-Alais, Castres and his other lands in the west. The younger Philip de Montfort had also been well known to Earl Simon, who in 1259 had made him his lieutenant in his county of Bigorre—an important fact hitherto noted in this connection only by Blaauw[1]. Now in 1265 the younger Philip de Montfort accompanied St. Louis's brother, Charles of Anjou, on his Italian adventure. Nobody was of greater assistance to Charles than he was during the next five years when the count of Anjou usurped imperial control in Lombardy and Tuscany and wrested the kingdom of Naples and Sicily from the last Hohenstaufen. In 1265 Philip helped to negotiate the submission of some of the princes and cities of North Italy, and in November he did the same service at Vercelli. After the battle of Benevento,

[1]Blaauw, p. 339, note 4. The document was printed later in the *Layettes du Trésor des Chartes*, vol. iii (ed. J. de Laborde, Paris, 1873), p. 456, no. 4476. It is dated the Wednesday before Easter, 1258, *apud Nonacuriam* (probably Nonan-court in Normandy). As Earl Simon used the "Easter" style in dating, this is 6 April, 1259, according to modern usage, not 1258 as Blaauw thought. Simon was in France at this date, but not on the corresponding date in 1258.

Charles made him his vicar in Sicily and later placed him in
charge of the forces entrusted with the defence of the Papal
States. In 1267, together with a French civilian, he negotiated
the surrender of Florence, and on Easter Day entered the city
as the representative of the new King of Sicily and Imperial
Vicar of Tuscany[1]. In 1268, after the victory at Alba (as we
must now call the battle of Taggliacozzo) over the German
army of the young Corradino and the army of the Ghibelline
league under Henry of Castile, Philip was sent southwards
again to secure the royal power in Sicily; and, on this occasion, we are told, he had with him Guy de Montfort. To conclude this summary of Philip's life, in 1270 he accompanied
King Charles to join the crusading forces in Tunis. He is said
to have died in this year, and he was succeeded by his son
John, lord of La Ferté-Alais and Castres. John had already
made his mark. He was given the county of Squillace on the
Calabrian coast and other fiefs in the Kingdom of Naples and
Sicily, and from 1273–1300 he was chamberlain in succession
to his father-in-law, Pierre de Beaumont. John settled in Italy
and, in later years, was the best friend Guy de Montfort ever
had.

I draw the conclusion that the way to fortune in Italy was
opened to Guy de Montfort by his cousin Philip.

3

If any single event could be selected as the starting-point of
modern European polities it would be the rapid conquest of
the great part of Italy by Charles of Anjou, and it was this
far-reaching adventure which gave the third son of Simon de
Montfort the chance to re-establish the family fortunes. For a
few months, Guy, somewhere between 25 and 30 years of age,

[1]Charles was accepted as the *podestà* of Florence, and quietly displaced
Clement IV as ruler of the city and of Tuscany.

was a more powerful man in Tuscany than his father had ever been in Gascony, and stood as high in the councils of King Charles[1] as Simon had stood before the Barons' War in the counsels of King Henry III. He leaped into fame in a great battle. We do not know when he came to join Philip de Montfort in Charles's army, but he came in time to fight at Alba on 23 August, 1268. So far as I am aware, no modern historian has seen the significance of his achievement, although some writers mention his presence in the field. The story is told by the chronicler of St. Denis. After describing how, by a clever stratagem, Erard de Valery saved the day for King Charles, the chronicler continues: Guy de Montfort, if anyone, deserves praise above all others. He was first in the attack, like a wild boar among dogs. Raising his father's battle-cry, he broke through the enemy and, drenched with their blood, came back to his men. But by some mischance his helmet was twisted round, so that, as his visor was at the back of his head, he could neither see nor breathe. Like a blind man, he struck wildly right and left. Then Erard de Valery[2], seeing his plight, had pity on him, and came up to him. He took hold of his head with both hands, reversed the helmet, and retied its strings. At first Guy supposed that he was in the hands of an enemy and he struck a great blow which, by Christ's aid, did Erard no hurt. He was about to strike again, when he recognized his rescuer's voice. This story would make Guy's name known and would fix the record of his previous prowess in the memory of men.

The victory at Alba made Charles of Anjou King of Sicily in fact as well as in name. Corradino was executed, Henry of

[1]Charles, in his deeds, frequently refers to Philip and also to Guy as his *cognati*.

[2]The friendly relations at this time between Erard and Guy are suggestive, for Erard was a close personal friend of Edward and three years later accompanied him on his crusade.

Castile was imprisoned. The King was free to consolidate his power, and to distribute the lands of the *proditores*. Guy's future was assured.

In the settlement of forfeited lands which followed the conquest he and his brother Simon, who probably joined him at the end of 1268, were endowed with very important fiefs in the kingdom of Naples. These fiefs, Arienzo, Nola, Castel Cicala, Monteforte, Forino, Atripalda, which came to Guy, and the county of Avellino, which in December 1270 came to Simon, control the roads which converge from Naples and Salerno on Benevento. In the time of Frederick II and his successors, Conrad and Manfred, they had been held by such trusted servants of the Hohenstaufen as Berthold of Hohenburg and his brother Louis, and Conrad Capece.[1]

But a still more brilliant future than that secured by the possession of these Neapolitan fiefs was opened to Guy de Montfort. After a brief period of service with Philip de Montfort in Sicily he was recalled to central Italy. He was entrusted with a difficult and responsible task in Tuscany. Although the Ghibelline league had been crushed at Alba, the imperial party still held out at Siena and elsewhere. A strong hand was needed to maintain the authority of the conqueror, and Charles chose Guy for this duty. On 24 March, 1270, Guy was appointed his vicar-general in the whole of Tuscany. Six months later, on 24 September, Charles made him also his vicar, that is, acting *podestà*, in Florence itself. Writing from his camp by Carthage he says that this additional mark of confidence was made in recognition of Guy's services to himself and to Italy. He had heard of him from the citizens of Florence, and it was fitting that the city, which was first among the cities of Tuscany, should have a great personage at its head.

[1]See the Additional Note at the end of this paper.

The archives of Florence and Siena show us Guy at work. He moved about among the men and women who live again in the *Divine Comedy*. Dante himself, a child of five years, may well have seen him on one of his ceremonial visits to the city. For twelve months he held his own, maintaining the prestige which he won during the summer of 1270 when, backing diplomacy by force, he brought Siena to submission. More pliable and less scrupulous than his father, he fitted well into his surroundings. He was not too proud to take a bribe and learned how to turn the feuds of Tuscany to financial profit. He received 4,000 gold florins from the Florentines to let them do their worst at Poggibonsi and was present at the destruction of the unhappy place. On the other hand, he was competent and he was attractive. He clinched his good fortune on 10 August, six days after the surrender of Siena. On that day, in the papal city of Viterbo, where the cardinals had gathered to elect a new pope, he married Margherita Aldobrandesca. King Charles gave his consent. Siena sent a gift of jewels in a silver box.

If Guy had had more self-control and allowed Henry of Almaine to pass by he might well have established a prosperous dynasty on the triple foundation of his lands, his vicariate and his marriage. When he made his great mistake, his marriage saved him from destruction. Margherita Aldobrandesca, a young girl of 16 or 17, was the heiress of the most powerful man in southern Tuscany. This was the count palatine Ildebrandino of Pitigliano, universally known as Rosso, the red count. His house was an ancient one, well endowed with imperial liberties granted by the Emperor Frederick I and his successors. At this time his lands were held as an *emphyteusis* of the monastery of St. Anastasia *ad Aquas Salinas*, at Rome. One of Guy's daughters, Anastasia, owed her name to this relationship. In spite of his imperial title and traditions—he was careful to secure confirmation of his privileges from Rudolf of Habsburg before he died—the red count was an ally of the Florentine Guelfs against the Ghibellines of Siena. Siena was his neighbour; and his kinsman, the count palatine Ildebrandino of Santa Fiora, who shared the Aldobrandine lands, was his rival and a Ghibelline, a man from whose wiles Margherita must at all costs be saved. Hence the brilliant young vicar-general came as a god-send. In Guy the count saw a protector of his daughter whose interests would be identified with hers; in the count Guy found a man who could give him a great inheritance. King Charles had endowed him handsomely in the kingdom of Naples; but the Aldobrandine lands were a prize which, as we know from later history, popes and cardinals might well covet. They were extensive and they were safe. Stretching irregularly across southern Tuscany, where numerous rivers run their brief course to the sea on the one side, and the streams which form the Tiber have their source on the other, they came to a head in the difficult country north of Lake Bolsena. The headquarters of the patrimony were at Soana and Pitigliano.[1] Siena lies to the north, on the way to Florence; on the further side of the lake, in the old papal country, Orvieto lies to the east, Viterbo to the south. Intersected by valleys in all directions, dotted by numerous strongholds, the Aldobrandine country could not easily be overrun; and, as Guy was to find, it was a good hiding-place.

After the murder of his cousin in 1271 he lay there, passing from castle to castle, for more than two years[2]. Indeed, save

[1]Davidsohn's account of the Aldobrandine lands, and also of the life of Margaret (*Forschungen*, iv, 377–86), may be corrected and expanded by the work of the late Don Gelasio Caetani, *Domus Caietana: storia documentata della famiglia Caetani*, I, i, (Sancascino Val di Pesa, 1927), especially pp. 132–44, 216–20, and of the authorities whom he uses. Count Rosso died on 18 May, 1284.

[2]During the negotiations with Pope Gregory X in March, 1273, Guy seems to have withdrawn further north to be out of the reach of King Edward, who was

for a brief imprisonment in 1273-4, he was probably there until his reappearance in King Charles's service in 1281. He retained the good will of the citizens of Siena. When King Edward came to Orvieto, on his way back from the east, in February, 1273, and planned a campaign to capture his cousin in his fastnesses, the Sienese refused to help him. The *podestà* of Siena himself went to Orvieto to plead the cause of Guy. And when, a few weeks later, the dreadful bull of excommunication was issued by Pope Gregory X, and Guy was a beast rather than a man, deprived of all his rights on earth and his hopes in heaven, the city fathers permitted him to enter the city secretly by night to meet King Charles, while they publicly forbade him to come near. In those days any man who sheltered Guy was *ipso facto* excommunicate.

4

I come to the murder of Henry of Almaine at Viterbo—one of the famous crimes in history. After a careful examination of all the evidence, I have satisfied myself that only two facts are established beyond doubt. The time was 13 March, 1271, during Mass, and the scene was the parish church of S. Silvestro, now the Chiesa del Gesù, which stands on a little *piazza*, surrounded by towers and old houses, off the main street leading to the cathedral. The motive was a desire for revenge, but we do not know whether the crime was premeditated or was an act of sudden impulse. The dramatic details given in the papal letters two years later, and, in a different form, by Villani more than a generation later, cannot be controlled. Some are probably true, but they cannot all be true. It is fairly certain that, after the first blows were

with the pope at Orvieto. After the bull of excommunication (1 April, 1273) he fled still further north to the castle of Monte Gemoli, in the Cecina valley, not far from Volterra. This castle was an outlying Aldobrandine property. See Davidsohn, *Forschungen*, iv. 205.

struck, Henry's body was dragged out of the church and maltreated, but it is not clear whether Guy dragged it out in
order to get clear of the crowd, or went back for it after he had
left the church, nor whether Henry was already dead or
merely wounded when his body was dragged into the *piazza*.
King Philip III of France and King Charles of Sicily were in
Viterbo at the time and their letters, written immediately to
Richard of Cornwall, to Edward, and to the Neapolitan
officials, still survive; but it is clear that Philip and Charles
were ignorant of the details. They tell us nothing but the fact
of the murder. The few chroniclers who mention it had, with
one exception, no first-hand information, and only one or two
of them can be described as contemporary witnesses[1]. The
exception is Guido de Corvaria, who in 1271 was the ambassador of Pisa to Charles of Anjou and whose chronicle is a
kind of diary. Guido de Corvaria left Pisa for Tunis with his
colleagues on 14 November, 1270, after King Charles had
actually left Africa. He returned to Pisa *de ambasciaria* on 9
April, 1271 (according to the Pisan use, 1272) and, as he implies that the objects of the embassy had been discussed, we
may assume that he joined the crusading army, travelled back
with it through Italy, and reached Viterbo with it on 9
March. In that case he was in Viterbo when the murder
happened. Here is his account:

> On Thursday, 12 March, Guy arrived in Viterbo. On the
> Friday following, i.e., the 13th, Count Guy came armed
> with his knights to the church of S. Silvestro in the said city,
> where the lord Henry, son of Earl Richard, was hearing
> mass, and killed him with his sword. Count Rosso was
> present, and the Kings (Philip and Charles) were with their
> forces (*gente*) in the city. The papal see was vacant. . . . Guy

[1]N. Denholm-Young in his book *Richard of Cornwall* (pp. 150–1) accepts,
in preference to all other evidence, the account given by the well-informed
English annalist, Wykes.

and his brothers were immediately deprived by King Charles of all their honours and goods (*omni honore, beneficio et bonis*).[1]

Every word of this account can be accepted, including the reference to Guy's brothers, for Simon was with Guy[2], and Amaury was for some time supposed to have been concerned in the murder, though actually he was lying ill at Padua and knew nothing about it[3]. Moreover, all the evidence goes to show that the red count had come to Viterbo with his son-in-law, and that Guy and Simon rode back with him to take refuge in the Aldobrandine territory. Simon died in a castle near Soana not long afterwards, in his thirty-first or thirty-second year.

My own view is that the crime—an act of almost incredible folly—was not premeditated. Guy, as the vicar-general of King Charles, would certainly be expected to join the King at Viterbo and to report upon Tuscan affairs. He had with him a large force of mounted mercenaries, 300 or 500 in number, presumably the paid soldiers of the Guelf league, and he must have ridden into Viterbo on 12 March quite openly with his father-in-law and his brother. Moreover Count Rosso came off very lightly, although he had been present and had afterwards sheltered Guy. If the murder was not premeditated, he might be acquitted of the death of a man against whom he had no personal grievance; whereas, if the deed had been planned beforehand, his presence would suggest active complicity. It should be noted also that Walter Baskerville, an Englishman who was apparently serving with Guy, and was outlawed as his accomplice, was later allowed

---

[1]*Historiæ Pisanæ fragmenta*, in Muratori, *Scriptores*, xxiv, col. 679.

[2]This is definitely stated by King Philip of France in his letter to Richard of Cornwall, and in the later bull of excommunication issued by Gregory X in 1273.

[3]Bémont (ed. 1), Appendix, pp. 365–7, an attestation from the bishop, chapter and university of Padua.

to purge himself and to recover his English lands. I think that, when the brothers learned that their cousin was in Viterbo, they were swept away by their memories of Evesham, by the thought of their disinheritance and humiliation, and by the knowledge that Henry was in their power. So in the morning they sought for him. We must remember two things: first, that the maltreatment of Earl Simon's body at Evesham had aroused intense feeling; secondly that, since his desertion of the earl, Henry of Almaine had never been forgiven by the Montforts. His desertion had broken up the baronial party. He was a traitor who deserved to die. His body deserved the treatment which Earl Simon's body had suffered at Evesham.

The deed acquires an element of Greek tragedy when we learn that Henry of Almaine had come to Viterbo as a peacemaker. King Edward, when he talked to the pope at Orvieto in 1273, assured Gregory X that he had detached Henry from the crusading army, which he was taking on to Syria from Tunis, with this purpose[1]. Guy had made a name for himself at Alba and during the next two years. He had powerful friends, among them the King of Sicily and Philip de Montfort, who no doubt intervened on behalf of the sons of Earl Simon when they met Edward on the crusade in Africa. I see nothing improbable in Edward's statement that Henry was entrusted with a mission of peace. At Viterbo, Guy and Simon might well have been the leading actors in a scene of reconciliation. During those days in March, 1271, Viterbo was, for a short time, the centre of the western world. Charles of Anjou came north with his nephew, Philip of France, in order to persuade the cardinals, who for more than two years

[1] *Ad quos* (Simon and Guy) *restituendos ad carissimi in Christo filii nostri Edwardi Regis Angliae illustris gratiam, qua ipsos fertur eorum gravis culpa privasse, idem Henricus de voluntate memorati Siciliae ac cum mandato eiusdem Angliae Regum venerat*—(Bull of excommunication, 1 April, 1273, Rymer, I, ii. 501).

had been deliberating in the bishop's palace by the cathedral, to put an end to their bickering and elect a pope. The city was full; a meeting-ground of kings, princes, cardinals, with their households, and the army which St. Louis had gathered for his last crusade. The circumstances were sad and solemn. The death of the King of France on 25 August, 1270, had hastened the abandonment of the operations in Africa, and his son was bringing back his father's body to be buried in St. Denis. The remains of Philip's brother, the Count of Nevers, of his young wife, Isabella of Aragon, and of his brother-in-law, Theobald of Champagne, King of Navarre, were carried along with those of Saint Louis. The crusading host was a body of mourners in a travelling necropolis. And Guy de Montfort must needs break in to add yet another corpse.

5

For a time the fortunes of the house of Montfort were broken. Guy never recovered all the ground which he lost in one wild moment at Viterbo. Yet it is a mistake to suppose that he was a ruined man. Ten years later he seemed about to become as powerful as he had been in 1270. In 1281 he was restored to the favour and service of King Charles; in 1283 he command-ed the papal forces in Romagna; in 1284, on the death of the red count, he returned to secure his wife's inheritance against the attacks of her relations and neighbours; in 1285–6 he was again the champion of the Guelf league. He was then in the prime of life, about 44 years of age, the lord of widespread estates, and one of the best known captains of his time. Those of my readers who study Dante may like to remember that Guy de Montfort in 1283 fought successfully against the famous Guido de Montefeltro, and in 1285 by the side of Corso Donati. Then in 1287 the end came. Charles of Anjou was dead; his successor, Charles of Salerno, was a prisoner in

Spain. The regent of the kingdom of Naples, Robert of Artois, and John de Montfort, the captain of the forces, summoned Guy to organize resistance to the house of Aragon. Guy collected a fleet for an attack upon the rebellious Sicilians. But the Angevin fleet was broken in the Bay of Naples by Roger Loria, the ablest admiral of his day (June 1287), and Guy de Montfort passed the rest of his life as a captive in a Sicilian fortress.

The last twenty years of Guy's life (1271–91) are, indeed, very interesting. It would need another essay to describe his excommunication by Pope Gregory, his relations with the unbending Edward of England and with his friends, Charles of Salerno (King Charles II of Naples) and John de Montfort, the astonishing story of his wife and what is known about his little daughters, Thomasia and Anastasia, also about his brother Amaury and his sister Eleanor, the wife of Llywelyn of Wales. Here my object has been to show that, so far from being penniless refugees, the family of Simon de Montfort played no small part in European affairs, and that one of them very nearly gained a permanent place in history, as one of the founders of a new Italy.

Additional Note

Guy de Montfort's fiefs in the Kingdom of Naples spread from Arienzo to Atripalda. They protected the city of Naples in the direction of Benevento. The most easterly, Atripalda near to Simon de Montfort's fief of Avellino, lies about half-way between Benevento and Salerno; it formed a group with Monteforte, the old Norman barony from which Guy, by what was perhaps a deliberate coincidence, had his title of count, and Forino. Nola, which had been one of the centres of resistance to Charles of Anjou, formed part of a middle group, composed of Cicala, Somma, Palma, Ottaiano and other places, backed in the south by Mount Vesuvius. To the west Acerra and Arienzo lie on the road to Benevento through the Valle Caudina.

Guy was deprived of his lands on the day of the murder at Viterbo, 13 March, 1271. It is not yet certain when they were restored to him. Some of them were certainly administered, during Guy's captivity (from June, 1287), by *procuratores*, on behalf of Guy or his daughter, Anastasia, the wife (1293) of Romanello, son of Gentile Orsini. On 28 October, 1293, Anastasia was restored to Nola, Cicala, Atripalda, Forino, and Monteforte. On 27 May, 1294, a royal *privilegium* definitely granting them to Romanello was issued.

The detailed history of the conquest of Naples by Charles of Anjou and of the distribution of lands has not yet been written. Miss Evelyn Jamison has very kindly called my attention to some of the numerous preliminary studies which have appeared in local periodicals and which supplement the more general work done by G. Del Giudice, B. Capasso, Minieri-Riccio and others upon the registers of the Angevin kings.

V

THE ORIGINS OF FRANCE[1]

Shortly before the war of 1870, when he was still a student, Monsieur Jacques Flach chose as his life work the history of French law. The ambitious plan was soon modified, but, in its new form, has been none the less the chief task of M. Flach's life. When he succeeded his master, Laboulaye, as professor of comparative legislation at the Collège de France he had already convinced himself that a knowledge of the history of the tenth and eleventh centuries was the key to a right understanding of his subject, and especially to the comprehension of French legal history. Accordingly, he read without faltering, between the years 1872 and 1883, all the original documents, dating from these two centuries, upon which he could lay his hands. He ransacked the archives in the search for cartularies and the lives of saints. The first volume of his *Origines de l'ancienne France* appeared in 1886. It contains a plan of the whole work, and also a summary of the general conclusions at which M. Flach had already arrived, and which he proposed to display in the six or seven volumes still to come. He has kept his plan in mind ever since, and in the preface to his fourth volume, written thirty-one years later, he claims that, after labours pursued throughout a generation memorable in the record of

[1]This paper first appeared in *History*, iii. 129–136, 193–204 (October, 1918 and January, 1919). As a contribution to a great subject it is of little value. It dates. I reprint it here as a critical study in historiography which may interest those who would like to picture the state of learning at the end of the first world war. M. Flach's book was the medium through which I returned to the study of history during my fourth year in the civil service.

French scholarship, he sees no reason to change his earlier opinions.[1]

M. Flach describes his fourth volume as the centre of his work, "the nave of the building." Its publication, therefore, affords a fitting opportunity for a brief appreciation of a noteworthy achievement.

I

M. Flach takes a great deal of trouble to make his theme intelligible. He defines his position at every turn. His style possesses clearness and force. Yet his book is not an easy one. The truth in these matters is, of course, not easy. At the period in their national development when, to adapt a saying of Coleridge, men were more than usually in the dark about themselves, we are unlikely to find their history neat and systematic. At the same time the difficulties of M. Flach's readers are not due altogether to his admirable determination to let the facts speak for themselves. In the course of a generation his method has naturally been altered. The aim and conclusions are the same, but the emphasis is different. The first volume was a treatise, rather in the manner of Maine, upon the various forms of early medieval protection—the *mundium*, the vassal relation, forms of personal jurisdiction. The fourth volume is a piece of pure historical criticism. Again, the point of view changes with the passage from one influence to another. Thus, in the first volume, where M. Flach relied mainly on capitularies and charters, the stress is laid on protection, while in the later part of the second volume, under the influence of the *chansons de geste*, the stress is all on companionship. The book has been written in very different

[1] "*Les Origines de l'ancienne France Xe et XIe siècles*". Volume IV.: *Les Nationalités régionales. Leurs rapports avec le Couronne de France. Par Jacques Flach*. Paris, Librairie de la Société du Recueil Sirey, 1917. The three preceding volumes appeared in 1886, 1893, 1904 respectively.

moods. And, yet again, as the evidence has accumulated, the work has somewhat outgrown its earlier form. M. Flach tries at times to maintain the legal note, to arrange and interpret the evidence in accordance with the earlier mood, but the details do not readily submit. The old formulas seem somehow less satisfactory.

In M. Flach's devotion to his main theme there is no hesitation, no inconsistency. Throughout he is seeking to explain a living society.

> *Chercher au premier moyen-âge un système absolu, un système juridique, c'est chercher la quadrature du cercle. Les seuls principes généraux qui se dégagent sont des principes d'ordre naturel, tels, notamment, que le besoin de protection avec ses ramifications infinies, tels encore que l'instinct de sociabilité qui se fait jour dans l'organisation féodale et communale, tels enfin que les aspirations religieuses qui feront de l'Église un centre si puissant de renaissance.* (ii. 3).

The influences of geography and race are of extraordinary interest and importance, and M. Flach, particularly in his fourth volume, devotes to them many of his best pages, but he subordinates them all to the force of those impulses which compel men to express their relations to each other in legal forms: the desire of the weak for help, the sense of companionship which both underlies and transfigures the sense of obligation, and, giving direction to these, the urgent force of tradition, of the complex of memories and associations, which are themselves the outcome of early companionships. The empire of Charles the Great itself was a fusion of Roman, Gallic, and Frankish traditions. It expressed the undying sense of the unity of Gaul, without which it could not have existed, and its traditions in their turn shaped the growth of modern France:

> *Des figures presque surhumaines, comme celles d'Alexandre, de Charlemagne, de Napoléon, creusent dans l'âme des peuples un sillon que rien n'effacera plus et y déposent des semences indestructibles.*

Alors même que la féodalité eut mis l'État en pièces, l'empreinte persista. Le prince et le seigneur apparurent comme des images réduites et subordonnées de la majesté royale, le compagnon ou le communier comme un concitoyen de l'ancien empire des Gaules. Et ainsi, du roi et du prince au peuple, à tous les degrés de l'échelle sociale, sous les formes infiniment variées de la fidélité, de la foi, l'idée unitaire et la conscience nationale se conservèrent dans leur germe et évoluèrent à travers tous les obstacles jusqu'au plein épanouissement (iv. 315).

In M. Flach's view the dissolution of Charles's empire involved no real breach with the past precisely because it was so complete. This paradox has perplexed many of his readers, and it must be admitted, is at times beyond its author's control. Although it would be hardly fair, one feels now and then that his view might almost be put in this way—that nothing artificial remained. During the tenth and eleventh centuries a new public law developed, the new counts and seigneurs translated their newly formed personal jurisdiction into a new kind of territorial rule within new boundaries. But the springs of this new society were essentially old. There is no break between the Germanic *comitatus* and the circle of vassals. The Gallo-Roman *villa* emerges from the harrow of new petty despotism as the medieval village community, or develops into the town[1]. Yet clearly this distinction between the natural and the artificial is not a sharp one, and in any case does not fit all the facts as described by M. Flach. If the area subject to the Carolingian count disappears, the office retains more than its title, and carries to the adventurer who assumes it something of its old dignity. The robber in his fastness, who styles himself *comes* and gives parcels of land to the devoted ruffians who serve him is a great deal more than a savage in a top hat. The dues which he exacts when he administers justice or

[1] ii., 64 *passim*. The first part of the second volume, on the growth of village and town communities, stands apart from the rest of the book, and deserves special attention.

makes the tour of his neighbourhood are perhaps new and
onerous, but many of them are called by old names, and have
a certain sanction in the traditions of Frankish statecraft.
Nature and art are inextricably combined. Indeed, M. Flach
allows great weight to the influence upon the new France of
the ancient artifices of royalty, of the complicated traditions
which had gathered about its religious character, and the
ceremonies of the Court. He probably exaggerates the importance of this element in the society of the tenth century.[1]
But, so far as it did continue to exist, it stamps that society as
self-conscious and sophisticated; it suggests a doubt whether
the dissolution of the Carolingian state had, after all, proceeded so very far.

Perhaps it is better to hold to the distinction between personal and territorial as the clue to the new age. For M. Flach's
point is that the feudalism of the law books, being essentially
territorial, and defining the functions of the state and of its
elements in terms of tenure, marks the close of a long period
of development. The principles of the feudal state—for
example, of the Latin kingdom of Jerusalem—were not
guiding principles, but attempts to formulate the experience of
centuries. Some writers speak of feudal relations as though
they were Kantian categories, existing in juridical thought
before feudal society itself, and the conditions of its being;
whereas it would be nearer the truth to say that they never
reached full expression, and, when the legists began to define
them, had already begun their transformation into the relations of the national state. The Master of Balliol[2] has shown
how, in a similar way, the Papal system had begun to break
under its own weight at the very time when that great
canonist, Innocent IV, was teaching Christendom to realize

[1]Halphen, in the *Revue Historique*, vol. lxxxv., (May–August, 1904), p. 283.
[2]A. L. Smith, *Church and State in the Middle Ages* (Oxford, 1913).

all that it involved. Or, to take a modern parallel, the "feudal system" of the thirteenth century may be compared with Blackstone's *Commentaries*, the classical exposition of a British Constitution which never existed. M. Flach will have none of this theorizing. He holds that the history of feudalism must be sought in the history of the men who made it, just as we study the history of the canon law in the lives of Gregory VII and Innocent III. It was the outcome of personal relations, and its logical expression in terms of tenure was only possible in a strong centralized state which, by its very nature, was more than feudal. France was not really feudalized until the reign of Philip Augustus, when France became fully conscious of herself as a national state.[1]

Hence it is impossible to separate the growth of feudalism from the story of painful social change in the tenth and eleventh centuries. Feudalism is no extension of the Salic law, much less the creation of a foreign aristocracy from the other side of the Rhine; it is the sum of the cravings, the traditions, and the loyalties of a much-divided people, Gallo-Roman, Burgundian, Frankish.

One such craving was the desire for justice. M. Flach believes that the "justice territorial" of feudalism was not the outcome of the judicial system of Carolingian times, not a shaking together, so to speak, of the authority of the count, the privileges of the immunist, and the judicial rights attaching to the ownership of land. The process was much more violent. There was a general dissolution of public justice, so that men turned from it to the protection of their more powerful neighbours. Hence justice became personal, a thing which could be bought and sold; the persons who exercised it could divide their rights and distribute them as though they were

[1]Among other passages, see iv., 108. For Flach, as for Freeman, the battle of Bouvines is one of the turning points in European history.

coin, by inheritance, concession, usurpation. In this uncertainty and agony the principle of territorial justice asserted itself. The need for order and security was satisfied by it. The multiplicity of judicial rights, and the endless variety of customary payments, with fragmentary survivals from earlier Frankish usage, became privileges of tenure—a crystallized medley which the feudalists afterwards tried to reduce to a system. For the historian they have a deeper significance. They show how institutions are formed from a few simple elements, indestructible, and combined in an infinite variety of ways:

> *Leur diversité nait de leur emploi. La science de l'histoire consiste à dégager ces éléments, à les isoler, et puis à les suivre dans leur combinaisons infinies. Leur essence reste indestructible, leurs propriétés changent et se renouvellent au gré des événements.* (i, 313).

The feudal tenures to which these judicial rights were attached and in part gave meaning were the outcome of personal relations of a still more intimate kind. Feudalism was made possible by personal loyalty. In his second volume, published in 1893, M. Flach made use of the *chansons de geste* to explain the reconstitution of society. The chivalry of a later date was the sap, not the flower, of feudalism, and can be traced in the devotion of the barbarian *comitatus*. Three years earlier, in 1890, Fustel de Coulanges had issued his volume on the origin of the feudal system, in which any connection between the fief and *le compagnonnage* was denied. The fief, in Fustel's view, is the benefice, a temporary grant of land; the feudal oath is the expression of a contract, military service only one of several incidents to tenure; there is no trace here of self-surrender, of devotion till death. Flach urges that this is to begin at the wrong end. Homage is essentially personal—it precedes the gift of the fief and issues from the oath of fidelity; the vassal enters a family, *la parenté fictive du chef;* his lands are gifts, just as his horse and arms, and are his so long as he remains in the *clientèle* of his lord; his military service is not limited, but is one of his duties to the family. Only gradually did the conception of homage become distinct from that of fealty and give rise to the limited feudal contract, largely under the influence of ecclesiastical tenures. All this is clear, if we go behind the charters which reveal only the mechanism of the fief and of its concession, and in the pages of the *chansons de geste* learn how the vassal lived and felt. Even in its classic period feudalism depended upon companionship, which survived in full vigour *comme un organe de vie du régime seigneurial*.

In obedience to what impulses did these family groups come to form principalities and states? In answering this question Flach explains the ruling idea of his thesis. Some scholars still hold the view that during the troubled period which preceded the firm establishment of the Capetian house the unity of the French monarchy was maintained by ties of homage. However feeble the royal power might be, the juridical nature of the relations existing between the sovereign and the dukes or counts who were his vassals was unchanged. [1] But if, as Flach contends, the feudal relation of lord and vassal was the last stage in a long process, and could be traced but rarely before the middle of the eleventh century [2], some other explanation must be found. Flach finds the answer in the formation of ethnic groups under the guidance of princes who, while politically independent, often belonged to the Carolingian family, and in any case felt that their well-being was bound up with that of a wider whole. In other words, a twofold body of tradition was powerfully at work in the west-

[1] Ferdinand Lot, *Fidèles ou Vassaux* (Paris, 1904). The publication of this important essay forced M. Flach to give a controversial character to his fourth volume.

[2] See especially iii., 87–99, and vol. iv., *passim*.

ern parts of the Frankish empire. The *mundium*, or extended family circle of relations, dependents, and officials of the old Frankish chiefs became the monarchy to which all men owed the duty of faithful service. It absorbed the traditions and ceremonial of the later Roman principate; and through the teaching of the Church was invested with the religious symbolism of kingship. After the division of the empire of Charles the Great, the monarchy, richly endowed though it was both in conception and for action, lost its power. But it never lost its hold upon the minds and hearts of men; indeed, it gained in spiritual content, for it was gradually recognized as the expression of the unity formed by the mingling on a common soil of Gallic, Roman, Frankish traditions. The *principes*, who brought order out of chaos in the great province of France, and slowly welded these "regional nationalities" into compact feudal states, sought and found prestige in their connection with the house of Charles the Great. They were peers, of whom the king was the first. But, on the other hand, they were far away, and these kings of a day were very weak. Except when they obeyed the call to join forces against an invader, they took their own course.

These developments are described at length in M. Flach's third and fourth volumes. M. Flach, needless to say, does not think that the strong national state which we find in France in the thirteenth century was the creation of family sentiment. The French monarchy was not a vague federation of feudal states subdued by the patriarchal principle. The lawyer, steeped in the Austinian tradition, may trace the modern doctrine of sovereignty in primitive ideas of patriarchal authority[1], but the historian cannot find it in the much more

[1] See the argument of the Lord Advocate on behalf of the Chartered Company's claim to the ownership of unalienated land in Southern Rhodesia. (*The Times*, 3 May, 1918): "These tribes, like most other savage tribes, had their social life organized on tribal principles, and at the root of it all was the patri-

sophisticated traditions of Frankish royalty. We have seen how M. Flach will have nothing to do with the juristic conceptions derived from the *feudistes* of the seventeenth and eighteenth centuries—that the growth of the Capetian monarchy was due to the extension of ties of homage. He elaborates the judgment already expressed by Guizot that the king was something more than any suzerain. Yet to identify the royal power with the authority of a vastly extended *mundium* would be a juristic generalization even more difficult to defend than that of the feudists. M. Flach finds the solution of the problem in the distinction between *Francia* and the rest of Gaul. Over Gaul as a whole the Carolingians could claim supremacy, over the lands of the Franks in Lorraine and the valleys of the Seine and Loire they could claim the oath of fealty—service of the most complete kind. The Capetian kings succeeded to this authority in western *Francia*. The source of their power lay, not in the office of *Dux Franciæ* (which was not, as the feudists thought, territorial), nor even in their lands in the Île de France, but in the fact that they controlled the most important "ethnic group" of all. However divided this group might be, no authority could be exercised in it which did not in the end rest in the king, the chief of the clan, the head of the *mundium*. This was no hard and fast sovereignty, but the expression of national unity. Added to the supremacy over all the princes of Gaul, invested with the trappings of Roman power and the sanction of the Church, and wielded by a succession of powerful men, such authority was irresistible.

archal system. The rights of the natives were rights of dependence, not of independence. Lobengula was the patriarch . . . and it was clear that Lobengula disposed of the use of the lands. If that was so they were a long way from anything in the nature of ownership. The power of Lobengula was destroyed, and with him the patriarch disappeared—nothing was left of the patriarchate, of the kingship, of the chiefship".

At the same time, other ethnic groups found unity and consciousness within the limits of Gaul. Their administrative forms became more complicated. Churches and monastic orders were founded, and avenues of trade were opened. Feudalism passed inevitably from the personal to the territorial stage; and became most marked and firmly knit when the power of the prince was greatest. In all these states the king had a footing, through the possession of lands or by reason of the close relations between the crown and the Church. The claim to supremacy was translated into a claim to feudal homage as the traditions of one regional nationality after another were merged in the sense of national unity. France became a single feudal state when she became a nation.

2

In his fourth and latest volume—the nave of the building—M. Flach has set himself a threefold task: (1) He seeks in the first place to elaborate his conception of ethnic groups, to analyse the formation and diverse characters of the regional nationalities through which the rich and varied culture of modern France was given expression. (2) Then he traces the relations between these groups and the crown, showing that they were bound to each other by the tie—not of feudal homage and service, but of the recognition of traditions common to them all as parts of the Gallo-Frankish Empire. (3) In the third place he is led to pay peculiar attention to the political communities which had comprised the kingdom of Lothair, and especially to Lorraine, the *Francia* whose capital was Metz; for these districts were divided and redivided between France and Germany. Were their ethnic affinities or preferences with east or west in the tenth century, with Aachen or Reims?

M. Flach, of course, does not treat his subject in this cut-and-dried way. He is an independent apostle of what, since he began to write, has come to be called the "regional survey", and no believer in the regional survey would adopt the scholastic method. The regional state is almost a living organism, whose essential attributes depend on each other and must be considered together. Rather unfortunately M. Flach overstates this part of his case, and distinguishes too little between the facts and the conclusions which he draws from them. He regards freedom from the tie of homage to an external authority as an attribute of the political life of a "regional nationality" in the tenth century; but it is doubtful if the significance of his description of provincial development is seriously affected by the question whether his views on homage are right or wrong. When the inevitable controversy on this matter has passed, the book will remain as the best—indeed, the only—connected survey of France during the tenth and eleventh centuries. One wishes that the historian had mastered the jurist earlier. Stimulating though the first three volumes are, one would gladly have had them compressed, if those which are yet to come, "devoted to the description of society under all its aspects, material and spiritual", were now in sight.

Ethnic groups must be carefully distinguished from racial groups. Previous writers have disputed about the *rôle* of *races* in the formation of France, and have overlooked the fact that man is subject to an evolution which is not biological. The student of racial characters considers man as a member of a zoological group, the student of ethnic groups considers him as a member of society. The ethnic group may contain various racial elements; its unity consists in community of language, customs, belief, traditional institutions. Such common characters distinguish Frankish Gaul, giving it a national unity denied to the rest of the Frankish settlements; such characters also distinguish the secondary or regional nationalities of which Frankish Gaul was composed, and whose political origins are studied in this latest volume. M. Flach, as one expects, lays stress upon the significance of common activities rather than upon geographical influences. He does not try to interpret regional characters in terms of soil, situation, climate; although he is far too keen a student of the new geography to overlook the co-operation of nature and history.[1] Take, for example, from the opening pages of the book the analysis of the growth of Flemish nationality:

> Point d'arrivée des grandes voies de commerce qui faisaient communiquer l'Italie et l'Allemagne avec la mer du Nord et que son trafic maritime prolongeait jusqu'en Angleterre, la Flandre maritime devint le noyau d'une nation de marchands et de marins, antagoniste de la société seigneuriale et féodale qui occupait la France, et rivale de la domination normande. Mais, ouverte à l'envahissement des flots de pirates nordiques, elle dut pourvoir à sa défense par des digues militaires, par une armature puissante. Ne cherchez pas ailleurs le trait distinctif de la nation qui éclôt et qui s'implante entre la Germanie et la France. Il est tout entier dans l'intensité de la vie municipale, que l'agriculture nourrit, que le commerce alimente et que le château fort sauvegarde.

And he proceeds to display the significance of this union of town and castle, the successors of Roman military stations and great Frankish abbeys. The fortresses were not merely lines of defence against invaders, they were like a coat of mail thrown over the country. The prince had the country in his hand. He took the lead in establishing the institutions of the peace and truce of God, and taught the peasantry to grow the vine. The national life of Flanders, *terra valde populosa*, was fostered by rulers, successors of the Baldwin endowed by Charles the

[1] M. Flach makes full use of the great work of M. Vidal de la Blache. The English reader will find an excellent "ethnic" survey of France in Professor Fleure's little book, *Human Geography in Western Europe* (London, 1918), p. 54 *seqq.*

Bald, whose independence was in turn maintained by a poor and half savage nobility, living on scattered farms, and by the communities of merchants and fisher folk, full of self determination, who lived under the walls of the *castella* on the river banks.

The history of Flanders is a comparatively well-worked field, and M. Flach is able to describe the relations of its counts with the crown against a background of more or less coherent detail. When he turns to the other provinces, he is confronted by a more tiresome task. The patient reader who accompanies him will find many a searching or vigorous page, many a pleasant resting place, in the course of an arduous journey. M. Flach's enthusiasm and keen sense of reality will save him from tediousness. But the road is undoubtedly gritty.

In later volumes the social conditions of the time will be examined generally; in this volume M. Flach tries to show how the various states were formed. Brittany, for example, was the outcome of a fusion, in the face of external peril, of two rival traditions—the Breton and the Gallo-Frank—of two houses, Nantes and Rennes. The political unity of Aquitaine was due, not to the gradual victory of Poitou over Auvergne, but to the existence both in Poitou and in Auvergne of a sense of a common Aquitanian life—a historical memory. In the resistance of Aquitaine to Pepin the Short's annual invasions (760–768) Auguste Molinier, "in spite of his habitual abstention from generalities", saw a proof of local unity and common aspirations. These never died away, and William V, the Great, who in the eleventh century had all the prestige of a king, was able to direct as Aquitanian movements the Peace of God, the revival of letters, and monastic reforms.

The workings of these regional impulses are everywhere obscure. Now and then a great man becomes real to us, as in the splendid pages upon Richard the Justiciar, the founder of the duchy of Burgundy (880–921). Very rarely, some gigantic and shadowy figure, otherwise no more than a name, starts into momentary life and blows his horn—[1]

non sonò si terribilmente Orlando.

But M. Flach's description is in the main technical rather than picturesque. It is an elaborately critical and argumentative study of the sources. The provincial groups are not capable of equal treatment, for the nature and extent of the available evidence varies from place to place, and from period to period. Moreover, at every turn M. Flach has to meet the contention, formulated at length by M. Ferdinand Lot in his essay *Fidèles ou Vassaux*, that these principalities were fiefs bound to the crown of France by ties of homage. M. Flach puts each bit of evidence, charter, chronicle, or life of saint, to one test—its value, namely, as a means to explain the precise nature of the relation in which a particular *princeps* stood to the person who happened at the moment to occupy the Carolingian throne. By this method he reflects, on the whole with success, the confusing variety and spontaneity of provincial society without losing sight of what he calls the dominants of French history. One does not feel so sure, however, that the result justifies another favourite idea of M. Flach's. He likens sound historical writing to the building of a medieval cathedral; every document—in however casual or haphazard a way it has chanced to survive—is a stone to be tested, shaped, and fitted into a definite place. This view, I fear, rests on a fallacy. All such work as this must give the impression rather of an excavation than of a cathedral. A few scattered pieces of workmanship and ordered lines of foundations are revealed *in*

---

[1] iv, 476. When Saint Pardoux was dying he heard, as though sounded by an archangel, the trumpet which Eudo of Aquitaine, the last independent duke of the eighth century, used to blow in summons to battle.

situ; the rest of the find is scientifically exposed in the local museum.

3

Since M. Flach began to write historical study in France has made great advances. There has been a busy and orderly revolution. How does *Les Origines de l'ancienne France* stand the test of the new learning?

In one sense the question may seem impertinent. M. Flach is one of the teachers of the new learning, and when he is not a teacher, he is an eager student. He has grown with it and keeps abreast of it. One can see, in this latest volume, how clearly the results of recent work are dovetailed into pages drafted some years ago. But on the other hand the outlook of 1918 is not that of 1870. If M. Flach were beginning his work now he would plan it differently. As the book stands, the emphasis differs in each volume, although the original plan is preserved.

Perhaps the change is most apparent in the attitude of French scholarship to Germany. M. Flach remembers 1870. He saw with his own eyes the destruction of the famous library at Strasbourg. Like so many of his fellow countrymen who followed Renan into the study of the *origins* of our civilization, he was determined that Frenchmen should henceforward look at the facts for themselves, free from all prejudices or foreign generalizations. In a well-known essay published in the *Revue des deux Mondes* (May, 1872) Fustel de Coulanges challenged one such generalization—that the formative element in French history was Teutonic. Flach attacked another side of the same problem, and, starting from what he considered to be the exaggerated significance of Salic law, investigated the legal and social origins of feudalism. He set himself against the orthodox view that feudalism came from Germany[1]. But since 1870 the Franco-German problem has naturally changed. To the best minds it has, of course, always been a scientific problem. Hard work, Renan had said[2], would be the salvation of France, the hard work of minds hardened by a new and stimulating scepticism. As time went on and the results of scientific work began to have effect, new issues arose. On the old field much which had been debatable became common ground. Nobody believes now that feudalism came from Germany, or that Roman and Gallic elements did not contribute to the life of modern France. Before 1870 two or three German scholars of singular greatness, such as Rudolf Sohm, had in several ways modified the current view. French and German scholars have worked together on the influence of Roman law, the significance of the immunity, the origin of towns, and a dozen other problems common to the history of all parts of the Carolingian empire. Then new ground was contested and, if German thought has been blighted by the conception of race, French scholars have, sometimes too eagerly, turned the tables on their adversaries and tried to show that medieval Germany owned its inspiration to France[3]. In architecture, poetry, chivalry, learning, political thought, France gave more than she received. Now, if M. Flach's last volume, revised since the war began, be compared with the preceding, I think that a certain sense of strain, due to this change in the Franco-German problem, can be traced. In the early volumes the stress was laid upon the continuity, under new and powerful influences, it is true, of the royal

[1] For this view Duruy's *History of France* might be cited.

[2] See the interesting recollections of Mrs. Humphry Ward in the *Cornhill Magazine*, April, 1918.

[3] Reynaud, *Les Origines de l'influence française en Allemagne* (Paris, 1913). In his delightful essay, *L'art allemand et l'art française du moyen âge* (1917), M. Emile Mâle quotes some astonishing arguments of a racial kind from German scholars, *e.g.*, pp. 111-2.

mundium, the Teutonic *comitatus*, the Frankish ethnic group which lived along the valleys of the Seine and the Loire. These forces, as we have seen, were transformed on French soil, but they were links between the Teutonic invasions and the Capetian monarchy as well as the formative elements in feudal society. In the fourth volume the stress is rather upon the cultural affinities which bound together the peoples west of the Rhine in opposition to the barbarians of the east. The traditions of the Carolingian empire are allowed no influence among the eastern Franks. The Carolingian dynasty is claimed as essentially Gallo-Frank. Charles, by descent, physique, interests, is discovered to have been as much a Celt as a Frank.

Although M. Flach does not always remember his own warnings against the argument from race, and has expressed his views with an anti-German emphasis which would not have appeared in times of peace[1], this extension of his argument was well worth making. But I doubt if the application of his thesis to the history of Lorraine will find acceptance. The relations between Lorraine and the other Frankish lands should be considered from the standpoint of fact rather than of right. In civilization, language, outlook, the kingdom was in no sense German, and always retained its individuality so long as it remained part of the medieval empire. The evidence for this view may be found in the excellent books of M. Parisot. "Lotharingia" was more than *Francia media;* it could be described simply as *Francia*, as distinct from *Gallia Celtica* or *Germania*[2]. Scholars have noted in the letters of Gerbert, and in the annals or hagiographies of the tenth century, a distinct

[1]Thus he argues that Charles the Great was brachycephalic (iv. 314, note 3), and finds in Otto the Great the qualities of modern Prussian militarism (p. 396).

[2]Wilmotte in the *Revue Historique* for January, 1918 (Vol. cxxvii., p. 10). Of course, *Francia* was also used of the lands west of the Rhine, as opposed to *Germania*, even in the tenth century.

almost conscious, mental attitude, which sharply separated the valley of the Moselle from the lands east of the Rhine. The final answer to modern German pretensions to Lorraine is that, after the union of Alsace and Lorraine with France seven or eight centuries later, this provincial temper responded to that of France, so that sympathy combined with statesmanship to form an indissoluble sense of unity. Now M. Flach reads that later sense of unity into the records of the tenth century and also seeks to give a *juridical* value to the facts. He has no difficulty in showing that the claims of modern German writers are unfounded, and that the later Carolingian and early Capetian kings of France tried with more or less success to get recognition in Lorraine. But his counterclaim that the chief men of Lorraine definitely preferred union with the West Franks will be found to rest upon a very slight foundation. Indeed, it rests at bottom, not upon any demonstration of national preference, but upon the dogma of Carolingian rights. Thus, after repeating his view that the rights of the Carolingians passed to the Capetians, he argues that, even if they did not, the *suprématie franque* was unaffected :

> *Elle (i.e., la suprématie) n'était pas attachée à une dynastie, mais au* regnum Francorum. *Supposez que la Lorraine fût restée un tel royaume, fût restée une France, et que le royaume de France occidentale eût disparu (absorbé, par exemple, par les Normands), c'est le roi de Lorraine qui aurait hérité de la suprématie sur la Gaule. Si, d'autre part, la Lorraine a cessé d'être une France, elle n'a pas cessé d'être une entité ethnique sur laquelle les droits du* rex Francorum *ont survécu* (iv, 289).

The same scholastic note disturbs what is, perhaps, the finest part of the book—the analysis of Burgundian history. M. Réné Pourpardin has prepared the way here, as M. Parisot has done in Lorraine, but as English scholars have helped to show[1], much good work still remains to be done. M. Flach's analysis is hard reading, but a student who had refreshed his memory of a certain appendix in Lord Bryce's *Holy Roman Empire* and had armed himself with a good atlas, would find it very interesting. M. Flach shows how Roman culture remained as the roots of social life in the valleys of the Rhone and the Saone and how the brilliant renaissance of Burgundy was directed by the great abbey of Luxeuil and afterwards by Cluny. The geographical structure of the country made political unity impossible for any length of time, and M. Flach describes the formation of the future duchy as a distinct entity around the dominating centre Autun, "the Celtic Rome". Richard the Justiciar, the founder of the duchy, was connected with the Carolingian dynasty, and had both great wealth and great military prestige. Similarly, the county of Besançon, which ultimately became the Free County of Burgundy, was separated from Jurane Burgundy, and its count, who was a son of Richard the Justiciar, refused to recognize the claims maintained by the Saxon emperors. So Jurane Burgundy, the kingdom of the Rudolfs, fell apart. The Transjurane state, Burgundy proper where Saint Sigismond in 521 had founded the abbey of Saint Maurice of Agaune, the home of the sacred lance, was united to Provence and the march of Vienne, as a result of events which form part of the history of Italy. It was this extended kingdom of Burgundy, wrongly called by historians the kingdom of Arles, upon which the Saxon and Salian Emperors set their ambitions. M. Flach investigates these developments with great wealth of detail. He destroys the structure erected by German scholars on the Rudolfine sur-

---

[1] See Dr. R. L. Poole's "Burgundian Notes" in the *English Historical Review* for 1911 and 1916, and Professor Previté Orton's paper on Italy and Provence (900–950) in the same *Review* (April, 1917).

renders and the alleged donation to Otto the Great of the sacred lance of St. Maurice[1]. He shows that, so far as opinion was expressed in annals and prophesy, it was definitely against the emperors. His examination of the charters proves that the mention of the reigning emperor in the date had no real significance. In short, the German element had no influence in Burgundy, which gradually fell apart into its constituent elements. All this M. Flach shows admirably; but his constructive argument in favour of French supremacy is not so convincing. Again he falls back upon "juridical consolidation".

There is, indeed, a curious dualism about the book. M. Flach has done as much as anyone to show us the danger of generalities as inconsistent with a clear-sighted investigation of facts in all their natural variety. It will, I think, be impossible to maintain any longer M. Lot's thesis that the provincial states were great *fiefs* in the tenth and eleventh centuries. M. Flach's demonstration of their haphazard relations with the crown is complete. He proves clearly from his amazing knowledge of local charters that there was no hierarchy in France. Nothing can be made of the use of such terms as *marchio, princeps, dux, comes*, etc[2]. I think, also, that he shows, if less clearly yet sufficiently, that the unity of France grew from and with the growth of organized regional states conscious of common traditions. The issue between M. Lot and M. Flach reminds one of the old legal discussion whether religion holds society together by the administration of oaths or because it contains the most powerful sanction for good conduct. M. Lot thinks that the tie of homage kept France together, M. Flach insists that it was something much deeper and less definite. So far one agrees with M. Flach. But, beside

[1] iv. 368, 408 *seqq*. The misconception is originally due to Leibniz.
[2] pp. 247-8, 338-341, 508-9.

this stream of thought, we find in his book a persistent strain-
ing after formulæ—a sort of juristic simplification. If a great
man was astute enough to claim relationship with the Carolingian house, or strong enough to gather together broad
lordships, we are invited to watch the *personal* or the *domainial*
factors in sovereignty. When, in a fit of energy, a king asserts
a successful claim to supremacy, we hear the word "consolidation". This is what the critics mean who say, very unfairly,
that what is new in M. Flach is not true, and what is true is not
new. There is a great deal that is both new and true. No one
else, for example, has got so much matter from the saint's
lives, and, as M. Flach justly claims, he was one of the first to
study the *chansons de geste* as historical documents. But it is just
to say that as the years have gone by French scholarship as a
whole has caught M. Flach up, and in many ways modified, or
even anticipated, his conclusions; also, that his work is least
convincing when he clings to his formulas.

A few examples will suffice. M. Flach has shown that an
ordered feudal system was of very slow growth, and that
feudal homage is rarely found before the eleventh century.
Luchaire and other writers are inclined to agree. But he
refuses to recognize any instance whatever of a vassal relation
between the crown and a regional prince before the second
half of the twelfth century. This is not so certain; for the texts
are very obscure, and M. Flach has to depend upon a hard
and fast interpretation of phrases (*e.g.*, *se committere*), which
he cannot always maintain[1]. Moreover, as we learn more
about early feudalism, we are faced by several objections to
the view that it developed from a society which was first

[1] See an important review of Flach's fourth volume by Louis Halphen in
the *Revue Historique*. cxxix. 90–96. This appeared while the present paper was
in the course of publication (1918).

broken up and then reconstructed on the basis of comrade-
ship. If we work backwards from the twelfth century, as M.
Halphen has done for Anjou, or Professor Haskins for
Normandy, we find that strictly feudal institutions, such as
the knight's fee and the service limited to forty days, can be
traced back almost to the tenth century. Or if we work for-
wards from the days of Charles the Great or Louis the Pious,
or even from the Merovingian period, we find that there was
more continuity than M. Flach seems to allow. Of course, if
the system of Charles the Great had been as ironcast in its
consistency as the prevailing school of thought imagines, then
the disintegration which followed it would doubtless have
been complete. But it is far more likely that the growth of law
and custom and of tenurial arrangements was continuous,
and that the organic diversity, so emphasized by M. Flach,
existed in Merovingian times[1]. That there was a period of disintegration may be granted, but that the feudalism which
emerged from it was the expression of new personal relationships, judicial, administrative, and military, is improbable.
Earlier legal fictions and immunities carried over into the
new order old territorial relations. M. Flach must compromise with that fine scholar, Guérard, who wrote *ce qui
forme la base de la société féodale, c'est la terre.*[2]

If this be so, it is unnecessary to find a base for the
Frankish monarchy in a hypothetical ethnic group, a *Francia*

[1] The best survey and criticism of the extensive literature on this subject is
Die Wirtschaftsentwicklung der Karolingerzeit, by Professor Alfons Dopsch, of
Vienna. This work was published in Weimar (1912–13) in two volumes.
Dopsch's main contention is that the prevailing view, of which von Inama
Sternegg was the chief exponent, is based upon a false interpretation of both the
nature and contents of the evidence, particularly of the *Capitulaire de Villis.*
There was no conscious striving after a systematic organization of the *Grundherr-
schaft* in early Carolingian times.

[2] Guérard's view is repudiated by Flach, ii. 427.

of the Seine and the Loire[1]. The monarchy had its roots all over France, broken and disturbed, no doubt, but not all dead. And, although M. Flach is surely right to insist upon the importance of personal ties, scholars would now hesitate to see the Teutonic *comitatus* in the feudal *maisnie* of the epics. A great deal more is known both about the *chansons de geste* and about the conditions under which feudal companionships were formed than was known when M. Flach published his second volume. The *chansons de geste* reflect French society of the twelfth century, not of the tenth. The feudal brotherhoods of the crusading age were a *renaissance*, like the chivalry of the fourteenth century, not a survival[2]. No doubt they can be traced in the tenth century, as they can in all times when war and adventure go together beyond considerations of the state. But they have to be fitted into a more of less ordered and sophisticated society. The more we know about western society in the tenth and eleventh centuries, of its thought, its architecture, of the activity of its monastic life, the less does this period appear as a chaotic breach in European history.

4

M. Flach stands somewhat apart from his contemporaries. He belongs, it is true, to that group of French masters who rescued scholarship from the asphyxiating influence of the Second Empire, and are a link between the labours of Renan and Michelet and the brilliant work of the École des Chartes and the École des Hautes Études. But since 1870 he has been engaged in a great adventure, the study and teaching of com-

[1]M. Louis Halphen has argued forcibly that, among the many meanings of *Francia*, this one, to which Flach attaches most importance, is unhistorical (*Revue Historique*, lxxxv. 275).

[2]The four volumes of Bédier's *Legendes Epiques* mark an epoch in the study of the *chansons de geste*.

parative legislation, a subject which is ancient, medieval, and modern, Asiatic, American, European. Between 1870 and 1886 M. Flach published a historical study upon minority, a study upon the administration of mines in the first century of our era, various essays upon Irish agrarian and political history, including an appreciation of Jonathan Swift's labours on behalf of Ireland, an essay upon Cujas and the Bartolists, and several works upon problems of Roman law[1]. The only publication bearing directly upon the work which was absorbing most of his time was his *Notes et documents sur l'origine des redevances et services coutumiers au XIe siècle* (1883)[2]. As the years passed, the interests of comparative legislation far exceeded the traditional developments of Roman or of feudal law. They embraced the excavations in Mesopotamia and Asia Minor, the intricate growth of modern political communities with their imperial and domestic obligations, and the new contact of eastern and western civilizations. Hence, M. Flach tells us, the delay in the publication of the fourth volume of *Les Origines* is mainly due to the discovery of the Code of Hammourabi and to the rise of Japan, events regarding which his pen has not been idle.

These preoccupations help to explain the detachment of M. Flach. They also account, I think, for the fact that *Les Origines de l'ancienne France* cannot be described as great, or epoch-making or classic. It is not sufficiently coherent and

[1] Between 1886 and the publication of the second volume of *Les Origines* (1893), M. Flach went still further afield and published writing upon the origins of the Holy Alliance, Mirabeau, and the truth in art and history.

[2] Other works of later date supplementary to the main theme are his *Études critiques sur l'histoire du droit romain au moyen âge avec textes inédites* (1890) and *L'origine historique de l'habitation et des lieux habités en France* (1899). His recent writing upon mediæval Alsace, and the tenth-century Latin poem, *Waltharius* though bearing upon the subject of his fourth volume, are inspired by French national claims.

definitive. Future scholars will not build upon it, as they will build upon the work of Julien Havet and August Longnon, of Delisle and Duchesne. But it will remain as one of the most suggestive books of our time.

VI

ENGLAND AND EUROPE IN THE THIRTEENTH CENTURY[1]

The subject which I have suggested for your consideration today was suggested with a light heart. How could the purpose of these conferences—the comparative study of medieval developments in social life—better be met than by some reflections on England and her place in Europe during the century which, I imagine, we all feel to be medieval as no other time—not even the more vigorous and formative century which preceded it—is medieval? The subject seemed indeed to suggest itself. But, when I came to think about it, I soon began to feel hesitation and perplexity. I could only ask questions to which I did not know the answers. This has always, I suppose, been my subject. I have regarded all my other wanderings into the past as preliminary to it. Yet I can only ask questions, born of impressions, not of knowledge.

England seems to me to have settled down during the reigns of Henry III and his son. In these ninety years, England lived as she lived in the reigns of Elizabeth and Victoria, and between the War of the Spanish Succession and the French Revolution. By "settling down" I do not mean that the course of general life went on quietly beneath the turmoil on the surface, nor do I mean even that the country, in the process of its natural everyday life, adjusted itself, sometimes

[1]A paper delivered at the Harvard Tercentenary Conference of Arts and Sciences, September, 1936; reprinted from the tercentenary volume entitled "Independence, converging and borrowing in institutions, thought and art," (Harvard University Press, 1937).

unconsciously, sometimes deliberately, to changes or developments regarded as necessary to its well-being. Those definitions would be equally true of the fourteenth and fifteenth centuries, perhaps of all un-revolutionary periods in all changing and civilized communities. I mean something more than that. I mean that England was able to cope with herself. Of course, when we set side by side the England of Henry III and Edward I, and the England of Elizabeth or Victoria or Walpole and Chatham, we mean to suggest a common quality in very disparate material, not in the same England, and I must not forget that you in Massachusetts may be inclined to dispute the existence of a quality common to the England of Burleigh or Palmerston and the England of Lord North. Yet, with due recognition of these considerations, I confess to this first and, if it is true, all-important impression. Is it the case that England in the thirteenth century coped with herself as she did not cope with herself while she became a parliamentary country in the two following centuries or during the great social and religious disputes which divided her under the early Tudors and in the days of the Stuarts and in our own times? And, if we were tentatively to admit the truth of this impression, how did the truth emerge from or affect England's position in Europe?

In recent years the interest and significance of the history of England in the period between the death of Edward I and the Reformation have gradually been realized. American scholars, especially in the fields of administration and literary history, have helped to lead the way. It is my duty, speaking in this place, to give my testimony to the work of C. H. McIlwain and T. F. Plucknett, who once was here; and all of us are united in gratitude to that happy and gallant scholar, the late James F. Willard. In England, at the present time, much of the most vigorous and revealing work in history is concerned with this period. If I draw a distinction between it and the thirteenth century, I do not do so from a lazy acceptance of traditional preferences. Each is as important, as fruitful, as the other; and, further, each is as informed by intelligence as the other. When I confess to an impression that England in the earlier period coped with herself more successfully than she did in the later period, I mean that the *tempo* is more even, that the measure of agreement was greater, that the issues were simpler and more clearly defined, that the response to fresh influences or new tasks was clearer and, if I may use the word, happier. In spite of its incoherencies, the period seems to possess a unity recognizable by our thought and feeling. It is easier to turn a page at the death of Edward I than at the death of his father, not because the death of Edward was a more dramatic event, but because Edward and his father and their companions seem to us to have so much in common.

If we are to avoid misunderstanding and to try to discover together if there is any justification for this impression, we must keep clear of generalizations about the spirit of the thirteenth century and of mystical talk about architecture and art as expressions of the soul of the age. Personally I feel that the emotional response which many of us probably feel to the life of western Europe about the year 1250 is harmonious; that the personalities of St. Louis and his great contemporaries, with the achievements of the scholars, builders, craftsmen, and poets, have a quality in common; but Heaven forbid that I should try to analyse this feeling. In any helpful sense of the word, it has no *meaning*. It is the flower, not the root, of our investigation into the past. Like a piece of music it speaks no language but its own. Impressions have no value for anybody save ourselves if we cannot give a reasonable explanation of them.

In the first place, I would suggest that the level of public service in England during the reigns of Henry III and Edward I was unusually high. Public men were intelligent and not so distracted as their predecessors had been by the association of England with other large and important fiefs. There were intransigeants, like Fawkes de Breauté, and there were groups of self-seeking men; but, during the period as a whole, the attempt to maintain a high standard is remarkably consistent. One illustration of this fact is the difficulty which we experience in visualizing the bad government of which the barons complained so bitterly in the years before 1258 and in 1258, or in estimating the change which the energy of Hugh Bigod and his colleagues effected. The evidence which Professor Treharne has sifted with such care seems to me to testify, not to any peculiar enormity, but to the persistence with which abuses were investigated. Moreover, as the researches of Professor Cam and Dr. Jacob have shown, the tradition of investigation was continuous during the last half of the thirteenth century. Before the baronial crisis began in 1258, and for several decades after it came to an end, sworn enquiries, followed by judicial proceedings and legislation, were the usual means of controlling local and judicial administration. They had precedents in earlier times and in some respects corresponded to the procedure in ecclesiastical visitations; in the period now under our view they were the expression of political concern for the maintenance of the public well-being.

If, starting from this point, we go on to enquire how and by whom this concern for the public well-being was maintained, we find some very interesting data. The main facts are well known, but their significance is not always appreciated. With some risk of exaggeration, they may be summed up in the phrase that, for the first time in English history, we seem to be living in a period of political programmes, or perhaps I should say (since the word "programme" suggests long views) of sustained political reflection. We have advanced beyond the treaties for the public welfare, of which the agreement between the earls of Chester and Leicester in Stephen's reign is the best known, and the bureaucratic contrivances of Henry II and his advisers, and even the struggle for the Great Charter. These were more important, no doubt, and made advance possible, but they were transacted in a different atmosphere. Their later thirteenth-century parallels, such as the agreements into which Simon de Montfort, Gilbert of Clare, the Lord Edward and Richard of Cornwall, and others entered from time to time, the household management of Edward I, and the rebellious movements of 1263 and 1297, fit into a more intricate and better established framework of public service. It is easy enough to point out the defects in this system—the opportunities which it gave to graft and cruelty, the cumbrousness of it all, and so on—but the remarkable thing is that it existed, existed continuously, and was accepted by all sorts of men, just as we accept, however much we may wish to improve, our own institutions. At one end of the system were those local gentry who had learned, to use Professor A. B. White's phrase, "self-government at the king's command". At the other end was the king himself, and in between were all the elements reflected for us in the treatise of Bracton. After the separation of England and Normandy, political reflection was more purposeful, and therefore more constant, directed to the maintenance of interests which were not incompatible in the eyes of intelligent men because they were all capable of subordination to the interest of the *regnum Angliae*. I am inclined to give the credit for the realization of this to the little group of bishops—men trained either in the schools or in the royal administration—who helped to

119

maintain the crown during Henry III's minority. These men
corrected the one-sided rivalries of the great ministers and the
great families. The practice of episcopal and baronial co-
operation in the royal service was not a brief experiment,
but, as a characteristic of the thirteenth century, was the
natural outcome of the controversy with St. Thomas of
Canterbury, of the Great Charter and the Charter of John in
favour of the Church, and of the close relations which existed
in this time between the Crown and the Papacy. For the first
time the hierarchy was knit together under the leadership of
men like Langton and St. Edmund and Pecham, who regarded themselves as successors of St. Thomas, while on the
other hand the organization of the Church of England was
not yet the expression of an "estate" whose interests could be
regarded by itself and others as distinct from the general
interest. Archbishop Stratford, in the fourteenth century—
not civil servants like William of Wykeham or primates like
Arundel—was, for a brief time, the counterpart to Langton
and Boniface of Savoy and Pecham. These men were both
intimately related to the general life and had something big to
contribute. Moreover, in England as in other lands, the Franciscans and Dominicans, in their first freshness and vigour,
profoundly affected the temper of the court and the transaction of public affairs. Agnellus of Pisa, the first provincial of
the Grey Friars, died on a mission of political reconciliation.
John of Darlington, the king's Dominican confessor, lived
and worked at the centre of political discussion. Odo Rigaud,
the famous Franciscan archbishop of Rouen, came over to
England in 1260 to make peace between Simon de Montfort
and the court. Archbishop Pecham, another Franciscan,
sought to find a *modus vivendi* between Edward I and Llewelyn
of Wales. And what would we not give for a full explanation
of those mysterious passages in the letters of Adam Marsh, the

Oxford Franciscan, about Adam's experiences at court and his heart-to-heart talks with the king and queen on the one hand, and with the earl and countess of Leicester on the other, and about the plans of reform which Earl Simon had worked out under the influence of Robert Grosseteste, the great bishop of Lincoln? To use a favourite word of the German historians, the co-operation of lay and ecclesiastical minds in affairs of state was, in the broadest sense of the term, more "genial" in this period than in any period of English medieval history since the days of Lanfranc: it was less encumbered by inhibitions, was more natural and intimate, more frankly aware of deep differences of principle, than it was ever to be again.

Now I think that, when we turn to consider the lay elements in English society, we can find indications that they were affected, if not by clerical influence, by the influences which co-operation with the clergy transmitted. The layman at his best is described for us in the life of William the Marshal, the adventurer turned statesman, who believed in the life that he had lived and made others believe in his fitness for the life to come. One day in 1219, when the great earl lay dying at Caversham, one of his knights asked the question, could a man be saved who had not returned all his spoils in armour, horses, and ransoms. "Henry", replied the earl, "listen to me awhile. The clerks are too hard on us. They shave us too closely. I have captured five hundred knights, and have appropriated their arms, horses, and entire equipment, If for this reason the kingdom of God is closed to me, I can do no more for God than to give myself to Him, repenting all my sins. Unless the clergy desire my damnation, they must ask no more. But their teaching is false—else no one could be saved". The master of the Temple had already shown that, in his eyes, William was safe. When the dying man was admitted to the Order, the master addressed him thus: "Marshal, attend. It pleases me that you give yourself to God. He has granted you a great favour—that you will never be separated from Him. He has shown you this in your life, and He will do the same after your death. In the world you have had more honour than any other knight for prowess, wisdom, and loyalty. When God granted you His grace to this extent, you may be sure that He wished to have you at the end. You have been a gentleman, and you die one".[1]

It was Christian gentlemen of this type, men of prowess, wisdom, and loyalty, whom a generation later Matthew Paris regarded as the mainstay of the realm. Like many critical observers of their own age, he was convinced that they were dying out and had no successors. We can take a more charitable view without shutting our eyes to the defects of the men who imposed their counsel on Henry III and shared the confidence of his son. However degenerate they may have been, they do seem to have inherited a conception of the political system which, though simple enough and indeed implicit in the career of the Marshal, finds no expression in the Marshal's biography. This conception is summed up in the phrase *communitas regni*. King, magnates, judges, knights had now one common concern. They lived together in a small but prosperous land. They moved daily among men to whose minds the debates in the schools, the problems created by the union of local ecclesiastical traditions under a common head, the call of St. Francis and St. Dominic to new forms of Christian duty, still appealed with their first freshness and promise. And so they came to look upon England as a whole and were conscious of some form of general will which could be expressed by the whole body of responsible men summoned together to discuss the affairs of the realm—the body described as the *communitas regni*. In its well-known letter of 1258 about the

[1] I have adopted Mr. Painter's English version.

Poitevin relatives of the king "the community of earls, magnates and others of the realm of England" tell Pope Alexander IV that King Henry has submitted himself to the counsel of the magnates, "without whom he was unable to govern his kingdom". The republic is a body, whose members must be knit together; it grows by the benefit of God's working, is moved by the decision of the highest equity, and is ruled by the moderating guidance of reason. Even if the king and the greater men did not, the community of the realm would insist on the removal of the young bishop-elect of Winchester. Doctrine of this kind had long been familiar in the letters of ecclesiastics and the writings of political theorists; here it is found in a manifesto issued by the barons of England. The phrasing was doubtless due to clerks—it is worth noting that one of the clerks of the earl of Gloucester, John Sackville, had been a famous rector of the university of Paris—but the thought must have been approved by those who sent the letter. And the insistence upon deliberation and consent not as the outcome of individual right, but as implied by the nature of the realm, was henceforward to be a principle of English political life. It was simpler and wider than any theory of parliament, but it gave impetus to parliamentary institutions. Edward I accepted it as a matter of course[1]. It would be detrimental to the state of the kingdom—to that which gave the kingdom its meaning and validity—if decisions made by the king and his counsellors were not observed. The king himself was morally bound by these decisions. This suggests not a contractual but an organic conception of the realm. Bracton approaches the same idea when, in defending the principle of primogeniture and the indivisibility of earldoms and baronies, he observes that the realm is composed of earldoms and baronies. I wish to suggest that these simple but

[1] See above, p. 74

far-reaching statements should be allowed their full weight. They were intelligible to ordinary men; but if they are wrapped up in elaborate theories they are only too likely to be set on one side as the impractical or remote doctrines of the schools. The next step towards the divorce of theory from practice is a denial of any living principle in the development of parliamentary institutions. This in its turn leads to a separation between history and life, and so puts history at the mercy either of accident on the one hand or of impersonal evolution on the other. Reflection on English history seems on the contrary to confirm the position of Otto Hintze: the system of estates—variously described as the corporate state or as parliamentary institutions—emerged slowly from the feudal order only in the Christian lands of Western Europe. It assumed various forms but was the expression of a process of thought and experience common to these lands. This does not mean that it was in itself a Christian system but that it is found only in Christian countries, where its growth was strengthened and refined by thought and discussion informed by Christian experience. In France, with its highly provincial-ized life, its centralization was intermittent and on the whole strengthened the royal power; in Germany its diffusion helped to give emphasis to local bureaucratic states which could hold their own against the central power; in England—small, com-pact, centralized—it expressed the *communitas regni* under the direction of the crown, which could not be dissociated from the *communitas*. The parliaments of the fourteenth and fifteenth centuries had their roots in the *communitas* of the thirteenth, and the principle of their being is to be found in those simple conceptions which I have tried to illustrate. We may say, if we wish, that the history of the English parliament is bound up with the struggle for the Charters, or was a wider applica-tion of "self-government by the king's command", but we dare not say that it was inevitable or impersonal, and divorce it from the convictions of ordinary men and women, for these convictions gave it life.

In the letter to Alexander IV the *communitas* declared that King Henry had realized the impossibility of dealing with the "Sicilian business" alone, without the counsel of his magnates. This Sicilian business was Henry's greatest adventure, and marks a turning point in the history of England's relations with the continent. It is a mistake, I think, to dismiss Henry III as a weak king. He was, rather, a man of grandiose ideas, and very persistent. If there was a childish streak of vanity in him, there was also a boyish delight in his own plans and achievements. He was easily disturbed and could easily be frightened, but his nature was resilient. He loved state and magnificence because of the pleasure which they gave, not merely because they befitted a king; indeed, he liked to be informal and gay, just as his receptive and inquisitive mind and his taste in beautiful things made him lavish in the expenditure of time and money without regard to the more pressing needs of the moment. He was always busy about something, though it might not be the right thing. He was resentful, but not vindictive, and could be made to see reason, which is more than being brought to reason. And he won in the end. Now a man of this kind, especially if we remember his antecedents, could not be expected to be a national king. Whatever growth towards national feeling can be traced in his reign owed nothing to Henry. His world was his family, not his people, and his family was large and scattered, with interests all over Europe. England was his *regnum*, his base, to be used when possible for the reconquest of Normandy, but, in spite of his veneration for Edward the Confessor, he did not realize the opportunity which England gave. It was his son, another Edward, who pushed home to its natural conclusion the old quarrel with the princes of Snowdonia and saw the possibilities in Scotland and the Low Countries, and found in the Gascon inheritance a centre for asserting his responsibilities as a European statesman. By comparison with Edward, Henry and his brother Richard were adventurers, whose ambition was easily stirred by magnificent prospects. They were ready to fish in the dangerous waters of papal and imperial politics, and to see realities where they should have seen only tempting visions. In 1258 the new baronial council rescued Henry, rather to his relief, from the results of his Sicilian enterprise and hurried on a definite settlement with France. The treaty of Paris in 1259 was not, indeed, a treaty between nations, but it did mark the realization of a new state of affairs. It cleared the way for the conception of the national policy of a national state. If we except the fleeting inspirations of Richard II, Edward IV, and Henry VII, it revealed a capacity for self-controlled statemanship which we do not find again until the days of Queen Elizabeth.

I do not wish to be misunderstood. I do not suggest that the issues, as we see them, were clear, still less that the possibilities in England and Europe were weighted in favour of what was to happen, least of all that what was to happen was the best that could happen. We must try to see the politics of the thirteenth century as men saw them then. There was nothing in the consciousness of the *communitas* or in the closing of the quarrel with France and the withdrawal from the Sicilian adventure which was alien to the common sense of western Europe as a group of communities bound together by a common belief in religion and equity. And a few years later, it was as natural that Edward should be the crusader, the hero of troubadours, the arbitrator between his neighbours in the south, as that he should find arguments in history or natural law for his enterprises in Wales and Scotland. Moreover, within the general framework of thirteenth-century society, moral and political issues could be as puzzling and difficult as in other times. I am simply trying to suggest how and why Englishmen in this period seem to me to have shown an unusual kind of competence.

It is worth while to dwell a little on the circumstances which made the emergence of the *communitas regni* a significant and not an obvious fact, explicable on other grounds but by no means inevitable. For example, the social and intellectual interests which still bound the kingdoms of France and England together influenced their life in many different ways. Henry III's correspondence in 1243 allows us to peer into his mind and to illustrate my point. In the course of a dispute over an episcopal election, the king laid much stress on arguments of law and procedure. Each party was obstinate and there was a dead-lock. The king at last offered to refer the case to the masters of the university of Paris. He explained to the pope that his suggestion was made in all humility and with a regard to equity; if it were adopted, the bishop's pertinacious and ambitious will would be clearly seen. As things were the latter urged that his refusal to submit his case to Englishmen learned in the law was just, for—the bishop felt—no one in the realm would dare to give an opinion contrary to the royal wishes. Now the king was ready to leave the points at issue to the cognizance of the masters in that city which he hated—so he declares—above all other cities as the place ruled and frequented by his greatest enemies. A king, face to face with an intractable ecclesiastic, here appeals to the impartial judgment of a university in a hostile capital. An essay could be written on all the implications of this letter. It raises in the mind of the historian all sorts of issues—moral, political, ecclesiastical, legal, academic. But Henry's proposal would seem quite natural though rather unusual to contemporaries.

Or take the position of Simon de Montfort. As I have suggested elsewhere, Earl Simon did not pose as a patriotic Englishman and nobody in his day thought that he did. He was the cadet of a great French house, with hereditary rights to an English earldom. His rights and his marriage to the king's sister combined to distinguish him from the other royal relatives and their clientele, who were regarded as aliens because they had no prior interests in the kingdom. He and his wife clung obstinately to personal rights and claims which they considered to be well founded in feudal law and practice, and as important, legally and morally, as what we call considerations of state. His great prestige was personal, rooted in social distinction and maintained by his own ability and character. On the other hand, he had come under strong moral and religious influences; he detested incompetence and bad faith; he had long been wont to think out and discuss with his friends the ways in which to solve problems in secular and ecclesiastical government, so far as these were within the cognizance of the rulers of the realm. His sense of the power and ability in himself, and the proud belief in the justice of his intentions fostered by his secret and passionate self-discipline, urged him on. Then came the crisis in his career: at Amiens, King Louis, to whom he had agreed to appeal, cut the ground from under his feet. Earl Simon had taken his stand on the agreements of 1258; King Louis took his stand upon his conception of kingship. A real issue, long felt, was now seen as clear as day. Edward was later to solve the problem by making himself the leader and expressing the mind of the *communitas regni*.

These reflections raise problems, affecting the medieval state, which on this occasion I can do no more than state for your consideration. They might almost be reduced to one: what is implied by the gradual education of the responsible

layman in the art of shaping a body politic? Political theory
can give suggestions but it cannot answer this question, for
the medieval state, in all its various forms, was not deliberately
conformed to patterns of statecraft. It was, so to speak, the
outcome of its own experience. Did the responsible layman
rely upon custom, which changed in spite of him, or was he a
legislator? Did he live aloof from the experience of the church
acquired in cathedral chapter, monastic organization,
ecclesiastical assemblies, and of the schools, reflected in the
writings of theologians, philosophers, and glossators of the
civil and canon law, or did he—in ways hard for us to trace—
share in this self-conscious and sophisticated experience? Was
his outlook confined to the maintenance of his rights and the
claims of contractual obligations, or was he aware of himself
as a citizen? How did he respond to and help to transmit the
influence of literary and artistic forms and economic developments in trade and finance? These are some of the questions
which are suggested by reflections upon the *communitas regni*.
They cannot be answered by reference to the categories of
later history. They ought not, in my view, to be answered in
terms suggested by those who see nothing in the thirteenth
century but the fight for a new nationalism. There was, I feel,
a sense of Englishry, going back to pre-Conquest days, penetrating and influencing from top to bottom the England
which we can dimly see, but it was a responsive, not essentially
an anti-clerical, anti-foreign thing. It was to find its full
expression later, in Chaucer and Langland and the great
English mystics, in More and Colet and Spenser and Shakespeare—not in the growlings of churlish defiance. No: our
questions will only be answered, so far as they ever can be answered, if we throw our net wide in the thirteenth century
and try to give its full value to everything that we can find.

VII

REFLECTIONS ON THE MEDIEVAL STATE[1]

The literature about the medieval state is enormous. Many very distinguished scholars, especially in Germany, have given their ripest thought to the problems which the word "state" suggests when it is applied to medieval society. In recent years several manful efforts have been made to extricate the subject from the trammels of law and philosophy. In Germany, for example, Georg von Below, Fritz Kern and, latest of all, Heinrich Mitteis, have, each in his own way, tried to deal with it as earlier writers, like Waitz, Ranke and Ficker, dealt with it. They have approached it from a political or social or economic point of view, and have made themselves independent, so far as they could, of the categories of the jurists and the generalizations suggested by a study of medieval political thought. Even these exceptional men have not found it easy to avoid categories of their own. If we concern ourselves with something more than a description of institutions, we cannot disregard legal and political ideas, yet it requires more insight and ability than most historians possess to treat the impressive law books and political treatises as raw material, which has no greater claim upon our allegiance than a charter or a chronicle. We in England have so far had only one great scholar of whom it would be hard to say whether he was greatest as historian, lawyer or philosophical thinker. This was Maitland. No wonder, therefore, that the

[1]A presidential address to the Royal Historical Society, delivered 13 February, 1936. For the original form, here modified, see the society's *Transactions*, 4th series, xix. 1–18.

ordinary man feels uncomfortable when he is asked to take account of legal and political ideas by people who are neither lawyers nor philosophers. He prefers to pick the brains of the lawyers and philosophers who have condescended to write legal and philosophical history with due regard to the history which he does understand; and, indeed, he has been well served. Brunner in Germany, Maitland himself in England, Olivier Martin in France are, for example, great and good guides to the political historian, and if the political historian wishes to pillage the rich storehouse of medieval speculation, other good guides are about him everywhere .

At the same time, I feel—and I should be surprised if others did not feel—that by co-operation of this kind, political, legal and philosophical historians will never succeed in explaining the medieval state. The impressive treatises may satisfy the mind, but they do not help us much to see the medieval state. We continue to repeat generalizations about what we think we see which bear little relation to what we know for ourselves. "All medieval law was supposed to be custom"; "the medieval state was not a national state"; "the division between the clerk and the layman was fundamental"; "the feudal system was based on a series of private contracts". "There was no conception of sovereignty in the Middle Ages". Do we really know these things? Are they as a lamp to our feet as we try to pick our way along our own chosen tracks? I doubt it.

We are often content to draw the conclusion that, as we are not polymaths, and do not wish to be humbugs, the safest course is to leave this problem to settle itself. There are two objections to this prudent attitude. In the first place, we cannot as reflective beings altogether disregard the wider issues raised by our studies. In the second place, we have to distinguish between what is possible for us and what should be possible for our successors. For example, we now all agree, I imagine, that, unless the divorce between linguistic and historical studies is ended, work on medieval history may well come to a standstill. The student of pre-Norman English history has learned to face philological problems; and the political historian of the future will have to take an equally intelligent part in the use and criticism of medieval texts which most of us now either disregard or study timidly at second hand. The same is true of legal and speculative literature. Our successors will be safe and able to stand on firm ground just in so far as they are able to use this literature without being frightened by it, or distracted by it, so long as they can follow the lead of the expert without the suspicion which is born of incomplete understanding. The distrust of legal categories and abstract ideas is good if it is the deliberate and clear-headed result of an informed comparison between established facts and contemporary or modern theory; it is not good, if it is the result of ignorance. Whatever we may mean by the state, we do mean that it is a condition only possible to intelligent beings who possess a faculty which we call the power of choice. If man were nothing but a creature of instinct, the "state" would endure unchanged in historic time, like the organization of the ant or the bee. However intricate it might be, it would have reached a stage of arrested development and could have no history. But intelligent and self-directing beings respond, within the environment possible for existence in historic time, to the changes in circumstances and the movements of thought which their own energy has helped to create. There is constant interplay between creation and response in political as in every other kind of human development. Hence, in dealing with that development, we have to take account of abstract ideas, and, as a matter of fact, however sceptical we may be, however anxious to confine our attention to what we honestly know, we use abstract terms at every step. Take two sentences from two of our best scholars, men whose concrete attitude to history is beyond dispute and is sometimes even aggressively expressed. "Those private charters of the twelfth century in which the characteristics of Anglo-Norman feudalism find their most authentic expression"[1]; "the evolution of civilized government is reflected in the history of the charter, which is the vehicle of the King's will and pleasure."[2] In order to understand these sentences we must attach clear meanings to the abstractions: private, feudalism, authentic, evolution, civilized, government, to say nothing of characteristic, expression, reflected, vehicle, etc. And both writers wish to emphasise the changes resulting from interplay of thought and circumstance. The one speaks of the evolution of a new order from the ancient simplicity of social relations. The other refers to the development of a variety of forms in accordance with the new uses to which the charter was put. Their language is steeped in Aristotelianism and Darwinism. They are making their contributions to the history of that abstraction, the medieval state. At the same time, there is all the difference in the world between the attitude of these scholars, commenting on definite bits of parchment, and the attitude of men who insist on interpreting the Middle Ages from such an acquaintance with glossators, theologians and publicists as can be derived from their systematic exposition in modern treatises. I am urging here that the political historian, if he really wishes to understand the development of the state, can no more afford to neglect the glossators and the publicists than he can afford to neglect the charter, the plea roll and the

[1] F. M. Stenton, *The First Century of English Feudalism* (Oxford, 1932), p. 6.

[2] V. H. Galbraith, "The Literacy of the Medieval English Kings", from *The Proceedings of the British Academy*, vol. xxi, being the Raleigh Lecture, 1935, p. 18.

chronicle; but I am also urging that he must use them in the same spirit of critical detachment. If we deal, as we must, with the interplay of facts and reflection, we can set no arbitrary limits to the range of our inquiry; but, on the other hand, we must treat all the material alike. The more an historical theme is concerned with abstractions, the more incumbent is it upon the historian to realize that history depends upon direct and sensitive observation. He must avoid the "unsubstantial day-dreams, inspired evasions of the real problems," which tempt him, just as they beset the poet and the artist.

When we speak of the medieval state we do not intend to use a technical term, but we do imply more than a complex of institutions. We think vaguely of organized public life, of the relations between men which enables them to discuss, plead and act together in councils, law courts, armies and business. Although we find associations of this kind in every stage of development, and though what nowadays we describe as functions of the state can be performed by primitive groups of men, the word "state" does suggest to us something self-conscious and sophisticated. One word for the public community in the Middle Ages was *civilitas*, and we associate the state with civilization. Now, if we are considering groups of this kind, we must allow the men who inherited and elaborated them the capacity to be influenced in their normal daily life by abstractions. They will not necessarily use big words of Greek and Latin origin, but there will generally be some relation between their thinking and talking and the speech of the clerks who do use abstract terms to express contemporary ideas. Take, for example, the word *utilitas*. It is true that this word is found in Frankish charters merely as part of the pompous and redundant vocabulary in which the clerks delighted. It occurs frequently in the sense of "worthiness", as in the formula *Noverit itaque sagacitas et utilitas fidelium nostrorum.* But it also frequently occurs in such phrases as *utilitas regis* and *utilitas regni*, to signify the purpose of public policy. When a king and his counsellors are considering affairs with a view to the well-being of the kingdom, they have got a long way from the predatory instincts of the war-band and the conception of kingship to be found even in the noble poem *Beowulf*, where the king is "the giver of treasure." We have no right to assume that the phrase, Roman, abstract, clerical though it is, did not reflect some regard for the general well-being in the minds of those whose decisions are described. We have here the expression of a simple conception of statesmanship in a rudimentary state. Again, if we turn to a much more sophisticated period in the Middle Ages, the reign of Philip the Fair of France (*c.* 1300), we can see, in the discussions of the royal court, a precocious familiarity with the subtleties of political speculation. It seems to me quite impossible to suppose that contemporary political pamphlets, which sought to justify the king in his quarrel with the pope, did not repeat, in a more systematic form, the arguments used during the debates in the king's council. The men who took the lead were knights as well as clerks, lawyers rather than theologians. They emphasized the duty of the laity in times of stress; their Latin and their French were easily convertible into terms of each other. If this be so, then the lords and knights about Philip the Fair were familiar with a conception of *utilitas* which carries us very far in the theory of statecraft. They could express or at least appreciate the expression of public utility in terms of *necessitas*, and by necessity they meant more than the public need. They meant the right and duty of the king and his agents, indeed of the ordinary man, to override positive law in the common interests for which they were responsible. The word "necessity" had had a long history in ecclesiastical literature. Pope Gregory VII had asserted that the pope in case of necessity could make new laws. A century later we find, applied to policy, the phrase "necessity knows no law." Innocent III speaks of *necessitas regni*. The law of the Church admitted the duty of clerks to come to the aid of the lay power in case of necessity. St. Thomas Aquinas developed a theory of necessity. He argued that, in certain circumstances, necessity knows no law; also that a tyrant can be removed on the ground of necessity; and he justified this view by an appeal to Aristotle's discussion of *epieikeia* or equity, when he says that gaps in the law must be filled from the standpoint of equity. In the meantime the argument had been taken up by the civilians who expounded the case of the Emperor Frederick II. The emperor must maintain the integrity of his charge. He could not allow himself to be crushed at the expense of the general well-being. The call of necessity was a call of nature. The legists of Philip the Fair gave a more positive direction to the argument. Necessity, in their mind, was more than a sanction of self-protection; it was a call to assert the power of the king, over and above the limits set by custom and tradition, in the interests of his kingdom and of the Christian community of which his kingdom was a responsible part. It proclaimed that the king, in the interests of natural law, was above positive law; he could revoke old laws and supply their defects by new laws. He was responsible, in all matters affecting his and his kingdom's well-being, to no other power, and at the call of necessity could exert his authority to maintain the spiritual power against the head of the Church itself, to oppose the Church in the interests of the Church. The next step was to identify the natural law of necessity with the natural impulses of a political community, its rights to natural frontiers and self-assertion, or even to identify necessity not with natural law but with the dictates of history. In their frontier policy, the French kings from Philip the Fair to Louis XIV seem often to be hovering on the edge of assertions of this kind in the course of their elaborate legal arguments and the practice of their elaborate legal devices.

Here I am concerned, not with these anticipations of the modern state, but with the way in which medieval political groups, as they grew in complexity and in the capacity for orderly and self-directed expression, were compelled to think and to think abstractedly. We cannot define the medieval state in terms of political categories; we can only describe it or suggest descriptions of it in its varied and elusive development; and, if we try to do this, we cannot afford to separate legal and political thought from the humanity about it and set it on one side as irrelevant or remote, for, however abstract it might become, it was essentially an expression of contemporary life. In its turn, it must be used, though not slavishly interpreted, to illustrate the development of what is often called a "political sense" in the men who had counsel with kings, devised the constitution of city-republics, sat in judgment, transacted local affairs or attended parliaments. These men had brains as well as experience, and they were not dumb. They did not continue in the indulgence of their savage appetites until civilization came to them like manna in the wilderness. They gradually civilized themselves; in becoming civilized they neither consciously adjusted themselves to some type of civilization nor shut their ears to the guidance which clerks and lawyers were ready to give to them out of their stores of experience and learning. They did not say, on the one hand "We insist on being civilized," nor on the other, "We refuse to listen to anything that these hypocritical self-seekers and pedants say." It is easy enough to collect instances to justify the dictum that "laymen are notoriously hostile to clerks," and illustrations of perfectly useless dialectic—it would perhaps be even easier to do so in our own age—but this is not the point. If it were, the study of history would be a much simpler thing than it is.

The use of the word "state" in medieval times helps us to understand how, in an increasingly intricate network of social and economic relations, the growth of a body-politic was directed by what may be described as moral considerations. In Greek and Latin the word meant stand or stance, as when the rhetoricians take their stand on a particular line of argument. It implies something central, fundamental, a ground or basis. Hence the word "state" could come to mean that which gives validity to a thing, and in due course validity in itself to a thing, so that it is more than fleeting or capricious. This seems to be the meaning which in medieval times survived most commonly from the multiform usages of classical Latin. When Eginhard says that Charles the Great went to Rome in the year 800 *propter reparandum . . . ecclesiae statum,* he means something more, I think, than we should mean by the state of the Church. Of course, he did not mean anything concrete like the papal patrimony, but he meant more than the gentlemen do who write letters to *The Times* deploring the state of the Church of England. What exactly he, or rather Charles, meant is still a matter of controversy; many volumes have been written about it.

The word recurs incessantly in medieval documents and treatises, and there always lies in it some such implication as I have noted. The preamble or *arenga* to a charter of Hugh Capet in the late tenth century begins: "The sublimity of our piety cannot have a due and orderly stand (*recto stare valet ordine*) unless it does justice to all and in all things and observes with intelligence (*mentaliter*) the just decrees of former kings." There is here, of course, no conscious and technical use of the verb. A king states his stand on the thoughtful administration of justice. But usually we find the noun (*status*) either accompanied by another noun in the genitive or alone, with a more deliberate intention. So far as I have noticed, it is never used in our sense of the word, as a geographical and political entity. We can say, "the well-being of the state"; but the medieval ruler spoke of the state of the commonwealth, *status regni* or *status republicæ*. When the word is used by itself it is charged with the significance of our word "condition," with a sense of value.

When a king maintained his "state" he did so with a due sense of moral responsibility. He did not assert a naked right to exist or to assert himself. Edward I, in replying to a clerical petition in 1280, explained that he could not answer otherwise, without completely departing from the advice of his magnates, a thing which would be in no wise profitable either for himself or the church, or for the state of the realm of England. In the next year he told the bishops that they must not presume to take council together about any matter which affected the crown or touched his person or state or the state of his council. The first passage helps to explain the significance attached to the word *status*, whether of king or of council or of kingdom. It would be detrimental, says Edward, to the state of the kingdom if decisions made by the king and his counsellors were not observed; he himself was bound—he means, I think, morally bound—by these decisions. In other words, the maintenance of the state of the kingdom implies deliberate, orderly and effective action, action which is not arbitrary. The word "state," as contemporary thought shows, was charged with moral significance. For example, there are two kinds of perfection, personal and *secundum statum;* a man may aim either at the perfection which comes of serenity and a clean conscience or at the perfection which is demanded of his "state," in the exercise of power and jurisdiction[1]. A really good man will aim at both, but they are not the same; indeed, it was sometimes maintained that the standard of personal perfection to be expected of a layman was not so exacting as that to be expected of a man of spiritual state. A king had, so to speak, a duty to his own state. If this is healthy, his judgment will be healthy. "The straight (*rectum*) is judge of itself as well as of the crooked," just as a man with an undefiled palate will distinguish between savours correctly. The thoroughgoing papalist argued that there were grades of perfection in states of this kind, and that the judgment of the higher had the right to correct the judgment of the lower; but he did not deny that each state had its own perfection, and that its possessor had the power and the opportunity to attain it. This conception of human responsibility to whatever state a man might possess explains why the plea of necessity was not divorced from a regard for equity. The state of the realm itself, impersonal though it was, was instinct with obligation; it was something to be maintained in accordance with principle, and was not conceivable to a barbaric mind, for the idea of it implies a capacity for abstract thought which goes much further than the instincts of shame and fidelity in which it is ultimately rooted.

The "state" in our sense of the word is possible when the ruling power has firmly established its authority over the "states" of other classes or persons, and when the range within which this power is exercised is naturally and normally expressed in territorial terms. The state of the realm comes to be the expression of corporate activity within a definite area; but, when this happens, and the word "state" is used without any qualification, as, for example, by Machiavelli, its moral

[1]Aegidius Romanus, *De ecclesiastica potestate*, lib. i., cap. 2; edited R. Scholz (Weimar, 1929), p. 6.

content tends to drop out. Its complexity survives; it means more than *regnum* or *civitas;* but it loses much of its life. It is debased in quality, though it is charged with more meaning. How this happened, first I suppose in Italy, has often been discussed, but I am not concerned with the development here.

In the light of the discussion of *utilitas, necessitas, status,* I should like to approach one of the *clichés* or commonplaces with which we are so familiar. This discussion does seem to make it unlikely, to say the least, that law was fundamentally the expression of custom. The insistence by medievalists upon custom is in itself largely due to a conscious reaction against the Austinian conception of sovereignty as applicable to medieval society. Scholars felt, and felt rightly, that whatever the medieval state was, it was not inspired by that hard abstraction. But the conception of the sovereign state in its stark nakedness now stirs in our minds the revulsion which we feel at the thought of the "economic man." Both historians and theorists see that its realization, if it ever has been realized, is a perversion, and that recent attempts to embody it in practice are a calamity. Hence they are now prepared to find both that the reverence for custom is not so remote from modern political life as was implied, and that the idea of sovereignty is not so modern as was supposed. Sovereignty does not necessarily require an articulated state and regard for custom is not necessarily inconsistent with legislation. When, in one of Miss Sayers's books, an old lady protests that the law could never have allowed parliament to make a certain change in the rules of succession to property, she is not speaking as a strange survival from the medieval world, but as an ordinary indignant conservative-minded and rather foolish person of any civilized age or country. Similarly, when a medieval churchman or lawyer said, "I never thought this change could be made, but as it has been made, we must accept it as right," he was not speaking as a man born centuries before his proper time. A changing society, driven forward by new spiritual and economic opportunity, cannot exist, whether it is medieval or modern, without both a regard for custom and the recognition of an ultimate authority, which can enforce change. A political society, however crude it may be, which can appreciate the political value of conceptions like utility, necessity, and states of social activity, has reached this stage.

The reverence for custom is, indeed, one of the essential characteristics of medieval life. We have to start from it and never forget it. At the same time, it was not a religious dogma, but a very practical way of maintaining the social realities. I have already quoted a charter of Hugh Capet. Here is a passage from another: "It is the function of kings, after a sagacious survey of the laws (*iura*) of their kingdoms, to take anxious care to cut away the harmful and to give wide effect to all that are profitable." A custom might be a bad custom, and to commit it to writing was not advantageous. For example, one of the supporters of St. Thomas Becket expostulated with King Henry II for giving a longer life to evil customs by putting them into writing as the Constitutions of Clarendon. The word custom did not necessarily mean something which had ancient use. We read in the record of the great arbitration of 1258 between the archbishop, Conrad of Hochstaden, and the citizens of Cologne that "the city officials, meeting in the city hall, decree whatever they like without the archbishop's knowledge, and a statute of this kind they wish to be observed as a special custom and right (*pro speciali consuetudine et iure*) without any archiepiscopal authority." In the history of any community, at any time, custom might be challenged in the name of some higher law or maintained as in accordance with some higher consideration.

In the year 1131 some Benedictine abbots of the province of Reims formed themselves into a kind of congregation. They met in chapter and agreed to enforce a stricter and simpler life than that required by the Cluniac customs under which they had been living. The papal legate, Cardinal Matthew of Albano, a strong Cluniac, tried his hardest to stop the movement. The abbots replied: "We do not profess the customs of Cluny but the law and rule of St. Benedict. Do we then destroy the customs by the rule? God forbid. We establish the customs."[1] When the English barons said that they did not wish the English law of bastardy to be changed, they were not mere reactionaries, holding to custom for its own sake; they were guided, rightly or wrongly, by considerations of social expediency—were maintaining their state, shall we say?—just as Grosseteste in his denunciation of them appealed to the higher law of the Church. The truth is that our incurable habit of thinking in categories makes us slow to realize how readily medieval society responded, in its legislation, to social needs. Legislation was, from our modern standpoint, comparatively rare, not because it was distrusted, but because, in a slowly moving and more agrarian manner of life, it was less needed than it is to-day. The hard and fast distinction which we draw between administration and legislation, and between customary law and the civil law, has blurred this fact. We are apt to dismiss a great change as merely administrative, forgetting that it might fundamentally alter customary law, and so go on to deny that it was legislative. I believe, on the contrary, that the assizes of Henry II, the ordinances of St. Louis, the acts of Frederick I at Roncaglia and of Frederick II at Melfi or in the German diets, were legislative, and that the judgments in the medieval courts, at any rate in the

---

[1] See Dom A. Wilmart, *Une riposte de l'ancien monachisme au manifeste de Saint Bernard*, in *Revue benedictine*, April-July, 1934, pp. 299, 300.

thirteenth century, implied a practice of conscious adjustment
to circumstance, an attempt to cope with new problems. The
plea rolls of King John's reign in England, for example,
abound in cases where suitors seek the considered opinion
(*consideratio*) of the court. A man holds a tenement by servile
custom. His holding is in villeinage. But he makes an arrangement by which he can render an annual payment in cash for
all services and he does this for twenty years. Has his tenement become a free tenement; does an action lie against his
lords for disseisin? Or again, can an action be brought against
a "simple hospitaller" acting on behalf of his prior? I pick
out puzzling points like this at random; they show how the
judges were suddenly called on to deal with problems of
prescription and agency and the like, whose solution would
help to shape the law and to define social relations. The right
solution was often hard to find and was certainly not dictated
by custom alone. Martin of Pattishall, as we have recently
been reminded, changed his answer to the question whether
a layman could or could not bring an action under the assize
utrum, and finally decided it in a way which Bracton deplored.
Where the local custom differed, as in the cases where the
rights of commoners were hard to reconcile with the tendency
to agricultural development, one custom had to be preferred
to another: so the famous Statute of Merton adopted the
"law of Arden." [1] Outside England, we find that the civil or
Roman law was frequently used as a model for new practice,
or to meet unusual circumstances or to guide national custom
along a coherent path. In the later twelfth century it began
to affect Lombard feudal law; in the middle of the thirteenth
it served as an example for the introduction of general legisla-

[1] D. M. Stenton, *Rolls of the Justices in Eyre . . . for Lincolnshire*, 1218–19, *and
Worcestershire*, 1221 (Selden Society's Publications, vol. liii, London, 1934), pp.
xxxii–iii, lxvii.

tion in the French monarchy. Philip Augustus had disliked it because he feared the emperor; Philip the Fair welcomed it because he felt more independent than any emperor; indeed he defines the relation between custom and the civil law with exactitude. Schools of civil law are required, he says in an ordinance in favour of the university of Orleans (1312), to encourage the principles of equity and reason which are applied in the litigation of this kingdom, "when the judgments, customs and ordinances of our forefathers and ourselves, which we regard as superior to all custom, are defective and no custom exists by which judgment can be given."[1]

Now, behind all this, we have the consciousness of a living, changing, yet continuous society, of a society which does not depend upon individual caprice, does not die, and has its own "state" and traditions. This quality in feudal society impressed the Moslem world as soon as the Latin states of Syria were established. When Jocelin of Courtenay, count of Edessa, was captured in 1122, he was offered his freedom on condition of surrendering his county. An Arab historian records his reply: "We are like laden camels; when one falls, the baggage is transferred to another; our possessions have already passed to other hands." The Moslem world lacked stability because it denied custom the power to adjust itself. I cannot close this part of the discussion better than by quoting two passages from the legist, Pierre Dubois. They illustrate the difference between West and East. In the first passage Dubois, referring to methods of warfare, urges his readers to deliberate with diligence and sadness of heart on the spiritual and temporal dangers which adherence to custom involves. In the second he says:

Does not Averroes say that the Arabs have suffered greatly

[1] M. Fournier, *Les statuts et privilèges des universités françaises*, vol. i, no. 27. See especially E. M. Meijers in *Tijdschrift voor rechtsgeschiedenis*, vol. i (Leiden, 1921), pp. 108 ff.

from their belief that laws are universally and externally binding? Was not every law made for a good and expedient end? The laws and statutes of men differ as places, times and persons differ. Many philosophers have taught that this is right, for *utilitas* obviously requires it to be so. The Lord God changed many things in the New Testament which he had decreed in the Old.

In these reflections I have tried to find a "stance" from which, as it seems to me, the various aspects of a great subject should be examined. It is from this point of view that we should regard the development and the variety of feudal custom, the relations between rulers and vassals or subjects, the maintenance of public law, the rise of corporations, the growth of parliaments, the attempts at majority-rule, the belief in divine right and in the right to resist. Instead of trying to define medieval public life as idealists sought to define it, we should examine its different expressions and try to explain the "state of the case"; and in doing this we should be prepared to realize the importance, in everyday life, of what we call abstract ideas, but what I prefer to call man's capacity to think. We should not confine the influence of religious thought to ecclesiastical circles, of legal ideas to those who practised in the courts or sat in the schools, of political conceptions to the theorists. If we do, me may find ourselves building walls in our reflections on the past which did not exist in the past itself. The problem might be summed up in a sentence as that of the education in political experience of the ordinary man, and especially, though not only, of the layman. Starting from the words spoken by Marsiglio of Padua, "the things which touch the well-being and the ill-being of all men ought to be known and heard of all," we should go on to inquire how far, in this place and that, in this time and that, they actually were known and heard. In a forcible and stimulating lecture, which I have already

quoted, Mr. Galbraith has invited us to remember the layman, but he seems to imply that, so long as the layman could
not read or write, his political experience was acquired in
isolation, apart from the movements of thought about him—
movements which, in Mr. Galbraith's view, have very little
relevance to the essentially formative factors in history or
even, if I understand him aright, to our conception, whatever
that may be, of civilization. Now it is true enough that the
layman could not fully come to his own until public business
was transacted and recorded in the vernacular; but, on the
other hand, we must not minimize the importance of the
vernacular as a vehicle of thought in those times when the
educated man wrote in Latin, nor the extent of its use behind
the screen of Latin. The fact that we have to approach the
layman through this screen is one thing; whether he himself
was cut off from mental intercourse with the kinsfolk and
neighbours who can talk to us is a very different thing. As yet
we know far too little about the individual layman and his
vernacular thoughts, of the influences which played upon him
in his assertiveness, as he became conscious of the validity,
the duty, the opportunity which lay in his "state," whether
he was a peasant in a manorial court or a baron debating
with bishops and kings. Yet I am sure of this, that the more
responsible he felt, the prouder he was of his position in life,
the more determined to face the issues about him in his own
way, the more use he made of the experience and thoughts of
others. "The evolution of civilized government is reflected in
the history of the charter." No doubt; but the charter is not
the measure of civilized government. The hawk does not soar
by this wisdom, and stretch her wings towards the South. The
common store of proverbial wisdom and the traditional ex-
pedients of practical life cannot, when men talked together,
have continually been enlarged and adjusted to changing

circumstance without some give and take between the active and the contemplative, between the shrewd stay-at-home and the wanderers among the riches of space and time. In Chaucer's wealth of English speech the results of centuries of mental intercourse were precipitated. One of the most profound and enduring conceptions of the layman's place in a mysterious universe was reached, in the days of Pope Innocent III and Hubert Walter, by an obscure German knight— as he says, a bit of a poet whose poem fared without the aid of books. Yet Wolfram von Eschenbach was, in the best sense of the term, a very sophisticated person. Who of us could set bounds to the influences which stirred his imagination as he meditated on the story of Parzival?

VIII

BOLOGNA, PARIS, OXFORD : THREE *STUDIA GENERALIA*[1]

In medieval times, the most comprehensive description of the learned society which is now described as a university was *studium generale*. As we shall see, every *studium generale* was required to have high authority to give it legality, but this does not mean that every *studium* was the outcome of deliberate creation. The three subjects of this paper grew gradually; they were not made by a single gesture. Yet the most convenient way to approach them is to begin by saying something about the earliest *studium generale* in imperial territory, the university of Prague, which began its career with full credentials from pope and emperor in 1348.

The *studium generale* of Prague was founded by Pope Clement VI in response to a petition forwarded by Charles, King of Germany and Bohemia, the illustrious Emperor Charles IV. In his charter of April 1348 Charles conferred upon the new studium all the privileges of the two greatest *studia generalia*, Paris and Bologna. Although its constitution was copied from Paris rather than from Bologna, the influence of the Italian university upon the students of Prague was considerable. While Charles had memories of study in Paris, the archbishop of Prague, who in the papal bull of foundation was given the authority exercised in Paris by the chancellor of Notre-Dame and in Bologna by the archdeacon,

[1]Reprinted, with same changes, from *Prague Studies* (Oxford, The Clarendon Press, 1949).

was a former law-student of Bologna. From its earliest days
the university of Prague also looked with a particular regard
to the masters of Oxford. A statute of 1367, passed only
twenty years after the foundation of the university provided
that scholars who dictated books to their fellow students
should confine themselves to works put together by well
known masters of Prague, Paris or Oxford; and, as we all
know, the relations between Prague and Oxford became very
close during the next half-century. Moreover, apart from
these considerations, the three great *studia*, if not so illustrious
as they had been a century before, were never more active
nor more conscious as corporations of their busy and assertive
life than they were in the middle of the fourteenth century,
when an ambitious emperor of a generous and constructive
mind decided to give the Empire its first *studium generale*, and
to found it in his new capital, with a prestige and *éclat* which
should establish its claim to be from the first one of the most
important centres of learning in the Christian world. Prague
was to be another Paris, another Bologna, another Oxford.

Neither the university of Paris nor that of Bologna nor
that of Oxford was *founded*. Each grew from beginnings which
are still obscure. The university of Prague, on the contrary,
was the outcome of a deliberate act, and also of a joint act; it
was founded by the pope at the instance of the emperor. And,
in a second charter, Charles IV conferred upon it all the
privileges ever bestowed by the emperors on any university.
Before we can discuss with any approach to certainty the
origins and development of the three great *studia generalia*
something must be said about the parts played by ecclesiastical and secular authorities in the history of medieval universities. No greater tribute could have been paid to the influence of Paris and Bologna than the facts that, as early as
1224, the Emperor Frederick II founded the university of

Naples, the first university to be founded at a definite time by a definite charter, and that, as early as 1229, Pope Gregory IX founded the university of Toulouse; for in their respective foundations both emperor and pope expressed a conscious sense of the far-reaching significance of systematic learning and teaching and asserted the will to avail themselves of them in the interests of high policy. There was a close connexion between the foundation of Naples and the imperial court. Frederick desired to erect a powerful rival to the university of Bologna which, in a Guelf city, was not so faithful to imperial views as it had been in the great days of his grandfather, Frederick I. When the doctors of Bologna tried to thwart the new *studium* at Naples he rated them for their resistance to the statutes of their prince and their disregard of imperial unity and ordered all teaching to cease at Bologna within four months. And there was a close connexion between the foundation at Toulouse five years later and papal policy in the heretical lands of the Midi. Pope Gregory, following up an idea of his predecessor Honorius III, made the provision of salaried teachers at Toulouse part of the final treaty between the conquered Count Raymond and his orthodox conqueror, King Louis IX of France. Masters from Paris were lecturing in Toulouse before the year was over. Now it is true that, neither in Naples nor in Toulouse was the impetus given by the actions of emperor and pope sufficient to establish the new *studia* on a firm basis. In a sense, the circumstances of their creation were too fortuitous. The university of Naples did not begin to "enjoy a really continuous existence and a modest prosperity" until the days in 1266 when Charles of Anjou, the French conqueror of the kingdom of Sicily and Naples, was able to refound it with the support of of a friendly pope, Clement IV. The university of Toulouse passed through troubled times before its "spiritual garrison in the heart of the conquered land of heresy" could feel quite secure. These early difficulties, however, do not concern us here. The creations of Frederick II and Gregory IX, in an age when local schools of learning which might naturally develop ambitions to become recognized *studia* or even *studia generalia*, were so numerous in Western Europe, in Italy, in France, in Spain, paid homage to the prestige of Bologna and Paris and, at the same time, did much to define the relations between the *studium* and the secular and ecclesiastical authorities described in medieval thought as the *regnum* and the *sacerdotium*. In Dr. Rashdall's words: "a very peculiar combination of circumstances suggested to the pope the idea of reproducing artificially in the city of Toulouse the institution or system of institutions which had spontaneously developed themselves at Paris and Oxford. And this precedent in turn suggested the notion that the pope could 'found' other *studia generalia* at the request of a ruler or a city, in the same way as he had founded Toulouse for his own special purposes; and from that notion it was but a step to the development of the theory that a *studium generale* could only be founded by the pope or his rival in the government of the medieval world-state, the Holy Roman Emperor."

From this point of view, we might well describe the foundation of the university of Prague as the culmination of a joint supervision of medieval developments in education by pope and emperor, and see in it a triumphant expression in practice of medieval theories about the unity of the Christian republic. Little reflection is needed, however, to moderate so sweeping an interpretation of Rashdall's analysis. As his words show, Rashdall was dealing with "notions" and "theories", and the melancholy history of the university of Prague in the first century of its existence in itself would refute any easy-going conclusions about the œcumenical temper of life in a medieval *studium*. The racial and theological feuds which divided the masters and scholars of Prague illustrate, with the peculiar intensity occasioned by exceptional local conditions, the truth that the university everywhere reflected the disorders and incoherences no less than the spacious idealism of a greater world. The emperor, whatever right he had to establish universities or to grant existing universities the status of *studium generale*, took little part in the development of academic life. Outside Germany and Italy his intervention was not sought nor would it have been regarded. Indeed, it is significant that Prague was the only imperial creation with the single exception of the still-born university at Treviso, which in 1318 received a foundation-bull from an imperial claimant to whom Treviso at that time happened to adhere; and that the sole evidence of imperial activity is to be found not in Germany but in Italy, and in imperial bulls issued by the founder of the university of Prague. Siena in 1357, Pavia in 1361, Florence in 1364 were strengthened or revived by bulls of the Emperor Charles IV, the only emperor who, in the two centuries after the death of Frederick II, was able to maintain, in fitful co-operation with the Holy See, something of the prestige which for a time had been won by the Ottos and Henrys and Fredericks of the past. Not one of the German universities founded after Prague owed its existence to imperial authority, though each of them in turn, whether founded by prince or bishop or town, was quick to acknowledge the rule that a new university required the authorization of a papal bull.

One vestige of imperial influence survived from medieval into later times. This was the constitution known as the Authentic *Habita*, issued by the Emperor Frederick I, in 1158. It won general recognition, casually admitted by the famous English lawyer Blackstone as late as 1765, not by reason of any power surviving in the Holy Roman Emperor, but because the text of the privilege had been comprised among the additions to the Code of Justinian made by order of Frederick I and his grandson Frederick II. The Authentic was part of the body of law studied in every law school and the protection which it gave to scholars was admitted as a right sanctioned by the civil law.[1]

The constitution granted by Frederick I marks one of the great moments in the history of medieval learning. The emperor, in the course of his assertion of his royal authority and his investigations into the rights of the crown in north Italy had owed much to the scholars of Bologna and especially to the four famous doctors, Martinus, Bulgarus, Jacobus and Hugo. The redress of the grievances of scholars was a fitting acknowledgement of the debt. The intellectual ferment of the age was intense. This was the heyday of the wandering clerks or scholars who, in the words of a contemporary monk, "are wont to roam about the world and visit all the cities till much learning makes them mad." The call of adventure, mental curiosity, weariness with convention, and the breach of social attachments produced this strange mixture of serious purpose and irresponsible vagabondage. The *studia*, as organized centres of study, did not exist, but the cathedral schools and the places, like Bologna, where, by whatever course of events, masters were wont to teach, were the rallying points, the cores, so to speak, of serious endeavour in the fleeting

[1]See H. Koeppler, "Frederick Barbarossa and the Schools of Bologna" in *English Historical Review*, liv (1939) 577–607. Cf. Blackstone, *Commentaries* (eleventh edition, 1791) iii. 84. The word *authentica* was given, perhaps by the famous Irnerius, to the twelfth century translation of the *Novellae*, Justinian's last collection "promulgated after the publication of the second edition of his Code". It was then restricted to extracts from the *Novellae* which were transferred to relevant places in the Code, and so applied to the laws incorporated by the medieval emperors in the Code. The title *Habita* is the first word of Frederick I's privilege.

movement. Now the purpose of the Authentic *Habita* was primarily to protect "all scholars and especially professors of the divine and holy laws, who are pilgrims for the sake of study (*causa studiorum peregrinantur*)." The constitution was the charter of the deserving, made exiles by their love of knowledge, too often impoverished, exposed to danger, subjected to the wanton assaults of evil men. The constitution expressed the will of the emperor that the scholars should have safe journey to and safe living in the places in which they studied, be immune from injury, and in particular from the custom of reprisal, by which the debts of one could be recovered from another who belonged to the same district (*provincia*). The ruling authorities in the places of study were required to make a fourfold restitution if they had not prevented reprisal; and they could be deprived in perpetuity of their qualification to hold office. Later commentators on the Code interpreted these privileges to cover the return journeys of students, and freedom from tolls, duties and customs both for students and their attendants, so that, for example, their precious books should be free from exaction. The conditions of the age and the difficulties in which the alien students at Bologna might so easily find themselves made these forms of protection the main intention of the imperial constitution, but in course of time it became better known and was perhaps more regarded on account of its last clauses, concerned with the right of jurisdiction over scholars[1]. The earlier clauses were forgotten and the last clauses remembered. To make the members of another political community responsible for the debts of one

[1]Koeppler, developing a suggestion made by Giesebrecht, argues that the privilege was granted without the last clauses in 1155, and that these clauses were added at the instance of the masters of Bologna when the privilege was formally issued as a constitution at the Diet of Roncaglia in 1158. He suggests that, owing to political changes in Bologna, the need for these clauses was more obvious in 1158 (*op. cit.*, pp. 604–5.)

of themselves was a crude and unjust device; it was hurtful to neighbourly relations and was denounced by the Church; moreover, it was mainly used to recover trading debts or to punish attacks upon traders. As public order increased, reprisals tended to disappear. The problem of jurisdiction over scholars, who were clerks or regarded as clerks, was, on the contrary, a continuous preoccupation of the Church, and of daily and vital importance to academic societies. In England, for example, it survived the Reformation and vestiges of the system to which it gave rise still survive in Oxford and Cambridge in the authority of the proctors and in certain legal, if unexercised, powers of the chancellor's court. The Authentic *Habita*, which, it should be remembered, was confirmed by the Pope, defined current practice in this matter of jurisdiction. Current practice recognized the natural right or duty of the master to maintain discipline or to castigate his pupils as members of his "family"; and it recognized the ecclesiastical right or duty of jurisdiction over clerks. On the other hand the settlement of groups of wandering scholars in a city was obviously not a matter of indifference to the local authorities. Justinian had recognized this six centuries before the time of Frederick I when "he charged with the jurisdiction over the students of Berytus the bishop of the town, the professors of law and the head of the local administration". Frederick, however, lived in an age in which clerks were subject to ecclesiastical authority and he wished to establish the rights of his learned advisers in Bologna. Accordingly he decreed that, in cases in which a scholar was involved, he might choose as judge either his own teacher or the bishop. Anyone who tried to bring a suit against a scholar before another judge was to lose his action, however just his cause might be.

The circumstances of this privilege are obscure, and do

not concern us. The point is that the privilege was enshrined in the Code, had papal sanction, and in due course was accepted as a definition of the rights of any master and, what was to become much more important, of the rights of the university authorities who acted in the place of the bishop. The imperial and local origin of the Authentic *Habita* was independent of the general consent which maintained it. To later minds it might serve as an indication that secular power was the source of academic privilege, but arguments of this kind belong to the time when academic privilege, however venerable, required the explicit sanction of the state as part of the law of the land.

Here we come to the true ground or source of academic development, a common desire shared by all kinds of authority to foster and take pride in it. The early universities were not created. They grew as a natural expression of spiritual, intellectual and social energy. Their fame would have invited imitation even if the temporary migrations of bodies of masters and scholars as protests against local grievances had not sown the seeds of other *studia*. One of the obligations of a good prince was to promote centres of learning. St. Thomas Aquinas, for example, includes this among the duties of a prince; and, indeed, fifty years before his time, and some twenty years before the imperial foundation at Naples and the papal foundation at Toulouse, the kings of Castile had begun to encourage by their grants and protection the centres of teaching in Spain. In Italy it was the civic authorities who generally took the lead. The German universities established after the creation of Prague were founded by dukes, bishops, and municipalities. Yet this development of the academic life was anything but artificial. Where it had no roots and struck no roots it withered away, however august its patrons might be. It was a true efflorescence, sustained by the influence or traditions of Paris and Bologna, and disciplined by its subjection to the oversight and guidance of the Church and especially of the Holy See, and also, it should be added, by the interventions of the secular authority. If we consider the history of the medieval universities as a whole we can see that they were exceptionally favoured by the powers of Church and State. They were treasures, sources of pride, objects of general beneficence.

The universities, like every other expression of social life in the middle ages, can be treated, it is true, in terms of conflict. In the three great *studia generalia*, for example, disputes between the university and the local ecclesiastical or municipal authorities, between "nations", between scholars and masters (at Bologna) between secular masters and the friars, (at Paris and Oxford) frequently occurred, and these disputes mark convenient stages in university history. Also, though not so frequently, the universities of Paris and Oxford had to face angry kings and the university of Bologna an angry pope. Yet, for the most part, the normal activities of masters and scholars, both under the Parisian and the Bolognese systems of organisation, were not pursued in conditions of strife. Medieval institutions were rooted in impulse, custom, tradition, loyalty, rather than in the conscious contrivance which helped to give shape to their structure and to direct their energies. The universities belonged to a Christian world of learning: but each university had its own life. Hence we find in them order in diversity, general principles modified by local feeling. What is known as the *jus ubique docendi* gives a good indication of this fact. As we have seen, no new *studium generale* could win recognition unless it had been approved by the pope, and in course of time a mark of a *studium generale* was that its masters had the right to teach in any other, the *jus ubique docendi*. Yet this right might not be allowed in particular cases or in the relations between one university and another[1]. Thus when Pope Alexander IV granted the right to Salamanca in 1255 he excepted the universities of Paris and Bologna. A master of Salamanca, in other words, could not lecture in Paris or Bologna without satisfying the masters there and receiving their licence. The exception was not made by the pope in an arbitrary way. It was a recognition of the attitude of Paris and Bologna, universities so outstanding that the status of their degrees was beyond question, although they themselves did not ask the pope for the formal privilege to teach everywhere until 1291, thirty-six years after Salamanca had received it. Paris and Bologna had their difficulties, probably because they created difficulties for others. Paris complained that Oxford, Montpellier and other *studia generalia* would not admit a master or licentiate of Paris, however famous he might be, "to the exercise of magistral functions." Oxford and other universities, such as Orleans and Angers, passed statutes reserving their right to judge of the competence of masters from elsewhere and to impose tests. It is curious that, although Cambridge got a papal bull from Pope John XXII in 1318, Oxford at least twice, in 1296 and 1317, had sought the same privilege in vain. We may possibly see the reason for this failure to be put on the same footing as Paris and Bologna, in spite of the eloquent appeals of the kings Edward I and Edward II, in the rivalry between Oxford and Paris, the insistence of Oxford upon reciprocity between Paris and itself, and the desire of popes Boniface VIII and John XXII to please Paris. It was certainly not due to any distrust in the value of an Oxford degree. Nor need we assume that scholars of repute were not welcomed in other universities than their own.

The most likely explanation of the discrepancy between

[1]See George L. Haskins in *English Historical Review*, lvi (1941) 281-92.

local practice and the general acceptance of the *jus ubique docendi* as "of the essence of a *studium generale*" is that social conditions in western Christendom were making the wandering master something of an anomaly in academic life, except perhaps in the numerous civic universities of Italy. The wandering scholar was a student who went to a foreign university, and especially to Paris, as a stage in his career. The academic population of most universities tended to become more local as national life and feeling became more intense. This was the tendency in Oxford in the last decades of the thirteenth century. Paris was an exceptional university. The famous masters of Paris were not, as a rule, Frenchmen, but came from all parts of the West. They had generally taken their degrees in Paris, whereas the foreign masters elsewhere, as at Orleans, might as often as not have been invited. Moreover, the fame of a great master was spread, not entirely or even mainly, by his teaching in the schools but, increasingly, by his books. In recent years we have learned much about the medieval book trade, which derived from the activities of the stationers in the standardization of texts and the systematic methods of copying them and selling them. The invention of printing merely accelerated a publishing movement which had developed in the thirteenth and fourteenth centuries. In short, the *jus ubique docendi*, by the time that it became fashionable to acquire formal recognition of the privilege, was becoming a distinction, a mark of status, rather than a practical necessity. The West was still, academically speaking, cosmopolitan, but the wandering scholar was not so much one of a large floating population as a man with a purpose. The scholars of the orders of friars, Dominicans, Franciscans, Augustinians, Carmelites, were the exceptions which help us to realize the change in the position of the secular clerk; for the friars belonged to societies which paid less attention to frontiers, and whose centralized organization was familiar to them whether they were in Oxford or Bologna or in the missionary centres of Persia and north Africa. When we read of a master who taught in half a dozen universities, in Paris, Oxford, Bologna, Montpellier, Naples and so on, we are fairly sure to find that he was a man who was moved about from one friary of his order to another. He lived in a separate world. Such movements as the interchange of secular clerks between German universities or, for a time, between Oxford and Prague were due to special circumstances.

Here are two examples of the tendencies to which I have referred[1]. The archdeacon of Tournai in Flanders had contributed 500 pounds of Paris towards the support of Robert de Sorbon's "congregation of poor masters studying at Paris in the theological faculty", the later Sorbonne, and in 1266 the masters and scholars of Paris, "wishing to reply in kind to his benevolence", gave the archdeacon, and the bishop of Tournai or archdeacon of Flanders after his death, the right to place each year, in the house of the said poor masters, five masters studying in theology, men of good reputation who were familiar with the Flemish idiom, the language spoken in the archdeaconry of Tournai. The archdeacon's intention in seeking this privilege was to provide well-trained teachers for his locality. A prudent ecclesiastic sees the opportunity provided at Paris by Robert de Sorbon's new foundation to raise the standard of theological knowledge in his district and to provide good teachers who could speak to the people in their own tongue. My second example contains more subtle implications. A passage from a dialogue written by Leonardo Bruni reveals the attitude of Italian dialecticians in the later fourteenth century to the scholastic methods preferred by English

[1] I take them from the useful collection of sources made by Professor Lynn Thorndike in his *University Records and Life in the Middle Ages* (Columbia University Press, 1944), nos. 35, 102; pp. 74-5, 269.

disputants, and to the English scholars themselves. It reflects the local predilections of a humanism later than that expressed by John of Salisbury in his more general criticism of his contemporaries two centuries earlier. Leonardo Bruni makes a famous Florentine scholar, Colluccio Salutati press for the revival of the practice of disputation. In a reply Niccolò Niccoli bursts out as follows:

> But what of dialectic, which is the one art especially necessary for disputation? Does it still reign and flourish and has it suffered no calamity from this wave of ignorance? Far from it. For even the barbarism which dwells across the ocean has made an onslaught upon it. And nations, ye gods, whose very names I dread, Ferabrick, Buser, Occam, Suisset and others of the same sort, who seem to me to have derived their names from the cohort of Rhadamanthus. What is there, Colluccio, to stop jesting, what is there, I ask, in dialectic that has not been disturbed by British sophisms? What is there that has not been separated from that old and true method of disputation and dragged down to trivial nonsense?

This denunciation of the barbarians of Oxford was more than a piece of petulant humanism. The speaker in Leonardo's dialogue was affronted by academic developments which, in Paris as well as in Oxford, threatened the kind of education which he preferred. I cannot identify Buser. Ferabrick may just possibly conceal the name of the distinguished Oxford logician, Heytesbury, a fellow of Merton College (the name was usually softened down to Tisberus), and Suisset was the Italian version of the name of another Mertonian, Roger Swineshead. The Italians could not fail to know something about the great William of Ockham, but they knew Heytesbury and Swineshead, I imagine, only from the colophons of manuscripts, where their names were hopelessly corrupted by scribes before they were subjected to a euphonizing process by Italian lips. And it so happens that, in certain Italian schools of thought, these manuscripts were highly valued. Suisset's sophistical writings, for instance, were studied until the seventeenth century. Hence the passage which I have quoted illustrates national prejudice, the remoteness of Oxford, the dislike of a new philosophical movement, and the importance of manuscripts in the propagation of academic fashions of thought.

It is high time to leave these generalities and return to the three great *studia generalia* as types—or rather as archetypes—of university life two centuries or so before the Emperor Charles IV procured the papal bull which confirmed his foundation at Prague. Hitherto the terms *studium generale* and *universitas* have been used without careful distinction between them. If, however, we are to understand the differences in structure which were characteristic of the schools of Bologna, Paris and Oxford, it is essential to realize that, while they had in common the qualities of a *studium generale*, they comprised peculiar types of "universities". The *studium generale* was a school of general resort; as Rashdall says, "in its origin the expression was a wholly popular and extra-legal one. The question whether a particular school was or was not a *studium generale* was one settled by custom or usage, not by authority". The term expresses a relation to the outside world, it does not define internal structure which varied from place to place. The word "university", on the other hand, means a grouping or guild of persons brought together and consciously united by a common interest; it expresses, in whole or in part, the internal structure of a community, whether this be a body politic, a city or borough, a *studium*, or other entity; but, as it is impossible in a self-governing home of learning to separate the structure of the body of teachers and scholars from its nature and purpose, the term "university" gradually displaced the term *studium generale*. An institution established for purposes of higher learning is now described as a university, and it is convenient to refer to medieval "universities" without a pedantic and confusing adherence to chronological exactitude.

In its widest and most general sense the university was the society of masters and scholars. When the society issued a charter or open letter in its corporate capacity the writer began, "to all who shall see the present letters the university of masters and scholars at Paris sends greeting" or equivalent words of address, and correspondents addressed it as the masters and scholars; but less comprehensive modes of expression reflected the authority of or relations between elements within this wider body. Thus a condemnation of theological errors at Paris in 1241 was made by the chancellor and the masters teaching theology. Or again, a decree of protest in defence of an injured physician, Master Hugh (1281) was issued by the masters of all faculties gathered in Paris in the church of St. Julien le Pauvre "in the name of the university and for the university both of masters and scholars". Here in Paris legislation by various groups was issued in the name of, or for the sake or welfare of the "university", and the authority of the masters was emphasized, as when in 1244 "the masters of the university of Paris in the church of St. Mathurin at Paris in full congregation" made rules about the rental of class-rooms (*scholae*) and lodgings. In Bologna, on the other hand, the word *universitas* was appropriated by groups of students. It is probable that there were four "universities" at Bologna in the early years of the thirteenth century, as there were in the *studia* established elsewhere in Italy as the result of schisms or migrations from Bologna, although by 1244 there were only two, one of which was

164

divided into three sub-universities or "nations". These "universities" were guilds of students of law, and in course of time they acquired and were acknowledged to possess powers of legislation similar to those possessed by the masters of Paris and Oxford. The masters or doctors, grouped into a guild or "college" had no share in the deliberations of these student universities. This type of organization has too often been described as eccentric, and even amusing. It was so different from anything with which we are familiar that it has been regarded as a "freak", an anomalous expression of the medieval guild, but, as Rashdall pointed out half a century ago, it was quite a natural development of the conditions of student-life in north Italy. The scholars who flocked to Bologna after the days of Irnerius in the twelfth century came from Lombardy, Tuscany and Campania or rather (from whatever part of Italy and the lands south of the Alps they might come) they were grouped as Lombards, Tuscans and Romans. Almost as many more came from the north of the Alps, especially from the German lands; these formed another group, the Transalpine. These students did not find themselves under the protection of bishops or princes and of masters who themselves could safely rely upon such protection, but were exposed to the extortions and claims of civic communities. Although they and their teachers acquired the legal protection of emperor and pope and their juristic status as clerks subject to ecclesiastical discipline had been defined, they had to live from day to day, aliens in the midst of all the difficulties and disorders incident to the activities of a city whose efforts to maintain its self-government and, if possible, its political independence made it watchful, exacting, and jealous for its privileges.

Moreover, the city was proud of the learned doctors or masters whose fame had attracted so many strangers. The masters were citizens of Bologna, and through them the city had increased in wealth and prestige. In the course of time they were paid by the city. If they were attracted elsewhere or if the students in defence of their independence migrated elsewhere—a frequent form of academic strike—the city suffered; hence the city did its best to impose sanctions in order to keep its learned citizens and to prevent migrations. The outcome was not more cohesion but greater distinction between local teachers and foreign students. The former were more closely welded to the city, the latter formed themselves into larger and more powerful guilds or universities from which in fact if not in law the masters and students of local origin were excluded.

So we find a twofold form of organization. The doctors grew in social standing and wealth, but were outside the governing body of the universities. The universities of Transalpine students and of Cisalpine students—the latter, subdivided into three nations, the Lombard, Tuscan and Roman—controlled the administration of the *studium* and, though apparently without much result, even tried to subordinate the statutes of the doctoral colleges to their own. Under the university-statutes on the one hand and the city-statutes on the other, the doctor indeed paid heavily for his dignity. In their most developed form, these statutes controlled him in the exercise of his duties, though of course they did not interfere with or attempt to limit his freedom as a teacher and guide. He might be world famous as a professor of law, and be surrounded by enthusiastic pupils, but within the range of university life he was subject to the rector of the "university" which provided him with his hearers. "At any moment his lectures might be interrupted by the entrance of the bedel to serve a summons on the professor to appear before the rector. A professor requiring leave of absence even for a single day was compelled to obtain it first from his own pupils and then from the rectors and *conciliarii;* and if he proposed to leave the town, he was required to deposit a sum of money by way of security for his return . . . By the city-regulations, moreover, for each day on which he failed to secure an audience of five for an ordinary lecture, or three for an extraordinary one, he was treated as absent and incurred the appointed fine accordingly". Punctuality was enforced with extreme rigour. The professor had to begin his lecture when the bells of St. Peter's began to ring for mass and was forbidden to continue a minute after the bell had begun to ring for tierce.

All the same, developments in Bologna were natural and gradual, intricately related to the varied circumstances which gave occasion to them. The internal constitution of the *studium* should never be regarded as a clear-cut, logical, revolutionary creation ruthlessly imposed at the expense of the normal. In Bologna and other Italian universities it *was* the normal. In the beginnings of the movement which produced the European universities no precise way of advance was or could be anticipated. The association of students at Bologna was regarded by the citizens and authorities of Bologna as natural and by the pope as a necessity. It was not directed against the masters. If we could follow its progress with knowledge of every circumstance and influence, we should doubtless be able to see how, step by step, the complicated organism of universities, under their rectors, of nations and *consiliariae*, of statutes and procedure was devised in response to particular needs. Here, as in most medieval communities, co-operation was the normal, conflict the exceptional condition of life. Masters, students, civic authorities, pope, bishop and archdeacon combined in a life full of energy and colour, of function and routine. As new faculties of arts, medicine and theology—the last as late as 1360—and a new student university of medicine and arts were established, new adjustments were made without a pedantic regard for precedent. The new "university", while it claimed to exercise control of every non-juristic academic activity in the city, including that of the local grammar schools, was less powerful than the two universities of law students and, though a select body, apparently did not exclude local men. The professors of medicine, surgery, philosophy, logic, rhetoric and grammar were more loosely-knit together than the professors of law in their "colleges", the courses of study for degrees were more flexible than they were in canon and civil law. The faculty of theology, indeed, was independent of the local university system. It had its own organization of masters under the bishop of Bologna who was its chancellor, and its students were drawn almost entirely from the friars. In fact the *studium generale* of Bologna, in contrast to the *studium* of Paris was both more diffuse in its operations and more colourful an expression of the secular and ecclesiastical life of a busy city-community. It originated as a centre of learning in law, and in its subsequent developments, notably in the notarial arts and rhetoric and medicine, it was more intimately related to practical life than was either of the two other great *studia generalia*.

These features of university life at Bologna help us to understand more clearly the nature of the university of Paris. In Paris the organization of the *studium* was much more coherent, so that the distinction between the *studium* as a whole and the university which developed within it became blurred and was early obliterated[1]. The general congregation

[1]A statute of the faculty of arts in 1245 suggests that the rector and proctors of the arts-faculty, for the purposes of the statute, acted on behalf of a university "of artists" (*pro universitate*). The word, however, was here used in its more general sense.

168

of the university of masters included regent (and later non-regent masters) in all faculties; its decisions expressed, so far as was possible, the opinion of the *studium*. No clearly defined body of this kind could be summoned at Bologna. Again, from the earliest times the chancellor of the cathedral church of Notre-Dame was, in a real if ill-defined sense, the head of the *studium*. His authority was the source of all degrees and, although, as Rashdall and others have argued, the rejection of his claim to control the "university" gradually forced him into an external position, and his relation to the masters was certainly less intimate than that which existed between the chancellor and masters in Oxford, it would be incorrect to refuse him a peculiar prestige, dignity, and on occasion, influence in the life of the *studium*. In Bologna the archdeacon was "chancellor"; in the certificate conferring the doctorate in civil and canon law he described himself as acting "with the authority which I exercise as archdeacon and chancellor of this *studium*", but it would be absurd, when we remember the long list of eminent men whose academic distinction at Paris was inseparable from their official dignity, to regard the archdeacon of Bologna as equal to the chancellor of Paris. Moreover, as we have seen, the archdeacon of Bologna had no authority over the theological faculty whose chancellor was the bishop. However troubled and perplexing his relations with the university might be, the chancellor expressed the continuity and unity of academic life in Paris. And so we come to the third main difference between the constitution of the *studia* at Bologna and Paris, namely, the predominance of the faculty of arts, for the masters and students in arts, forming by far the largest faculty, had taken the lead in the resistance to the chancellor of Paris.

The technical use of the word "faculty", which had been used to imply disciplinary instruction (Boethius had used it of such instruction in dialectic), is found in the early days of the *studium*. The medical school of Paris would seem to have been organized as a faculty later in the history of the university, but the faculty of arts and the higher faculties of theology and law had a rudimentary existence in the later twelfth century. The cathedral schools of the north, however, were essentially schools of the arts, and in Paris of logic in particular. Graduation in the arts was the usual and became the statutory preliminary to study in one or other of the higher faculties. When the masters and scholars felt the impulse to organize themselves in order to maintain and extend their common well-being against the chancellor of Notre-Dame and other interests, the lead was naturally taken by the "artists". The history of this development, though fairly well documented as surviving medieval records go, is still obscure and it would be a mistake to read into its troubled phases any clearly defined object or anything but immediate intentions. It was always subordinated to the self-conscious interests of the *studium* or university as a whole. Few, if any, of the generalizations which have been made about it should be regarded as more than indications of tendency; all need qualification. That the chancellor was put outside the life of the university, that the faculty of arts was nothing but a federation of four independent nations, that the nations had no cognizance of masters in the higher faculties except as former students in arts, that the rector of the artists was much more than an executive officer, an *actor et procurator*, of university business, that the proctors of the four nations must be identified with the agents or proctors appointed, during the early disputes with the chancellor, to plead the cause of the university at the papal court and elsewhere,—all these generalizations give too clear-cut an explanation of constitutional developments. What *is* clear is that, as the masters—possibly at first the

170

scholars and masters—struggled towards the recognition of
their corporate independence, they gradually devised a
system of government which depended on the organization of
the arts faculty, divided into four nations, under the leadership of a rector who became the executive head of the university as a whole and on occasion the arbiter between the various
faculties. The rector, as the head of the whole body of artists,
emerged before 1249, in which year the four nations agreed
on the method of his election by their four proctors. By 1259,
ten years later, he was definitely recognized as the rector of
the university, that is, of the masters and scholars in all faculties. As a master in arts, he might, even during his period of
office, be continuing his studies in a higher faculty, but he
was head of the university.

About the same time the higher faculties were taking a
more precise form *as* faculties, with their deans, assemblies
and powers of making statutes. Voting in the great congregation was by faculty and was preceded by separate deliberations in faculty, each group of masters retiring to its wonted
place in the church or place where they all met. The rector
summoned the congregation, opened the proceedings, and
"concluded", pronouncing the collective sense of the house.
The rector, in fact, kept the university together, and both
symbolized and expressed its unity, as it acquired its complicated structure, just as the chancellor symbolized its
continuous life from the days when masters had opened their
schools under his protection and had enlarged the range of
the studies over which he had presided as head of a cathedral
school. The rector, compared to the chancellor, was a bird of
passage. His time of office lasted only three months, his powers
of jurisdiction were slight, he might or might not be a man of
academic distinction, yet, on the other hand, he kept the
whole university system in daily being. If we reflect upon the

variegated intensity of academic life in Paris during the century or so before the university of Prague was established, upon the ever increasing number of colleges and halls, upon the meetings of the nations under their proctors, of the faculties, of the congregation of masters in all faculties, upon the busy lecturing and disputations, and debates about all sorts of matters, small and great, sometimes upon matters affecting the well-being of the whole Church, we may well marvel at the way in which the university of Paris maintained its composite unity in spite of all the distractions which disturbed the most cosmopolitan corporation in Christendom.

The course of events in Paris was doubtless affected by the fact that the masters and scholars could generally rely upon the indulgence of the king of France and be sure of papal support. Although they were grouped in numerous nations[1] they were not sharply divided, as in Bologna, into local and foreign elements, nor constantly compelled, as in Bologna, to adjust themselves to the interests of the civic authorities. Masters and scholars alike came from all quarters of the West. Their main problem was their relations to the ecclesiastics of Notre-Dame. Only once during the early history of the *studium* were they at serious issue with the crown. This was in 1229, when a student riot was fiercely quelled by the provost of Paris and several innocent scholars were slain. Neither the papal legate nor the ecclesiastical authorities took any steps to protect the clerks and it is probable that the suppression of their violent outbursts, which caused general annoyance, was not unwelcome to those who had watched recent developments in the university body with concern. The outcome was a "great dispersion" of masters and scholars. Pope Gregory

[1]The best and fullest account of the "nations" at Paris and of the difference between them and the "nations" at Bologna can be found in a recent book by Pearl Kibre, *The Nations in the Medieval Universities*, published by the Mediæval Academy of America in 1948.

IX induced them to return in 1231. He took the opportunity, in a series of mandates, to make a comprehensive settlement. The young King Louis IX was required to confirm a royal charter of 1210 exempting the masters and scholars from secular jurisdiction. The bull *Parens Scientiarum*, the most important document issued in April 1231, has been described by Denifle as the *Magna Carta* of the *studium*. It defined the relations between the chancellor and the masters of the higher faculties in the admission to degrees, and put beyond cavil the existance of an organized body which could legislate about its own affairs. The university could no longer be regarded as an illicit conspiracy against the authority of the chancellor. At the same time the careful phrases of the bull make it clear that independence implies responsibility, and the obligation of all, king, chancellor, citizens and university alike, to co-operate with good will in a splendid task, worthy of the city of letters, the "parent of the sciences". The bull, as an expression of favour and protection, was the culminating point in the happy relations between the university and the papacy. Pope Gregory went so far as to say that, by their departure from Paris, the masters and scholars had maintained not so much their own case as the common cause. The maintenance of their privileges served the general need and utility of the church.

One outcome of the rapid development of the *studium* after the great dispersion caused a discordant note to disturb the harmony of pope and university. At the very time when Pope Gregory was clearing the air, the Dominicans and Franciscans were establishing their houses of study in Paris. As we all know, these newcomers gave an impetus to academic life which made the next hundred years one of the great moments in the intellectual history of mankind; but, unhappily, their presence also provoked jealousies and disorders which were fiercer and more lasting than the disputes between the masters and the ecclesiastics of Notre-Dame. The story of this controversy falls outside the scope of the present essay, but a few words should be said about its effect upon the structure of the university. The need to provide funds for the frequent appeals to Rome tightened the administration of the faculties and nations under the control of the rector by putting at their disposal the proceeds of fees and taxation. The faculties, notably the faculty of theology, were welded together more firmly within the constitutional framework as the secular masters rallied against a common danger to their control of the curricula. And, at a time when public affairs in Church and State and theological and philosophical movements of much consequence increasingly engaged the attention of the masters of Paris and increased their prestige, the quarrel with the mendicant orders disturbed relations between the university and the papacy. "The alliance between the Holy See and the mendicants", in Rashdall's words, "sowed the seeds of Gallicanism in the university which was to be its stronghold".

The *studium* of Paris, as we have tried to show, was different from that of Bologna, although it borrowed and adapted much in the Bolognese system. The Parisian system, on the other hand, was the basis of the academic constitution in Oxford, and the differences between the two northern *studia* at first do not seem very significant. In fact, however, these differences had deep roots and, as the Oxford system gradually developed, acquired much importance. In two respects, indeed, Bologna and Paris were more like each other than Paris and Oxford were. Both depended more upon foreign students; both had a strong and fundamental organization of "nations". Oxford, on the contrary, was from the first composed mainly of English masters and scholars and, in spite of the division into northern and southern groups, did not develop a system of nations as part of its constitutional structure. Moreover, it was less disturbed by the theological, ecclesiastical and political problems which made the university of Paris a microcosm reproducing the disputes of a wider world. When we compare the disputes at Oxford about the mendicants with those of Paris, we realize that Oxford was only "just touched by the storm which rent the university of Paris in sunder for so many years". The direct intervention of the university of Oxford in the controversies raised by the Great Schism was slight, and the influence of English academic opinion, by no means negligible, owed its weight, not to the heated convictions of the university as a whole, but to individuals who could make themselves felt in the English delegations at the General Councils. Any master of Paris who pursued his speculations untouched by the clamour and excitement about him must have been a recluse indeed; but one feels that life in Oxford was not stirred to its depths by the great issue at stake in the Church. Again, when all has been said, one feels that the Wycliffite movement was the expression not so much of strenuous academic reflection as of impulses in English life of which the Oxford master was the mouthpiece. His teaching found an echo in the lecture rooms of Prague but did not reverberate in the Oxford schools so much as give voice to the half-conscious prejudices and aspirations of clerks and laymen in the English midlands. Wyclif's logical processes and his use of the doctrine of grace had a scholastic origin, but his intelligence, like that of so many later Oxford reformers, worked under influences both more diffused and more deeply rooted in English social experience. Those who responded to him and applied his teaching in strange and unexpected ways formed but a small minority of his fellow countrymen, whereas his counterparts in Bohemia helped to make a national upheaval.

The peculiarities of the university of Oxford, indeed, require more subtle treatment than do the forthright expressions of the academic spirit in Paris. It is true that the Oxford masters owed nearly everything to Paris in the main organization of their *studium*. Their coherence, their strong faculty of arts, their intellectual interests were Parisian. The Best Oxford minds, with the possible exception of Roger bacon's, were at home in Paris. Many of the greatest teachers of Paris, such as Sackville, Shirewood, Pecham and Duns Scotus were Englishmen trained in English schools before they crossed the Channel. Most of the greatest teachers in Oxford had been students and masters in Paris. The dependence of English brains upon Paris began many years before the university of Oxford took organized form. Yet there was a *genius loci* in Oxford. As a French scholar has remarked of academic reactions to the Great Schism "the masters of Oxford and Paris spoke a different language", and though this statement would not apply to the thirteenth century or to the early fourteenth, it points to a general truth. From early days, for example, scholarship in Oxford seems to have been rather more attracted to science than to theology and metaphysics as it played upon the new learning made available in translations from the Greek and the Arabic. We must confine ourselves here, however, to academic life as expressed in social structure. Why do we feel that Oxford was different from Paris?

Behind the university movement—by which we mean the growth of academic corporations in centres of learning—lay the free, widespread and unorganized fellowship of scholars who in the course of the eleventh and twelfth centuries enriched and enlivened the life of the Church and became more and more detached from the monastic surroundings which had hitherto fostered adventures of the mind. Ecclesiastical discipline had on the whole kept pace with and indeed given an encouraging impetus to the revival of learning. The right to teach (*licentia docendi*), the duty of cathedral chapters to provide schools for the clergy, the provision, so far as possible, of free instruction by masters who need not be dependent upon fees, were regulated by the Church. As we study the careers of the "masters" of the twelfth century, we find ourselves in a world strangley parallel to that of the knight errantry of the romances, a world of chartered freemen, and indeed libertines, of the mind, who moved about from cathedral school to cathedral school, set up schools for themselves, and found a measure of security in the friendship and patronage of great men, princes, abbots and especially bishops. As papal decretals prove, the Holy See was well aware of its responsibilities towards a movement which was so useful yet might be so dangerous. There was no reason to suppose that the movement would coalesce into great centres of learning in which scholars or masters or both would settle down and gradually form powerful and highly protected corporations or universities, or if they did that Bologna or Paris or Oxford would take the lead. Laon, Chartres, Salisbury, Exeter, Lincoln and many a city in Italy might well have been the favoured places. There were still famous monastic schools. But Irnerius opened his law school in Bologna and a great bishop, Peter the Lombard, gave standing to the cathedral where he had pursued his biblical and theological teaching in Paris. Why Oxford took the lead in England is still an unsolved historical problem. Oxford was a royal borough situated at the crossing of important roads. Two big monastic houses were established there. Scholars had taught there. Parisian masters, in one of their migrations, may have found a resting place there. Whatever the causes were, Oxford became a famous *studium*, important enough to be regarded

before so very long as a *studium generale ex consuetudine*, in its
own right. From the time of the Norman Conquest to the
Reformation, Oxford lay within the diocese of Lincoln. The
cathedral city was far away. Hence, as the masters settled
down, they required a local head, for there was no local
chancellor responsible as at Paris for a cathedral school and
for the ordered activity of the independent masters. The
studium was given its own chancellor. In 1214 a papal legate
issued an ordinance which "is the first document in the
nature of a charter of privilege which the university of
Oxford can boast", and one of its clauses refers, in a casual
way, to "the chancellor whom the bishop of Lincoln shall
set over the scholars therein". Here, in the act which the
practice of Paris suggested, lay the main difference between
the schools of Paris and the schools of Oxford. A cathedral
dignity "was reproduced in a university town which possessed no cathedral". The chancellor of the masters was one of
themselves, elected by themselves. There was no need for the
masters of arts to take the lead in asserting themselves against
him. There was no need for a separate "rector". The inevitable disputes with the bishop of Lincoln about the *status* of
the chancellor were occasional wrangles with a distant lord,
not a perpetual trouble at their door.

In the compact kingdom which England was, all disputes,
whether with bishop or the borough, affected public order
and were subject to the arbitration if not the practical intervention of the crown. For the same reason, any tendency of
the rivalry between southern and northern scholars to develop
into a system of nations was soon checked—there was no
strength in it. The proctors in Oxford did not rule as the heads
of "nations" but as the executive officers of the university.
Pope, king, and bishops were alike concerned to foster the
studium and maintain its privileges. The king was both willing

to maintain the rights of the clerks and able to establish himself as their lord and protector. The university became a national institution, a home of institutional compromises between the secular and ecclesiastical authorities, a reservoir upon which the royal court could draw for its servants, a nicely balanced corporation which scandal and disturbance might shake but not overturn. It is a significant fact that, when for a few years early in the fourteenth century the disputes between the university and the mendicant orders were really serious, the solution reached by a body of arbitrators was imposed by royal letters.

IX

SOME PROBLEMS IN THE HISTORY OF THE MEDIEVAL UNIVERSITY[1]

The questions which, I imagine, are most frequently asked about the medieval university run something like this: What was the value of all this intellectual activity? Was there any sequence or permanence in it? What kind of degree did scholars take? Was it a mere form, or did in involve a serious mental discipline? We can best get some ideas about the answers to such questions—I do not say that we can ever get very satisfying answers—by looking at Paris in the middle of the fourteenth century.

By this time the university was fully developed. The four faculties of arts, medicine, degrees, and theology were clearly defined, each with its own statutes, organization, and records. Three of them, if not all four, were localized, that is to say, their studies and activities went on in definite areas of the university quarter. Just as at Bologna the jurists had their headquarters in the Dominican and the artists in the Franciscan church, so the artists in Paris lived in the neighbourhood of the church of St. Julian and in the Rue du Fouarre, while the decretists or canonists lived in the Clos Brunel. The use which the theologians made of the college of Robert de Sorbon was in all probability the result of a similar tendency,

[1]A presidential address delivered to the Royal Historical Society on 8 February, 1934, and printed in the Society's *Transactions*. 4th series, xvii, 1-18.

especially among the secular theologians[1], though it would be as wrong to identify the faculty of theology in the middle ages with the Sorbonne as to identify the jurists of Bologna with the Dominicans. The faculty of medicine, always more closely connected with the faculty of arts, appears to have had no definite centre; it is not known to have acquired a home until 1470 when it bought a house in the Rue de la Bucherie. But its precious commentaries, or records of faculty meetings, survive from the year 1395 and its distinct organization under a dean can be traced back at least to 1330. Each faculty, and each of the four nations which together made up the faculty of arts, had its parchment book of statutes, privileges and calendar, and its continuous paper registers which contained the minutes of meetings, and the names of scholars admitted as bachelors, or to the licence and the full mastership. The registers of the Anglo-German nation survive from 1332—a very precious record of academic activity from month to month in one society or corporation of the university. Until the commentaries of the medical faculty begin in 1395, and the registers of the faculty of decrees in 1414, they are the only record of the kind. Sometimes the registers tell us about meetings of congregation, the assembly of masters of all faculties. But the more important proceedings of congregation were described in reports and memoranda which, though sometimes they survive separately, are for the most part found in one or more of the chartularies of the university; and these chartularies seem to have been compiled as often for the use of nations and faculties as for the use of university officials assuch.

[1]The university used the Sorbonne for disputations from at least the early years of the fourteenth century; see the *Chartularium*, ii, 693, with Denifle's note, p. 695. The *Sorbonica* or disputation, held on Saturdays between members of the college, was carefully regulated in 1344. The statutes issued by the *provisor* of the college in this year suggest that this domestic exercise was a new departure, different from the disputations mentioned in the university statutes (*Chartularium*, ii, no. 1096).

Congregation might include as many as 200 masters; it usually met at St. Mathurin. No doubt customary meeting-places came in time to be used by the several nations and faculties; but there was no fixed rule. The English nation, for example, met in many different places, including the houses of officials and on at least one occasion in a tavern. The examinations *in camera*, which preceded the formal rites of inception or the licence, were apparently held anywhere, just as in our universities to-day examiners sometimes conduct oral examinations, discuss the written questions or decide the fate of candidates in private houses or college rooms. Official life in the university of Paris was not merely a series of solemn acts directed by solemn bedels, of formal public meet-ings and elaborate religious ceremonies, or of feasts and junketings. It was the life of men who did a great deal of academic work in informal ways. These men were crowded together in colleges, hospices, houses and lodgings. The "scholars" comprised men and boys of different ages and dignity and social importance. One gets the impression that the gradual passage from the status of scholar to that of bachelor and of bachelor to master was not the orderly affair which it is to-day, but might be accompanied by great dis-comfort; it was not easy to find *scolæ* or rooms for the exercises of the bachelors; men qualified for the licence might have to wait a long time and to use arts and blandishments to get it; masters could not be sure of finding a school in which to teach. This aspect of the medieval university has not been systematically studied and perhaps will always be a matter of surmise. We can learn a good deal about forms and constitutions on the one hand, and of the less academic sides of student life on the other ; but so far we can only form impressions about the heat, the intensity, the personal give and take, of everyday academic life. Yet this was the real life of the university, for in this combination of routine and scramble the masters and scholars gave or heard lectures, conducted or attended disputations, and found time and place for private study; it was in this atmosphere that they took sides on all the vexed questions of the day, from the casual incidents of a crowded and in every sense a very touchy companionship to the larger matters of academic prestige, public concern, theological or philosophical controversy, and high ecclesiastical policy.

The labour of recent scholars upon the manuscripts which contain the writings of scholastics—both the great men and those of secondary importance—have given the intellectual life of Paris a new perspective. The chief defect of Rashdall's *Universities of Europe in the Middle Ages*, to my mind—an inevitable defect no doubt—is that it fails to convey an impression of depth. I mean depth as a dimension, not as a metaphor for intellectual thoroughness. His picture of medieval Paris has extension but not depth. Hence it conveys little sense of coherence, of a closely knit, if turbulent, society actually alive and carried along by its own impetus. Yet we cannot realize the significance of a medieval university if we do not go beyond a classification of its activities and a summary description of its interests. Let me illustrate this point by a few definite considerations:

1. The university was intensely self-conscious and self-important. To what extent this was true of other universities requires investigation, but it was true of Paris and Bologna. The graduates of Paris were scattered over Europe and did not forget their colleagues at the *alma mater*. The regent masters felt that they were the centre and source of the intellectual life of Europe, the spring of the *studium* which refreshed the *imperium* and the *sacerdotium*, and was one of the three functions of the Christian society. When the project of a

council was under discussion during the schism, theologians and decretists of Paris insisted that the representatives of law and theology should equal in numbers the representatives of the hierarchy and monastic orders. Their arrogance shocked some of those who shared their conciliar views. Dietrich of Niem, for example, protested against it. Now this spirit was no new thing; it was merely an expression of an habitual attitude of mind, the attitude rebuked by the future Boniface VIII in November, 1290, when, as papal legate, he trounced the academic critics of Pope Martin IV's privilege in favour of mendicant orders. Certain masters had determined against the bull: he would have them know that the feet of the Church were *non plumeos sed plumbeos*. "You sit in chairs and think that Christ is ruled by your reasonings". One is reminded of Harnack's remark about the professors of Berlin, that they thought they sat at the loom of history. The confidence of the Parisian masters in themselves was not unnatural. It had been fostered by flattery and protection, and was kept lively by constant disputes over the judicial immunities of the Parisian scholars. During one of these disputes, a master seriously suggested that both the bishop and the provost of Paris as *conservator* of the university should be summoned before congregation as before a tribunal. During a controversy (1384) about the right of the canons of Notre-Dame to lecture on the canon law, the decretists maintained their claim to monopoly by elaborate historical arguments and by dwelling upon the advantages which concentrated study and teaching in a closely confined area possessed over the more leisurely and isolated performances of a clergyman in a cathedral close. Here we come to the heart of the matter.

2. The masters, we have seen, had discussed the bull of Martin IV in their lecture rooms. They had weighed the pros and cons and had "determined" upon them. The *scola* was

indeed the workshop of opinion; it was an intellectual smithy, to which metal of every kind could be brought. One of the hottest disputes of the fourteenth century (1385) concerned the duties of the chancellor towards bachelors who had qualified for the licence. The masters claimed that the real work was done by them: they examined the candidates and gave the necessary certificates; they decided who should or should not have the licence to teach. It was the duty of the chancellor not to discriminate or delay or accept large gifts which in reality were bribes. And the chancellor complained that one master had "determined" that he was a heretic, for he was obstinate in the breach of his sworn trust and so was rejecting the divinely disposed order of things. The appeal to the schools was no formality in the middle ages. When Thomas Cranmer, then a theological master at Cambridge, suggested that King Henry VIII should refer the problem of the divorce to the universities, he was not merely suggesting a way out of a difficulty. He was influenced by a tradition which had been immensely strengthened by use since, more than 250 years before, another King Henry had played with the idea of submitting his dispute with Thomas Becket to the judgment of the masters of Paris. Almost anything might be referred to the judgment of the masters. Their deliberations upon matters of ecclesiastical, theological, moral and public interest would fill many large volumes.[1]

In matters of heresy the joint commissions of theologians and the local authority, including the inquisitor, came to have executive authority in northern France. And the schools where the masters lectured or presided over disputations were the workshops of the opinion, which was expressed in solemn

[1] E.g., the sentences of censure pronounced by the faculty of theology before 1735 fill the three folio volumes of the *Collectio judiciorum de novis erroribus*, made by the bishop of Tulle, C. du Plessis d'Argentré (Paris, 1724–36; new edition, 1755).

judgments of the university. I am inclined to think that the preoccupation of historians with the general trend of medieval thought and particularly with the work of the Dominicans and Franciscans has tended to conceal the significance of this fact. Although another favourite preoccupation of historical scholars is the organic nature of medieval society, with its estates, corporations and guilds, the activity of the university as a social structure has been overlooked. In the medieval section of his well-known book, *Die Soziallehren der Christlichen Kirchen,* Ernst Troeltsch omits altogether any consideration of the universities as such. Now it is true enough that, in the thirteenth century, the Dominicans and Franciscans set the pace in the development of scholasticism, but the treatment of this fact in historical literature conveys a very misleading impression of academic life[1]. The Dominican priory at Paris, for example, was not a kind of beneficent cancer which absorbed the life of the university and drained the secular element of vitality. What happened was something like this. Two great centres of intellectual activity were fostered, partly by their own internal energy, partly by papal support and direction. One of them, the university of Paris, was centralized; the other, the system of Dominican schools, was a kind of distributed university, highly organized, pervading the whole order. Much of the more important work of St. Thomas was not lectured and written at Paris at all, but in the Italian *studia* of his order. The two movements naturally had to find a *modus vivendi* at the point where they met: the danger that the Dominican (and, a lesser danger, that the Franciscan) theologians might secure a monopoly was for a time a real one, especially as it coincided with a crisis in the history of the Parisian schools, but, once surmounted, it and other problems

[1]In his *Repertoire des maitres en théologie de Paris au XIIIe siècle* (Paris, 1933). Father P. Glorieux deals with 71 Dominican and 233 secular masters of theology.

incidental to the presence of flourishing mendicant priories were adjusted—uneasily, unevenly, with all the glamour and publicity which attend academic disputes—but they were adjusted. And in the process of adjustment each side strengthened the other. The mendicant philosophers and theologians had in Paris a sounding-board. The secular masters learned something from the organization of the new orders and got prestige from the fame of some of their new colleagues. St. Thomas, at Paris, like the Franciscan John Pecham at Oxford, probably put some method into the traditional system of disputations. But nobody at Paris in the thirteenth and fourteenth centuries would recognize the conventional picture of the medieval university in that city as the home of a few great men, followers of St. Francis and St. Dominic, surrounded by a crowd of garrulous dullards. This is a ridiculous travesty of the truth.

3. The intensive work, to which I have referred, upon the manuscripts of this period has done much to recapture the activity of the schools and to rehabilitate the secular masters. It has shown that the text-books—what we call "set books"— were the occasion of incessant discussion, so that there was gradually accumulated about them in the stationers' shops an important lending library of accredited commentaries and treatises. Each faculty had its prescribed texts, just as the theologians had the Bible and the Sentences of that very great man Peter the Lombard. Rashdall was puzzled by the *ars medicinæ*; he thought it was a book, whereas we now know that it was a *corpus* of texts, originally due to the famous teacher of Salerno, Constantinus Africanus, who lived in the eleventh century— a group of medical texts which medical students had to know. The artists had their exegetic lectures on logical and Aristotelean texts; they had lectures in the course of which "disputed questions" were dealt with under

the careful guidance of the master and his bachelor; they had sophistical disputations, corresponding, as Monsignor Grabmann has pointed out, to the *quodlibets* of the theologians, in which, according to fixed rules, all sorts of matters could be fully discussed and disputed, before the presiding master summed up and determined[1]. The decretists had the *Decretum* of Gratian and the Decretals of Gregory IX, Boniface VIII, and Clement V, masters lecturing on the *Decretum*, bachelors on the rest. In the faculty of theology the bachelors lectured on the Sentences, while the masters did the greater part of the teaching and lecturing on the Scriptures. Most of the surviving literature was clearly based on this teaching, or records these disputations, and most of the literature which does not reflect this experience was intended for the use of teachers and scholars. The catalogues of libraries, notably of the Sorbonne early in the fourteenth century, show conclusively that the university of Paris was much more than a society of boys who read a few text-books, of disputes which led nowhere, and of a few exceptional men who worked aloof from the life around them.

4. Time has done rough justice to this mass of learning. The wheat has been separated from the chaff. But the toilers of to-day, as they work among the chaff, have discovered many precious things. Undoubtedly there is much chaff. Indeed, when all this work is done, I imagine that its main value will be in the revelation of that continuous activity, in which the grain was sown from generation to generation, and the sowers were disciplined to scatter it at the call of popes and kings, councils, bishops, inquisitors, or to carry it away—a source of inward sustenance rather than of outward influence —in the service of church and state.

[1]M. Grabmann, *Die Aristoteleskommentare des Simon von Faversham* (from the *Sitzungsberichte der bayerischen Akademie der Wissenschaften*, Philos.-hist. Abt. 1933), pp. 11–13.

Yet this is by no means the whole story. Perhaps the best illustration of the point which I am trying to make is to be found in the history of logic. At first sight nothing is less helpful. We are told, for example, that a Durham man, William Shirewood, much praised by Roger Bacon, had great reputation as a teacher of logic at Paris; that one of his pupils, Petrus Hispanus, later Pope John XXI (1276), compiled a text-book of logic, the *Summulæ logicales* which was destined to be for centuries the favourite text-book in the subject; that in succession to him we find important logicians, among them John Buridan, who was rector of the university in 1327 and 1348 and wrote important commentaries on the *Physics* and other Aristotelean works. This does not take us very far; but if we can trust the experts, we have here the bare bones of a significant story. Peter Hispanus summed up a stage in the development of dialectic—the dialectic of the sophistical disputations in which the sceptics and Averroists of the thirteenth century, headed by Siger of Brabant, found expression. We find this dialectic flourishing early in the next century in Oxford, and though its work was soon forgotten in England, it lived on the continent. Meanwhile, logical exercises in Paris had been more fruitful; dialectical method was used, on the one hand, in the interpretation of Aristotelean science, on the other, to explain the direct observation of natural phenomena; the outcome was the teaching of Buridan and his followers. Their theories on physics, especially Buridan's theory of *impetus*, in due course influenced the great Italian scientists of the sixteenth century, who were not so independent of their predecessors as is generally supposed. In other words, modern science does not start with Leonardo da Vinci, Galileo and the rest; it began at Paris in the classrooms and studies in the crowded narrow streets of the artists' quarter, and the way to it was prepared by men, young and old, who had wrangled about logical terms and pored over the text of Aristotle and had gradually realized how important it was to observe facts for themselves.

Buridan was an Occamist, one of many. He did not hold with the "moderns", as they were called, who denied that the existence of God could be proved; but he and his successors, in what are often believed to be the barren years, were deep in those discussions about names and things which were to affect the history of the modern world. I am speaking of things which I do not understand and am warned by the facile generalizations of the latest philosophers of history. Yet there seems no reason to doubt that this period saw a turning-point in the history of thought. At bottom the issue between the Thomists and the new nominalism (and how recently the teaching of St. Thomas had itself been suspect) turned upon the possibility of believing in the essential reasonableness of the universe. If faith need not be divorced from reason, conscience need not be in a state of civil war, divided against itself; the sanctions of behaviour, whether political or religious, are not capable of fundamental discord. This is the Thomist view. But the Occamist philosophy, reflecting and justifying current tendencies, was different. Luther, who read the Occamists, and perhaps did not always understand them, was tortured by a sense of discord which he could not transcend. That facts were not in harmony might be transitory, but there was a fundamental lack of coherence in intellectual experience. A man, while intent on personal salvation, might have a duty, a moral duty, to sin in maintaining the sanctions of society and the state. The brutal instinct which sends a criminal to be broken on the wheel has its own authority. Luther's successors, and men and women in all countries, are face to face with this dreadful dilemma to-day.

In these notes on Paris in the fourteenth century I have

said enough, I hope, to show that the first group of questions with which I began are serious questions: "What was the value of all this intellectual activity? Was there any sequence or permanence in it?" And the next group of questions, "What kind of degree did scholars take? Was it a mere form, or did it involve a serious mental discipline?" are clearly very serious questions also. The point to be made here is that, in such an academic life as I have tried to suggest existed in Paris, intellectual earnestness and excellence were not revealed by a kind of accident; they were not in the nature of the case exceptional. They were encouraged. A keen student found incentive all about him. This after all is the main thing. It would be absurd to suppose that the students in the medieval university were, as a whole, an especially bright or conscientious set of men, though I imagine that circumstances selected them quite as carefully as they select university students to-day. As a medieval distich says: "You may send a little donkey to Paris, but if he is an ass here, he won't be a horse there". Whatever he were, he could find plenty of fodder. Rashdall, who was the last man to encourage any illusion on this subject, points out that the obligation to attend and, later, to take part in disputations, deprives the problem of efficiency in examinations of much of its significance[1]. A young man who had "determined" in arts, or a theologian who had reached the grade of "formed bachelor", had gone through a very severe discipline. The determiner, for example, had been required to display intellectual agility and persistence in disputations which lasted for several weeks. The formed bachelor had been required to lecture on the

[1]Since this paper was written, the publication of the volume *Oxford Theology and Theologians, c.* 1282–1302, by A. G. Little and F. Pelster (Oxford Historical Society, vol. xcvi, Oxford, 1934), has greatly facilitated the understanding of the academic exercises at Paris and Oxford.

Sentences and knew that if his lectures, when he had revised and published them, won esteem, his name would be made. The very conditions which would help a scholar to be idle or perfunctory, could encourage another to put out all his powers. Until 1452 lectures in arts and, both before and after 1452, lectures in law were given without notes and in a rapid or at least continuous voice, without pauses. A good lecturer had to be quite sure of himself and a good hearer had to have a retentive memory. There was a great to-do in the faculty of decrees in 1386 when a master, usurping the function of the bachelors, lectured to large and profitable audiences on the Decretals by the light of a candle, that is to say, read lectures which could be taken down. These particular lectures according to the statutes had always to be given by a bachelor at an early hour; no candle was allowed, and as the academic year comprised the period when the days were short, this meant that the lectures were given in darkness. Although the masters presumably lectured in daylight, it must have been very difficult to take their lectures down—a fact which may even help to explain the discrepancies and incoherences in the *reportationes* or texts made by the masters' bachelors. Now when we remember that these lectures were full of references, we realize that they might put a heavy strain upon the attention and memory of those who heard them. The relations between master and pupil and the importance of the memory in the medieval system of education are described very neatly in a short tract, *De regimine et modo studendi*, written in the thirteenth century by an Italian master, Martino da Fano. The tract is dedicated to his pupils (*dilectissimis scolaribus*). He advises them, in their judgment of a master, to consider whether he teaches the things which he ought to teach, is willing to answer questions, and draws out what is in the inquirer's mind. Does he suffer opposition sensibly and give reasons for what he asserts? Does he make an adequate impression upon his hearers and use effective illustrations to explain his arguments? Is he free from pretentiousness, really helpful, and more concerned with the truth than with fine tricks of speech. Then, turning to the scholars, Martin warns them to set a high standard before themselves, to see that they understand the legal argument so that everything fits and not to think they know unless they fully understand every part. "And finally, as you lie in bed or walk about the street, go over what you have learned and say, 'To-day I have learned so many laws, and these are the opening words of each'."[1] Again some of you will remember the story of Albert the Great, how while he was lecturing one day in his *scola* at Cologne his memory suddenly failed him and his reasoning would not come. He sat silent for a little while: then, flushed and comforted, he told his pupils that the Virgin had appeared to him long ago, and after she had anticipated a life of great learning for him, had warned him that this would happen to him, *in publico officio lectionis*. From this time he gave himself to prayer, and, though he could still remember his texts, the power to recollect *rationes philosophicæ* never returned to him.

He could still remember his texts. One version of the story defines this as the text of Scripture and philosophy. The implication is that Albert knew the Bible and a good deal of Aristotle by heart. If this is not interpreted pedantically, I imagine that it is true. A true medieval scholar knew the great texts of his subject and could refer to them from memory. Now anyone who has ever looked at a medieval commentary or a reading (*lectura*) in the civil or canon law can realize the

[1]Edited by L. Frati, in *Studi e Memorie per la Storia dell' Università di Bologna*, vi (1926), 25-9.

significance of this fact[1]. It suggests a mental discipline as astonishing to us as the physical discipline suggested by a suit of medieval armour. Picture to yourselves a young law student attending a lecture in the dark, a lecture given in a level continuous voice, without pauses. Picture him later, as a bachelor, engaged in disputations or in lecturing on the problems raised by a decretal. Think of the opponent ready to trip him up and on the alert for the least slip. A man who could go through this discipline and be certified as ready to undergo an examination *in camera* might well be permitted to pass on to his mastership after a very perfunctory test. I do not deny that there were ways of evasion and periods of slack administration; but, so far as I can understand the texts, the system was more or less as I have sketched it. In any case, before we safely conclude that every one passed his examination as a matter of course, we must know two things: first, how many scholars dropped out by the way; secondly, are the records, even when they seem to be complete, records of successful candidates only, or of all candidates, all of whom got through?

The impression that medieval examinations can be ignored, even if they existed, is untrue, and results from a hasty concentration on the more formal ceremonies, which fill so much space in the university statutes. The belief in a course of apprenticeship, followed by testing, is fundamental in early societies, as we may learn from the anthropologists, as well as from Tacitus and the practices of medieval chivalry, and of medieval arts and crafts. The examination system is very old and in the middle ages was widespread. There is a story of an examination in medicine at Salerno about 1200,

[1] Cf. the study of the references (*allegationes*) and abbreviations in legal texts, by H. Kantorowicz, *Die Allegationes im Späteren Mittelaltar*, in *Archiv für Urkundenforschung*, xiii (1933), 15–29.

when a rejected candidate went in disgust to Montpellier. Stray references in Buoncompagno's writings seem to imply examinations at Bologna about the same time, and the letters of Pope Honorius III to the archdeacon of Bologna enforced them. Grabmann has noted in two thirteenth-century manuscripts a collection of questions to be discussed in examinations on the arts course at Paris together with the answers.[1] At the papal court poor petitioners for benefices had to undergo examinations, and records of the reports of examiners survive, saying how one candidate sang badly, or another failed to satisfy in reading. It should be noted, by the way, that university graduates were excused this examination, and the fourteenth-century university graduates in the main depended upon the pope for provision to benefices. Our chief record of the graduates of Paris and Oxford, for example, is the *rotuli* containing the names of graduates submitted by the authorities to the papal court; and when the withdrawal of obedience at Paris during the papal schism, and the statutes of provisors and *præmunire* in England, seemed likely to interfere with the transmission of the *rotuli*, the consternation in university circles was very great. But my point is that at the papal court graduation in a university was considered to be a proof of competence; it excused applicants for papal provisions from examination.

In the statutes of the theological faculty at Bologna, edited by the late Cardinal Ehrle, we have precise regulations for examination. The statutes were compiled in 1364 and were explicitly based on those of Paris, which are now lost.

[1] *Revue néo-scolastique*, xxxvi (1934), 211–29. Virgilius Wellendorfer, who wrote a most interesting and detailed account of his studies at Leipzig (1481–7), gives a list of the questions which he had to answer at his preliminary examination (*tentamen*) and *examen* proper for the licence in 1487; see R. Helssig, *Die wissenschaftlichen Vorbedingungen für Baccalaureat in artibus und Magisterium*, especially pp. 80 *sqq.* (*Beiträge zur Geschichte der Universität Leipzig im fünfzehnten Jahrhundert*, Leipzig, 1909).

Here is the statute headed "on the procedure to be observed in the private examination." The candidates were bachelors who had been recommended for admission to the test which preceded the conferment of the licence, i.e., the mastership or doctorate in theology. I summarize the text: As effort wanes without reward, so distinction suffers if it is given to the unworthy. It is inconsistent with our duty to acquiesce in either of these possibilities, so we prescribe as follows. Three days before the examination the dean shall choose two subjects (*puncta*), that is, two *distinctiones* from the Sentences. He shall frame two very debatable questions, suggested by these, stating both sides of the case, and shall give these in writing to the candidate. A full day before the examination (i.e., two days later) the candidate shall give in writing to each master in the faculty his reasoned conclusions on each question, under four or five heads. On the next day at the eighteenth hour those masters whose schools are incorporated in the theological body (*universitas*) shall come together in conclave before the chancellor. First the dean, then each master in turn, according to seniority, shall dispute against the position taken by the candidate on the first *questio*, giving two or three reasoned arguments, which are to be sprung upon the candidate, or as we say, to be "unseen." The candidate must give three reasoned replies (*replicationes*) to the first argument and two to the second. And then the same process is to be observed in dealing with the position on the other *questio*. When all this is over, the candidate shall be sent out of the room, and the chancellor shall call on each master to give his honest opinion both of the moral character of the candidate and of his fitness for the degree. (In 1364 the decision of the weightier—*major vel sanior*—element prevailed; according to a later recension of the statutes the voting was by ballot and three adverse votes could fail the candidate.) Until his success is assured the candidate must on no account, on pain of perjury, offer gifts to his examiners; but later he may offer them wine and refreshment, provided that the cost of the entertainment does not exceed two florins. I doubt if I could ever have passed an examination of this kind.

X

THE MEDIEVAL UNIVERSITY IN CHURCH
AND SOCIETY.[1]

The medieval universities provided a vocational training for clerks in the broad sense of the term—for notaries, secretaries and the clerical handyman, for civil and canon lawyers, for medical men and for the intellectual *élite*, the theologians and philosophers. We should regard with caution two facile generalizations which are apt to colour our thoughts about university life. The first is that learning as such is an end in itself, the second that universities as such form a kind of estate and constitute a distinct element in society, and that each university necessarily speaks with a united voice because it issues acts under its own seal and expresses its life in corporate institutions. Both generalizations contain enough truth to give them currency, but both can be misleading, and not least if we apply them to the medieval university.

"Learning is an end in itself." The learned clerk in the sense of a man who devoted his life to learning and to nothing else, was a comparatively rare person, and the learned clerk who lived in seclusion, like a monk, was rarer still. It is true that, when colleges were founded, the college of Robert de Sorbon in Paris and of Walter de Merton in Oxford, followed by several more, the opportunities for retired and prolonged study must have been increased, and that the linking of Franciscan and Dominican priories with the academic life

[1]Based on a public lecture first given on 23 February, 1943 for the Bedford College for Women, then located in Cambridge.

gave much more stability to what we call research. Yet we know little of these men. The most vocal of them was, I suppose, the Franciscan, Roger Bacon. Most men of great learning and reputation for learning, whether they were friars or seculars, came to their own in the work of the schools as teachers, in their lectures on great standard texts—a book of Aristotle, the Code, the Decretals, the Sentences of Peter the Lombard, the Scriptures—and in disputations and exercises of the schools. They lived a busy, exciting, exacting life in which the fittest survived. This fact explains both the strength and the weakness of their work, its insight and vigour when it is good, its mixture of conventional thought and pedantic controversy when it is bad, for it was born of dialectic and bred in discussion. And these men were marked men. They were used, and no promotion, not even the papal throne, was too high for them. To come to the second generalization, since the university was an arena rather than a cloister, it could not speak with a single voice. It was indeed a privileged corporation, but its privileges, by their very nature, show that it lacked those material endowments which gave unity and stability to the most factious abbey. They were not the privileges of possession, but of protection. Kings and bishops had the duty to protect, and, in accordance with the canon or, it might be, the common law, to discipline these collections of studious men; for the scholars were exposed to the violence both of their own passions and of the townsmen, sometimes exasperated, sometimes exacting, among whom they lived. So the process began, the series of courts, supervision of markets, safeguards of independence, often against the bishop himself, which were built up into a dignified fabric of academic independence, and survive, where and so far as they still survive, as an archæological curiosity. But we should not be misled by the compliments of popes and princes, nor by the unblushing demonstrations of academic self-advertisement, into the illusion that the medieval university derived its strength from material endowments and garnered social prestige, "remembered in tranquillity." It derived its strength from its own turbulent life. It could, if need be, dissolve itself in a week. It could fold its tents and pitch them elsewhere. Its masters met for business in churches, hired rooms in religious houses or private houses for their lectures; its scholars lived in lodgings or licensed halls under the protection of masters. It possessed few books and little money. The young scholars spent money, brought and begged from home, the masters spent their fees, to the profit of householders and shopkeepers; and from a material point of view this was the chief purpose of a university in the thirteenth century.

Halfway between the battles of Lewes and Evesham, King Henry III, then under the direction of baronial councils, made a serious decision about a little settlement at Northampton which was showing signs of turning itself into a university. The scholars had migrated from Cambridge a few years before. They had no charters and no property, but the king had allowed them to remain. His account of his action, however, is significant. On 1 February 1265, he wrote as follows to the mayor and burgesses of Northampton. "We acceded to their request because we believed then that this would benefit your town and that advantage would accrue to us; but now we have learned on the testimony of men worthy of belief that, if the university remains at Northampton, no small damage would be incurred by our borough of Oxford, which is of ancient creation, has been confirmed by our ancestors, and is generally approved as a convenience to students. We should on no grounds be willing that this should happen, especially as all the bishops agree that for the honour of God, the advantage of the church of England and the well-being of the students, the university should be removed from Northampton". In spite of the opinion of the bishops, one feels that it was the borough of Oxford that really mattered; it had got the better of Northampton. The scholars sent home from Oxford by Henry in the previous year had been given permission to return, but perhaps they were not returning fast enough or in sufficient numbers. Even as late as 1265 they had not learned to feel that theirs was an abiding city.

I lay some stress on this point because the university was a function of the Christian society, not a separate order; it needed protection, or as King Henry, possibly with a touch of irony, put it, "peace and tranquillity", in order to fulfil its function, not in order to cut it off from the world. The author of a tract, *Notitia Sæculi*, written in 1288, put the matter in a systematic way. After dividing time into five ages and the world into three parts, Asia, Africa and Europe, he concentrates on the *populus christianus* in Europe. Europe has four realms, the Greeks in the East, the Spaniards in the West, the Romans in the South, the Franks in the North. The Christian republic resides especially in the two last, which together are subdivided into three provinces, Italia, Teutonia and Gallia, inhabited by three different races. By divine ordinance the three principalities in the Church are distributed to the keeping of these three races. "The *Sacerdotium* keeps the faith in Italy, the *Regnum* commands it to be kept in Germany and the *Studium* teaches it to be kept in Gaul". The symmetry of this exposition was, of course, highly tendentious and its artifice need not disturb us. The real point is that the author regards the Church or Christian folk in Europe as under three kinds of direction, the temporal (*regnum*) the spiritual (*sacerdotium*) and the educational (*studium*). How the Church regarded the work of the *studium* can easily be discovered. I take two texts at random. Here are the opening words of a privilege of Pope Innocent VI, dated 30 June, 1360 at Avignon. It confirms the creation of a faculty of theology in the university of Bologna: "As the tree of life in the paradise of God, and as a lamp burning in the house of the Lord, so is the faculty of theology in the holy Church of God. It is like a fruitful mother of learning for the irrigation of the barren earth". And here, slightly more prosaic, is a sentence from a letter to a pope from an English king, on behalf of certain privileges of the university of Oxford: "This university which we embrace as we should with the arms of intimate love, especially because by it the whole church in England is maintained".

The *studium* was given to France, because Paris had the most famous and influential university in Europe, and at least once in its history the masters of Paris took the lead in the Church. This was during the Great Schism, when the existence of rival popes deprived the Church of undisputed guidance. The university sent its embassies to and fro throughout Europe. Its influence was able now and then to bend the royal council and the assemblies of bishops to its will. If ever the university could be said to act as an organic whole, it was during these years; yet it was not even then united. I take one example from 1406, because it illustrates very well some of the points which I wish to make. The question at issue was whether the particular pope of Avignon at this time, Benedict XIII, should be recognized or not. A very great man, Pierre d'Ailly, bishop of Cambrai, was in favour, the university as a whole was not. The bishop maintained that the question at issue was a matter for the theologians, who had recently met in an assembly, not for the faculties of arts and medicine. A university champion, though himself a master or doctor of theology, made a speech in congregation. It reads very like a vivacious oration might today:

I am suprised that the bishop should maintain that the faculty of medicine and the faculty of arts should not concern themselves with this matter. To begin with, there are a thousand masters in the faculty of arts. Someone at the back says two thousand. Anyhow, there is at least a thousand, and two or three hundred of them are graduates in other sciences, bachelors in theology, in medicine, in civil and canon law; some, indeed, more than bachelors. A theologian is a member of the faculty of arts until he has the bonnet on his head, and it is not the bonnet that gives him his knowledge. My friend behind says—he seems to be afraid that I might forget it—that many a poor man in rags is a good and sufficient clerk. He is right. Learning trusts in poverty more than in riches. There are bachelors in theology to whom I always turn if I have any difficulty, men who see more clearly, perhaps, than many a man of great name in the world. Many good clerks are not masters. Guignicourt, who was regarded as the best man of his time, was never more than a bachelor in theology.

Jean Petit—for he was the orator—was discussing the most serious matter that a responsible body of men could discuss. Was a particular person to be recognized as the true pope? Yet, in a perfectly natural way, he talks as though this were some casual issue in academic politics. We are taken inside the university. The general congregation of masters in all faculties, regent and non-regent, i.e. teaching and non-teaching masters, is like a public meeting. It is "large, youthful, and fluctuating". It responds to popular oratory. The faculties have their rivalries. Influence does not depend upon reputation. No practical matter and few spiritual subjects are too high to be beyond dispute, back-chat, badinage. We are reminded that this famous corporation is a collection of individuals, grouped in various ways, crowded together.

The conditions of university life expressed themselves in different places in different ways. Institutions, the exercise of authority, the curricula were the outcome of local circumstance. Thus Bologna was, in a sense, a federation of universities. In its great law schools the governing body was the students, but, on the other hand, the teachers or doctors were much more dignified, more stable, more closely connected with civic life, wealthier, than the regent masters of Paris who were the governing body in their university. Hence, in spite of its growth in coherence and its occasional emergence into importance, the influence exerted by the *studium* was not corporate so much as personal, and was exercised as much through the masters who left it as by those who remained. From this point of view, the universities were important, not as close corporations, not as distinct organs of the Christian republic, but as the training centres of men who performed functions in the Christian society and stimulated its life.

A profession can both fit a man to advance its work and interests, and it can make him a useful member of society as a whole, as a counsellor or administrator or writer. The medieval master in theology, law, medicine, and in the arts (which, as well as being ends in themselves, were generally, though not always, preparatory to the studies in other faculties) might stay on in his university for many years or go out into the world. If he did the former, he had the opportunity to take part in deliberations upon public questions or, if he was famous enough, to deliver expert advice upon them when invited to do so. From the second half of the twelfth century, at least, if not earlier, the masters in Paris were consulted on all sorts of things, and we may be sure that they discussed them among themselves whether they were invited to do so or not. In either case they helped to form opinion. The subject might be a problem in dogmatic theology, like the Immaculate Conception of the Virgin or Pope John XXII's personal, as distinct from any formal and authoritative, views on the Beatific Vision, or it might be a problem in the relations between the spiritual and secular authorities, such as the quarrel between King Henry II and Archbishop Thomas of Canterbury, or Philip the Fair's appeal to a General Council against Pope Boniface VIII. Frederick I engaged four leading civilians of Bologna to define his rights or *regalia* as king of Italy. King Henry III, during a long dispute over the election to the see of Winchester, consulted the lawyers at Oxford and proposed to consult the lawyers at Paris. Perhaps the most interesting and not the least far-reaching matters discussed by the masters were those which, when deeply considered, raised issues affecting everyday life in the Church: for example, the ever-present problem of Christ's teaching on poverty, as it affected the clergy, or the theological and legal implications of the permission given to wandering friars to hear confession and, in doing so, invade the province of the parish priest. Just as we should not think of the universities merely as secluded citadels of abstract speculation, so we should not think of popes and bishops, kings and princes, as exercising their plenitude of power, whatever it might be, with an arbitrary disregard of the expert. Deep answered to deep. A great papal bull, *Unam Sanctam* for example, might reflect as in a mirror the teaching of a treatise, and would certainly take account of the opinions of the schools. Indeed it might have as its purpose the decision between conflicting opinions. And the same thing can be said of a great English statute, although in this case the "schools" were not the universities, but the gathered experience of the judges and common lawyers. "Who would have thought that a pope would have done this?," Stephen Langton once exclaimed in a lecture. He felt as Bracton sometimes did when he deplored some current tendency in English law, or as a distinguished canonist might feel, as he sadly corrected his teaching on the implications of a decretal.

But this meant that he had not had his way, not that the decision was arbitrary. In the closely articulated interplay of theory, law and practice, there was no end to the issues which some stately generalization might raise.

The record of academic intervention in ecclesiastical and social developments is impressive; yet the use made of university men outside the schools, if less spectacular, was probably more effective. Graduates were taken into the service of great men, popes, bishops, princes, city-states, and their trained minds helped to shape and direct action. I doubt if they often initiated action; rather they gave counsel and defined issues. They were, so to speak, super-draftsmen. Their training in arts made them masters of composition and rhetoric. Their study and teaching of the great texts, notably of Justinian's law books and Gratian's *Decretum*, with the later compilations of papal decretals which were circulated by the popes to the schools of canon law, enabled them to cope with practical issues. The Western Church was regarded as a republic within which disputes should be settled by discussion and arbitration, not—if it could be avoided—by war. Every issue depended on rights and the appeal to history, and, just as our later system of banking and exchange developed, to a large extent, through the co-operation between Italian merchant-houses and the papal financial system, so the later system of states found expression under the guidance of men trained in the civil law of Rome. The impetus came from elsewhere, but trained minds formed the methods of discussion and influenced the political arguments. What now-a-days we call state papers and propaganda, both of which became common in the thirteenth century, were profoundly affected—often initiated—by men of this kind who had entered the chanceries of popes, emperors and kings. Civilians, canonists, rhetoricians, notaries were the authors of the manifestos which appealed to opinion, from the days of the political propaganda of the Emperor Frederick II onwards. In France, for example, there was a flourishing law school at Orleans, and masters of this university were drafted into the service of Kings Philip III and Philip IV. Their lectures and commentaries show that they were ready for their work, for they abound in cases drawn from contemporary life, and showing the impact of the civil law upon circumstance. Indeed, the men of Orleans can be traced earlier. In 1262 Henry III went to visit King Louis to try to settle in his court the endless disputes which he had with Simon de Montfort. Before he left he wrote to Guido of Pavia, a prudent man and a doctor of laws at Orleans, begging him to come to him on a certain day at Paris to discuss the urgent business in hand; and Henry adds, "in this way the friendship between us may be drawn closer". As time went on, the employment of academic jurists by English kings became frequent, for, as a vassal of the king of France for his lands in Gascony, the king of England was constantly involved in cases in the Parliament of Paris and in tiresome arbitrations about piratical acts at sea and similar matters. Edward I's employment of the great civilian Accursius is well known. England, however, had not much need for civilians; it was a land with its own common law, and its own legal profession; but, like every community within the ambit of the Christian west, England did need canonists. Henry III generally had a little group of experts by his side, specialists in ecclesiastical affairs. The chronicler Matthew Paris compared them to hounds which could be unleashed against persons who did not see eye to eye with the king. For a short time, during the trouble of the Winchester election, when he was faced by his former friend and counsellor, William Ralegh, the bishop-elect, the most distinguished common lawyer in England, the king employed a bright young canonist from Savoy, a master of Paris. Such was the apprenticeship of Henry of Susa, who was to acquire in legal circles a reputation which has ever since given his title as cardinal, Hostiensis, an intimate significance. The history of the masters of the schools who entered the public service, and ended as popes, cardinals, archbishops, bishops, is a fascinating study; there is no end to it. They were everywhere.

Let us look a little closer at two types, the men at the top of the academic ladder, the theologians, and the dim crowd at the foot, the young men and boys who went to the universities and left as bachelors in arts, or after a few terms, without any degree at all. What parts did these play in the Church and society? I can say little about the clerical underworld. One looks down a pit, as Sir Max Beerbohm, in one of his essays, looks down on the users of popular guides to letter writing, and hears the interminable scratching of innumerable pens. One at least, François Villon, shot up to become a bright star in the heaven of poetry, but he was, indeed, an exception. And yet enough evidence survives to give us some idea of their fate. Some had livings waiting for them, some had been released by their bishops for a year or more in the hope that they would become fitted to hold the benefices which they already had. Some became schoolmasters. Some, I imagine, drifted into that large army of clerks which provided the medieval curate, the badly paid assistants of rectors and vicars, and the deputies of absent pluralists. More would be used in what we now call the civil services, in the offices of ministers of state, in the households of the great, for every household of any size implied the possession of lands and that in turn implied some sort of domestic chancery. On the whole, I do not much like to think about the clerical underworld in the middle ages, whether or not it was recruited from the schools.

The studies of recent scholars do seem, however, to be throwing light upon the influence of the universities and of the cathedral schools which preceded them, notably at Chartres, and existed alongside them, upon letters and the arts. I am not competent to deal with this difficult problem; but I do not believe that the unknown men who went through the schools, and were reabsorbed by the outside world, were necessarily isolated persons, who had a smattering of useless knowledge. They would create an atmosphere. And here lies the significance of Villon, rebel though he was, and of the lesser unknown men of his type and of quieter types, who had found reality in their studies. The poignant humanism which fed the mind of Heloise did not disappear entirely from the schools. Some scholars believe that the art of *dictamen*, of which the medieval letter, manifesto, state paper was the fruit, lies behind even the development of the language of courts in the vernacular—of what corresponds to our "King's English". Certainly, we could not explain, just as we cannot understand, Dante, the Romance of the Rose, Langland, Chaucer, and much of the lyrical poetry of the middle ages, without access to the matter and the form of classical literature and the later Latin literature which it inspired in every branch of expression. And the same holds good of the arts and of architecture. This is a very intricate, subtle, difficult subject; but we should not ignore it, for it points to a move-ment in social life which proves the academic underworld to have been capable of life and health.

The position of the theologians, with whom we may as-sociate the masters of arts, should be considered from two points of view. In the first place they were sought out as men of ability, or at the least were likely to receive benefices. If, as sometimes was the case, the bishops neglected them and local patrons were not forthcoming, the court of Rome had an interest in them. From the beginning of the fourteenth century *rotuli beneficiandorum* begin to appear, that is to say, lists of masters presented each year to the pope as suitable candidates for papal provision to benefices. A graduate, whose name appeared on the roll, was excused the examination to which the ordinary petitioner had to submit. He had a good chance of a benefice. This practice may help to explain the large number of masters who appear as rectors in the fourteenth century. Other influences, of course, were at work. For example, some of the distinguished men who adorned Merton College passed to good livings; but Merton was an exceptional society. The wealthy bibliophile, Bishop Bury of Durham, had a group of *Mertonenses* in his household, and the college produced three archbishops of Canterbury, including the great Bradwardine, the *doctor profundus*. Many university masters were recommended to princes and entered the royal household as royal clerks. The letters of that busy Oxford Franciscan, Adam Marsh, who knew everybody, show us how this was done. Walter de Merton himself, chancellor of England, bishop of Rochester, founder of Merton College, began his career at court as the result of Adam's intervention and testimonials. An able young master who caught the fancy of an influential man was sure of a job, and, if he did well, might rise high. And so it was with the theologians, whose "market value" was still greater and more dignified. A famous theologian might leap straight into a bishopric or even be made a cardinal. He might be an object of competition. John of St. Giles, an Englishman who startled the university of Paris by a dramatic entry into the Dominican order—the first secular master to take this step—was claimed in later years both by King Henry III and by Robert Grosseteste, the bishop of Lincoln. The one wanted his counsel at court, the other wanted his help in the government of a big diocese. The long training in theology was very comprehensive. It brought a good man, who looked out on the world about him, face to face with problems of the pastoral care and conscience and the rights and wrongs of administrative life in Church and State. In the thirteenth century such training was an exciting experience. In those great days, a group of theologians who became bishops shaped for a time the destinies of England. They have never been quite so influential since then.

This last reflection brings me to another point of view from which we may consider the position of the masters in arts and theology. The good men were intensely conscious that they were engaged as scholars in a mental adventure. Many of these men, more than those whose names are familiar to us all, were very big men. They brought order out of chaos and breathed life into it. When all is said, this incessant exercise of the human reason is the greatest contribution made by the philosophers and theologians of the schools of Europe to their own world and to the world in which we live. They restored dignity to the human mind, and made modern science possible.

A distinguished Cambridge scholar, the late Professor Stewart, wrote about Pascal's use of the conception of the three orders, the order of the flesh, the order of the mind, the order of charity—a scale of values familiar to medieval man. In Pascal's view they are discontinuous; there is no transition, no evolution from one to the other. "The greatness of men of the spirit, of the mind, cannot be seen by the kings, by rich men, by the captains, by any of the great ones of the flesh. It is seen not with the eyes, but with the spirit". And similarly the saints, in the order of charity, have no need of the greatness either of the carnal or the intellectual. They are seen by God. In this paper I have spoken of the scholars as men of the world, as men of service to the world; but they lived a life of their own, so far as they pursued their mental adventure, as the saints lived a life of their own. They did not speak much, as we so often do, of knowledge for its own sake. Perhaps they were too wise and had too much reverence for the order of charity to do this; but they spoke a great deal about the search for truth. They were not so perplexed as we are by the problem of freedom, for they believed that truth is one, and would be seen later. They had quite enough freedom to be contentious, and they liked controversy.

A new world is emerging, in which education will be an obligation on all, above every kind of specialism. The greatest problem set before human society will be the maintenance of freedom. Some say that discipline and purpose are the only things which will matter in a general education. Discipline and purpose are not the *only* things. The best safeguard of freedom will be the desire for truth. So long as men keep that desire and act upon it, the medieval university will not die.

XI

OXFORD[1]

A conference of inter-allied professors and lecturers in Oxford is an important event, and the more so because your Association is more than a visitor. Your members have been admitted to some of our rights and privileges. On 15 June last the Congregation of the University of Oxford formally accepted a certificate qualifying for admission to any of the universities which you represent as equivalent to our entrance examination, responsions, "if the holder has satisfied the examiners in either Latin or Greek". You yourselves contemplate many ambitious plans for the co-operation of universities in Europe, if not throughout the world, including a proposal for the creation of an International University Institute. We seem to be placing our feet in the path which leads to a very old ideal—an ideal which the jurists of the fourteenth century defined as a legal fact, but which has never been fully attained—the ideal which regarded students and teachers of one *studium generale* as citizens, so to speak, of all the rest, so that a student in one could carry on his studies at another without having to begin again, and a master who had the licence to teach from one could teach everywhere. I might suggest to you, as the main object of your gallant enterprise, the capture of that will of the wisp, the *ius ubique docendi*, and the translation of it into actual being, fixed in a legal respectability. For what a prospect this object would open before

[1] A lecture delivered in New College, Oxford, 16 July, 1943, at the opening meeting of a Conference of the Association of University Professors and Lecturers of Allied Countries in Great Britain; printed in *Polish Science and Learning* (December, 1944), pp. 23–30.

our eyes, and how long the road would be! It implies the subordination, though not the surrender, of local or national courses of university study to a common or general standard. It implies a language or languages understood and spoken by all university students and teachers. It implies an intimacy in the pursuit of learning which the scholars of Europe have experienced once and only once, in the first half of the seventeenth century; and even then the universities took little part in the movement. Then scholars lived in a gracious, but precarious and brief, companionship as friends. The true *ius ubique docendi* would be rooted in the statutes and activity of great institutions.

The university of Oxford in the course of its long history has not been idle in this matter; but as an Oxford man, I am bound to admit that it was more sensitive to European academic life and thought in the thirteenth and fourteenth centuries than it has been since. The *ius ubique docendi* implies too much to be an immediate object of co-operation. It lies at the end of the road. Even in the fourteenth century Oxford refused it, without conditions, to Paris, because Paris had refused it to Oxford. And yet the jurists who were trying to say what a university exactly was admitted that Oxford, which could not show the same credentials as Paris could, was so venerable, so firmly established, that custom gave it every privilege.

And so we come to Oxford. In spite of much ingenious speculation, no one knows why or when the schools which existed at Oxford, as in other places, grew into an outstanding home of study. The site of the town is propitious, for Oxford was the first place on the Thames, west of London, which was both an administrative centre, with a royal castle, a religious centre with two big monasteries, and a road centre. It lay on the great road between Southampton and Northampton and other roads diverged from it. Geographically, in fact, it was important, and its importance may be reflected in a traditional connection with London. Men gathered here, though the town was not large. Scholars who had something to say liked to say it here. Possibly some English students, who left Paris in 1167, settled here as they came north from Southampton. At all events it was known to be frequented as a place of learning, with a trade in books, by the end of the twelfth century. In 1209 the life of the scholars is revealed to us. In this year the first well known quarrel occurred between the clerks and burgesses. The mayor raided the hostel where a clerk, who had killed a woman, had his lodgings. Clerical immunities were disregarded. The students and masters dispersed and some of the emigrants went to Cambridge. Five years later the papal legate in England at that time made an award which is the first official regulation still extant of the schools at Oxford. Studies could be resumed, the rent of lodgings and the cost of victuals was to be moderate, the townsmen were to do penance and give satisfaction, the right of the bishop to do justice on clerks was maintained, and the bishop's representation or chancellor is mentioned for the first time. The earliest extant statutes of the university show that the methods of study in the various faculties and the subjects of study were well defined, on the lines which were followed at Paris.

We do not know when schools began at Cambridge; our first acquaintance with the place dates from the migration from Oxford in 1209. The university, as distinct from the presence of scholars, was first recognized by the pope in 1318, a hundred years later, by which time it had become large and vigorous. Naturally in later centuries the Cambridge men did not agree that their university was younger than Oxford. When Queen Elizabeth visited Cambridge in 1566 they claimed greater antiquity, and in his book on this subject published in 1568, a certain John Caius printed a charter granted by King Arthur, in A.D. 531. An Oxford champion, also called Caius—Thomas Caius—at once replied; and so a great controversy began. In 1602 one of our most famous antiquaries, William Camden, master of the school at Westminster, published an edition of the life of our great King Alfred written by the Welshman Asser. It was not a good edition nor a new book, for Camden reprinted with alterations of his own, the *editio princeps* of Asser made by the first Elizabethan archbishop of Canterbury, Matthew Parker; but he inserted in this text, as though it was a part of Asser's book, an account of the foundation of the university of Oxford by King Alfred. The forgery was soon discovered and denounced but it was so much more reasonable and natural than King Arthur's charter to Cambridge, that many people tried to believe until modern times that Alfred was our founder. After all, he lived four hundred years later than King Arthur and was a patron of scholars. What more likely than that he should found the university?

Now there is one very important characteristic of the medieval universities which we in Oxford and visitors to Oxford easily overlook. If a stranger asks an Oxford man in the street where the university is, there is no answer, except possibly the Clarendon Building, where the registrar and the secretary to the University Chest have their offices. There is no university in the sense in which you can point to a great building like the university of London or Edinburgh or Manchester and say, "there is the university". If a student wishes to join the university he cannot go to the registrar and be admitted, he has to go to a college. It is all very puzzling. The answer which I gave just now to the question "where is the university?" is historically very curious, for the Clarendon

Building was built early in the eighteenth century to house
the University Press, and it was only a hundred years later
that it was fitted up for lectures and university business. The
registrar who has his office there now does not appear until
the middle of the fifteenth century. The extensive and complicated financial system of the university, centred in the
offices of the chest, developed very gradually, as its name
implies, from the time when the masters in congregation, who
had no home of their own but met in a church, had control of
various chests or boxes in which records or books or money
were kept. The money was generally held in trust; it was not
university cash. The earliest ordinance, dated 1240, was made
by the bishop of Lincoln for the foundation of a chest for poor
scholars, and this chest was known as St. Frideswide's, because it was kept in the great priory whose church still stands
as our cathedral in Oxford. The chests of this kind were kept
in various places and their keepers or proctors were elected
in congregation. So, to return to the Clarendon Building, we
find as the only real centre of university business in Oxford a
place which was built for a printing and publishing depart-
ment in the reigns of Queen Anne and George I. The room
in which the chief committees of the university as a whole
meet is called the Delegates' Room, because it was retained
as a meeting place—as it still is—by the delegates or board of
control of the University Press. Fairly soon a room was allotted for university business and this got the nickname of
Golgotha, "the place of skulls or heads of houses", showing
that the heads of colleges—some called wardens, some masters, some provosts, some presidents, some principals—were
now important in university administration. Some lectures
seem to have been given at one time and lectures in music
are still given in the attics of the Clarendon Building. Then
the building came to be used by the chief officers, the regis-

trar, and the financial officer. The proctors, two officers elected annually—first by the masters, now by the colleges in rotation—have a room in the building, and their little police force lives in the basement. Of course in the meanwhile buildings were erected from the fourteenth century onwards—a library alongside the choir in the Church of St. Mary, with a place for congregation in the vaults underneath it; then in the fifteenth century a very beautiful divinity school for lectures and disputations in theology, with a new library over it; then in the seventeenth century a quadrangle adjacent to these to contain various schools, and Sir Thomas Bodley's munificent extension of the library—the Bodleian. A little later a western arm was built with a convocation house and the court-room for the administration of our branch of ecclesiastical law on the ground floor, and an extension of the library above them. The Sheldonian Theatre close by was built on a part of the old town ditch by that great architect Sir Christopher Wren and was inaugurated in July, 1669. It was intended for the greatest ceremonial and academic gatherings, so that the Church of St. Mary need no longer be used for what were now regarded as secular purposes. Since the seventeenth century the development of the examination system, of the Bodleian Library, of the Press, of museums, of literary and scientific departments immediately subject to the university and needing special equipment has led to the erection of big buildings, some beautiful like the Ashmolean Museum, some not so beautiful. Yet still it is hard to answer the question "where is the university?" Most of the time the Convocation House and the Sheldonian are in the hands of caretakers. One does not find the university in an examination school or a library or a museum or a laboratory. The answer is still the Clarendon Building; and with all proper respect for the registrar, a poor answer it is. The vice-chancellor himself has no official home. He does most of his business in the lodgings allotted to him by the college over which he presides.

Why is this? For, of course, Oxford is, and since the reign of King John, always has been, a great university. Some of you may have tried to read our statutes based, with ever more voluminous additions and changes, on the great *corpus* made early in the seventeenth century at the instigation of the chancellor, Archbishop Laud, or you may have studied the reports of the great royal commissions for university reform from 1850 to 1919—there are five of them—or sought to follow the intricate contents of the university *Gazette*. If you have, though the task may have given you a headache, you must have no doubt that this is a very active university. Yet why can we not say where the university is? The answer is very simple. The medieval university was a corporation either of students as at Bologna, or, more usually, of masters, as at Paris and Oxford. It was a personal thing. It had little or no property either in money or buildings. It did its business in churches, its masters taught in religious houses or hired rooms. It could fold its tents and migrate in a night. If a distinguished master was dissatisfied he could go elsewhere. If the university felt a strong sense of grievance it could migrate. The university of Bologna migrated four times between 1204 and 1321, the university of Paris—not to mention the exodus of English students in 1167-1168—was dispersed in 1229 and dissolved itself after excommunication in 1255. The university of Oxford was forced to disperse for a time in 1263, and partial migrations or secessions to Northampton, Salisbury, and Stamford occurred in 1228 and 1334. By its very nature, since the university was a corporation of masters and not a local institution like a monastery or collegiate church, it had no "abiding city". Its early privileges, granted by popes and

219

kings and bishops were protective, giving it self-governing rights, recognizing its freedom from secular jurisdiction, regulating prices and rents, authorizing some supervision over markets and the like—they did not grant endowments or bestow lands. The administration of the meagre finances of the university was in the hands of the proctors and, by a statute of 1549, of three masters whose accounts were audited each year by three other masters. The present financial administration is modern and is the outcome of royal commissions. Until recently the university owned little property. The total disbursements in 1871 amounted to £43,000 while those of the colleges and halls were £369,000 or nearly nine times those of the university, and twenty years earlier the annual income had been only about £7,500. The increase was largely due to special endowments for professorships and other objects. As these figures suggest, Oxford had become a place of colleges. The social life of the university and most of the teaching were centred in colleges rooted in the ground and the owners of landed property. The development had not been peculiar to Oxford and Cambridge. There had been more colleges in Paris before the French Revolution than there were in Oxford; but the type of college which ultimately prevailed in Oxford was different and more stable than the normal Parisian college. The original idea of benefactors had been the provision of a fund for the support of poor scholars. And the earliest benefactions of Oxford were funds of this kind which gradually led to the establishment of University College and Balliol College. They did not imply buildings or even highly regulated corporate life. They did not grant self-government to the beneficiaries. They were rather what we should call trusts. The first college of the stable, endowed, self-governing type in Oxford was Merton College, which took shape under the direction of its founder, Walter de

Merton, and of two archbishops of Canterbury in the second half of the thirteenth century. Merton set the standard for the later foundations in Oxford and Cambridge.

Events were to prove that the possession of firmly fixed revenues controlled and administered by the fellows of colleges was the essential condition of later academic life; but, of course, developments in Oxford, so different from those in continental universities, were due to circumstances peculiar to England, and these circumstances affected university growth very gradually. Until the Reformation a visitor to Oxford and Paris would not have seen much difference between the two universities. The colleges, though they differed in some respects from each other in constitution and personnel, were mainly occupied by scholars—companions or fellows—who were in the later stages of their academic career or had become teachers and men of learning. As scholars and teachers these men were concerned with the public exercises in the university. One of our academic historians has said that if every college had been abolished by Henry VIII the life of the university would have been little affected. And this would have been the case in Paris if, let us say, King Francis I had proceeded from his creation of the Collège de France to abolish all the Parisian colleges. If, however, we imagine a visitor to Oxford and Paris on the eve of the French Revolution, he would have found the contrast between the two universities more striking. The colleges of Paris were then still numerous, but compared to the Oxford colleges they were fragile institutions. Indeed, the abolition of tithes in the early years of the revolution is said to have crippled them. I am not talking to you about Paris, but as you know, after the abolition of universities in France, it was possible to reconstruct the university in Paris on lines which could maintain a great tradition, though the colleges disappeared. And elsewhere in Europe—more than in Paris—the close connection between universities on the one hand and the government of princes and of towns on the other had devised types of university life, so that the answer to the question "where is the university?" would have been easy. Oxford, on the other hand, could not have been imagined without its colleges. Queen Elizabeth's statutes had made every student live in a hall or college, and as the numerous medieval halls or hostels kept by masters were reduced to a few survivals, this practically meant that the colleges had become places where undergraduates lived with graduates. The distinction between scholars and masters, between undergraduates and fellows became clear. It was a duty of the fellows henceforward to look after the undergraduates. Only one college in modern Oxford—All Souls—consists only of fellows, and its history is regarded as quite unique, indeed almost a curiosity. For a long time the tuition of undergraduates was not the most important duty of the persons who were given charge of them. The fellows with this duty were primarily regarded as custodians and moral guides; but by the seventeenth century the "tutorial" system alongside the lectures, exercises and disputations required by the university statutes, was well established. The university exercises and the teaching of "regent" masters declined or became farcical, and the old system was reformed at the end of the eighteenth century. Our modern examination system took its place, and the need of tuition increased. It is a long, slow, complicated story, but at last we arrive at present-day Oxford, in which the university system of teaching, the professors and readers and lecturers, the Boards of Faculties, the conduct of examinations are new things, and the college life is the old thing. The maintenance of traditional forms, the continuity of the university constitution conceals this development, but the fact remains. The greatest problem of Oxford, a problem first realized in all its complexity in the middle of the last century, when the first Royal Commission took evidence, is the adjustment, in a smooth, friendly co-operation—I should prefer to say organic unity—of the college system which developed from Elizabeth's times to the academic institutions which, in spite of their appearance of a venerable antiquity, have painfully emerged during the last hundred years. And now, perhaps, you may understand a little better why it is so hard to answer the questions, "where is the university?" It is nowhere because it is everywhere.

I turn to a subject which is more closely related to the peculiar development of our academic life than one might think—the contribution of Oxford to the history of Western thought and learning. If we except the great period, from about 1250 to 1350, when the university of Oxford was one of the organs of expression of a new movement of philosophic thought, the answer to the question "what has Oxford done for thought and learning?" is rather like the answer to the question "where is the university?" The influence of Oxford has been everywhere and nowhere; and I say this in no critical spirit, for probably the influence of Oxford has been the wider and more penetrating just because it is so hard to define it or even to trace it.

In the thirteenth and fourteenth centuries relations between Oxford and the continental universities were close, though the passage of scholars and books was by no means confined to the universities. Some great men passed from our academic life to other fields. The greatest Oxford man in this age, probably the greatest in any age, was Robert Grosseteste, bishop of Lincoln, but though he owed, as he gave, much to Oxford, his work was done and his reputation made as much after as while he was in Oxford. He became a figure in the Church as a whole, almost worthy to be one of the doctors of the Church. Another famous Oxford man, Roger Bacon, was always something of a free lance. The influence of Oxford men as teachers and masters in the university is to be found at work in the fields of philosophy and mathematics under the inspiration of the "new" Aristotle. Here Oxford and Paris met. Master John Blund, who had been at Paris, taught in Oxford in the first decades of the thirteenth century. His *De Anima*, the first of many treatises and commentaries on the same subject, was the first to display the new learning. His successors, Master Adam of Buckfield and Master Richard Fishacre, were acquainted with all the works of Aristotle then known—the greater part of what is now known—before 1250, and had developed a mature technique. Others followed, with glosses, then with questions and discussions, until the fourteenth century, the flowering time of Oxford learning. And here we see the result of the establishment of Merton College, which provided its scholars with leisure and a home. The logical, dialectical, and scientific work for which Oxford was famous was largely centred at Merton. The highly technical lectures of Merton men survive, so far as they do survive, especially in continental libraries. As two modern scholars, Pierre Duhem and Father Michalski have shown four at least of these men, Richard Kilmington, Thomas Bradwardine (afterwards a theologian and for a year or two archbishop of Canterbury), William of Heytesbury, and Roger of Swineshead, contributed to that powerful dialectical movement which, especially through Paris, prepared men's minds for the discoveries of modern science. Two of them at least had such difficult names and yet were so widely studied that their origin seems to have been forgotten. Heytesbury as Tisberus and Swineshead as Suisset became citizens of the academic world, and were influential in Italy throughout the period of the renaissance. How important this activity was I cannot say. Discussions go on still between the advocates of traditional influences and the advocates of innovation in the mental life of fifteenth-century Italy; and much minute work remains to be done, but one fact is certain, that Oxford men were a force, and may even have been a creative force in the academic thought of France and Italy during the later middle ages. Towards the end of the fourteenth century the emphasis changed though the wide range of studies remained the same. The Austin Friars were the medium of a theological interest, and Bradwardine, in his last years, had contributed a powerful Augustinian influence of his own in his famous work against the Pelagians. One outcome was the work of John Wyclif, who turned the doctrine of grace against the papalism which it had formerly been used to maintain. We used to think of Wyclif as the source of a great religious and theological movement in Bohemia, but, though relations between Oxford and Prague were undoubtedly close, we are now told that John Hus had his Bohemian predecessors and that the most permanent and living elements in his thought were due not to Wyclif but to himself and to his refusal to be a blind follower of the Oxford scholar.

All the same, the age of Wyclif following the time of great doctors like Bradwardine and Fitzralph saw the culmination of the prestige of the university of Oxford in European life and thought. This was the time of the Great Schism and the conciliar movement, and although the university did not take the lead which Paris took in the formation of opinion on the great issues raised by the schism, it gave its views on the matter and, through some of its sons, exerted some influence upon conciliar proceedings. From this time onwards it became increasingly insular and receptive, and so, on the whole it has remained to this day. It has produced great scholars who have won a world-wide reputation and, what is more important, have advanced the study of their subjects—orientalists like Pococke and Jones, astronomers, classicists and, later, historians—but only one Oxford man, John Locke, has influenced the world as Duns Scotus and William of Ockham influenced it; and Locke's work was produced not at Oxford, but when, after periods of travel and of government service, he was nearly sixty years of age. He wrote as a man of affairs and a friend of European thinkers, rather than as a former student of Christ Church. Like so many others, including Gibbon and Adam Smith, who owed less than Locke to their colleges and university, he had disliked or been repelled by Oxford studies and Oxford ways of life. Too many Oxford men throughout the past four centuries have been shocked by what John Morley called the mental dilapidation of the place. The history of Oxford, as a home of learning, has its melancholy periods; it is always fascinating, often diverting, sometimes moving, but it reveals few periods of formative vigour and intensity. Yet we must remember, on the other hand, that during the period between the Reformation and the French Revolution most of the greatest European universities seem to have been in worse case. No one can read the second volume of Stephen d'Irsay's history of universities without being struck by the frequency of this fact. The richer, more constructive, movements of thought and learning took no root in the universities and, so far they had corporate expression, found it or made it in academies and societies of their own. Even the Collège de France at Paris became loosely attached to the university of which it had been a part. In many ways Oxford was happier than the ancient universities of France and Italy.

I have presented the Oxford of these centuries as insular and receptive. I do not mean to suggest, when I use the word "insular", anything derogatory in itself. I use the word with a descriptive intention. I mean that Oxford became an expression, sometimes a reflection or microcosm of England in the world of thought and learning. It has been called the home of lost causes and with some justice, but the phrase is misleading; for Oxford never ceased to be a place of debate and controversy. Its conservative majority has always been harassed by radical minorities; its complacency has bred its own critics, its abuses its own reformers. Authority has been an impetus to revolt, as when some colleges became Whig, or some theologians Puritans or, later, deists. When the heads of houses frowned on Locke's great essay, some tutors had a particular pleasure in advising their pupils to study it. This has always been the case. It gave poignancy to the Oxford Movement and vivacity to the work of the royal commissions. Hence it is not surprising that Oxford men have always been found to start new as well as to protect old causes, that Oxford is the home of the two most persuasive and influential movements in our religious and social life, the Methodist and the Tractarian or Oxford Movement, and that Oxford men have been the pioneers in constructive work for the betterment of the lot of mankind, and in our own day for the furtherance of a wise imperialism and an international outlook on affairs. This quality in our academic life has been strongly expressed in the studies of the place, particularly outside the orthodox curricula and fashions of thought. I am sometimes tempted to think that learning here has had two distinct foci, the schools and the Bodleian Library. In the seventeenth century, for example, the Bodleian became the home of precious manuscripts—oriental, medieval, scientific—and certainly some Oxford men were foremost in the antiquarian, philological, legal studies which made English learning illustrious at that time, and many were in close touch with the newly formed

Royal Society. The study of our antiquities continued throughout and the investigations of our literary memorials were diligently pursued by the famous Warton in the eighteenth century. I cannot tell this story, it would be too long, but it is part of the story of England. As always happens, new studies, if only officially recognized much later, tended to become fixed and to give a tone to the place where they were formerly novel. A good instance of this is our school of law, now notably associated with the study of English law. The first lectures in English law were planned by Sir William Blackstone in 1753, five years before he became the first Vinerian Professor in this subject. His famous commentaries contain the substance of his lectures. "Notwithstanding the novelty of such an attempt in this age and country," he wrote in the preface, "and the prejudice usually conceived against any innovations in the stablished mode of education, . . . his endeavours were encouraged and patronized by those, both in the university and out of it, whose good opinion and esteem he was principally desirous to obtain."

Oxford has always been receptive. In this it is like England. More than three hundred years ago that masterful Oxford man, Archbishop Laud, deplored the English habit of preferring whatever came from abroad to what was said by Englishmen. The Aristotelian studies in the thirteenth century, the dialectic of the fourteenth, the interest of Oxford scholars in the revival of classical learning in the fifteenth, the theology of the sixteenth, the reception of continental scholarship in the seventeenth and later centuries, the facilities offered to foreign scholars at all times, all illustrate this quality in our academic spirit. The reception is not general and it is not uncritical. It has to be digested before it is able to enrich and strengthen thought. It is passed on in all kinds of unobtrusive ways and much of it is wasted or after a time rejected. It feeds our insularity, it does not make us cosmopolitan. Yet it is there. The use which we make of it is, I think, largely dictated by the most receptive yet most English element in our life—the college tutorial system. For this element is very sensitive to what Englishmen think and need. It is influenced not so much by the claims of learning as by the service which learning can render to English society. Teaching, discipline, and social life are subordinated to this service and so must be whatever we receive and absorb. In one respect this preoccupation has had a healthy effect upon our scholarship. It may tend to keep us amateurs, but it also tends to check pedantry and professionalism. It may limit our outlook and put obstacles in the way of scholarly adventure, but it gives form and understanding and a sense of values to what we do know. We try to go to the heart of the matter and learn how to put in a few terse paragraphs what the pundit will spread over a thick volume.

And now Oxford, still strongly entrenched in traditions and prejudice, yet more open to receive than ever before, has to face the world. Unscathed, she has to build up the wounds of learning. She will increasingly have to satisfy people like you. How far she will succeed who could say? May I venture to remind you in conclusion that, whatever changes may come, she will insist on being the same? She has to be understood and she deserves to be appreciated. She has nurtured, willingly or reluctantly, every element in our national life and in our work overseas. She has inspired great poetry, great prose, great music. Her buildings at their noblest are shrines of the arts. Her libraries give shelter to the lore of the ages. Her beauty can both soothe and exalt the minds of her children.

XII

MASTER SIMON OF FAVERSHAM[1]

Both by example and by precept M. Ferdinand Lot has done
more than any living scholar to define the canons of a sound
and fruitful historical treatment of medieval French literature.
And during his lifetime his fellow countrymen have taken their
share in extending the scope of the historical method in the
study of medieval Latin literature, the work of theologians,
preachers, philosophers, scientists. The Benedictines laid the
foundations when they planned the *Histoire Littéraire de la
France*, Hauréau and Renan put this great enterprise on a new
footing, and their successors are co-operating with the scholars
of Belgium, Germany, Italy and Poland in following the
growth of medieval thought in detail, with due regard to the
lives of the men who wrote and to the influences and traditions which affected their writings. So far, unhappily, England
has done little. Yet the English field is a very large one. The
British Museum, the Bodleian Library and the colleges of
Oxford and Cambridge possess hundreds of unexamined
manuscripts, which contain the works of many unstudied
authors. All the great continental libraries, notably those of
Paris and Erfurt, preserve the writings of some English

[1]First contributed to the *Mélanges d'histoire du moyen âge offerts à Ferdinand Lot*
(Paris, 1925). Here revised in the light of recent investigation; see especially
A. G. Little and F. Pelster, *Oxford Theology and Theologians,c.*, A.D. 1282–1302
(Oxford, 1934), pp. 262–5, 365. Between 1930 and 1933 Carmelo Ottaviano
in Italy and Martin Grabmann in Germany described other manuscripts (in
Milan, Munich, Leipzig and Vienna) which contain works or commentaries
on Aristotle by Master Simon. Their articles are noted in Little and Pelster,
p. 365.

philosophers and scientists. Since the sixteenth century
Englishmen have had, in the books of Leland, Bale and Pits,
more complete lists of English medieval scholars and their
writings than any other country can claim, and these lists
were carefully revised and rearranged by Thomas Tanner,
bishop of St. Asaph, in his *Bibliotheca Britannico-Hibernica*
(1748). Moreover, the official records of the English state in
the middle ages are the most detailed and elaborate in
Europe and have suffered little from fire or war. The Reformation caused no break in the administrative records of the
English Church, so that in our episcopal archives many
registers and wills survive. Hence much can be done to trace
the history of academic thought and teaching in the days of
Roger Bacon, Duns Scotus, Bradwardine and Wyclif, by
scholars who are able to read and understand the manuscripts, and also are able to use the political and ecclesiastical
records, which tell us something about the men who wrote
the books which the manuscripts contain and about the
people who owned them.

Even those of us who have no special knowledge of
medieval thought and find a difficulty in understanding its
technicalities can do a good deal if we care to keep our eyes
open. As an example, I propose in this short paper, to say
what I have been able to find out about an Oxford scholar,
Master Simon of Faversham, who lived in the reign of King
Edward I.

Simon of Faversham was an Aristotelian. Several of his
commentaries and *questiones* on the books of Aristotle survive
in at least two manuscripts, the one in Merton College,
Oxford (O.I. 8), the other in the Amplonian library at
Erfurt (F. 348). Both manuscripts contain Simon's work on
the Physics, as "reported" by Robert de Clothale (Clothall,
Hertfordshire); and on palaeographic grounds, both would

be assigned to the beginning of the fourteenth century. But the tradition is that Simon of Faversham lived later in the century about 1370 and this tradition has been so generally accepted that the learned editor of the Amplonian Catalogue hesitated to follow his palaeographical impressions and supposed that the Erfurt manuscripts must have been written a hundred years or so later than he would have supposed. Yet a little investigation in English records is sufficient to show that tradition is wrong and that Simon lived in the last half of the thirteenth century and died in 1306.

We may first take Robert of Clothall, the author of the *reportatio* of Simon's *questiones* on the Physics. We find that Robert of Clothall, chancellor of the cathedral church of St. Paul's, London, between 1309 and 1319, had been connected with Balliol College, Oxford. No other Oxford scholar of this name is known, and we should expect him to have reported the lectures of a master older than himself. Hence we must look for a Simon of Faversham who taught at Oxford about the year 1300.

He is not difficult to find. In the year 1304 he was chancellor of the university. Later documents in the university archives refer to decrees, which regulated the university chests in the time of Master Simon of Faversham, *quondam cancellarium Universitatis*. So there was a scholar of this name, who held the highest office in the university early in the fourteenth century. Now, if we look around elsewhere in other records of this time, we find that a Simon of Faversham was ordained sub-deacon in 1289 and deacon in 1290, in which year Archbishop Pecham presented him to the church of Preston near Faversham; also that a Master Simon of Faversham was rector of the valuable living of Harrow in 1304 and died about 1306. As a previous rector of Harrow had died in 1299.

Simon was probably presented to the living by the patron, Archbishop Winchelsey, about 1300.[1]

Can we identify the incumbent of Harrow with our scholar? It is almost certain that we can, for it is possible to show that the latter also died in 1306. Here we must turn to the chancery records of the English kings and to the register of the archbishop. On 22 September, 1305, Master Simon was appointed archdeacon of Canterbury by the archbishop, but he was compelled to surrender the dignity in favour of a papal nominee. A few months later, 12 April, 1306, King Edward I refers to this disappointment in a letter to Pope Clement V. In this letter he commends Simon of Faversham to the pope as a doctor in theology, *assidue studiis virtutum pervigilans*, who had surrendered the archdeaconry of Canterbury and was now very much afraid that he would be disappointed also of the living of Reculver in Kent, owing to the papal provision of a man much his inferior in merits and goodness. Simon, anxious not to suffer again from papal provisions, had evidently decided to go to the papal court to protect his cause. On 24 May the king issued letters of protection for him on the occasion of his journey to the "court of Rome". The end of the story comes very quickly. On 23 August King Edward presented his physician, Nicholas of Tingewick, to the church of Reculver, void by the death of Simon of Faversham.[2]

[1] In a law suit of 1313–1314, the king's attorney stated that Simon had been presented during a vacancy of the archiepiscopal see in Henry III's time, *i.e.* in 1272–1273; but A. G. Little has shown that this was an invention.

[2] Nicholas of Tingewick, a village near Buckingham, was the physician of King Edward I. In the height of his last controversy with Archbishop Winchelsey, in the very letter in which he discussed with Pope Clement the way of dealing with this troublesome ecclesiastic, Edward did not forget to plead the claims of Nicholas to papal favour. He begged that his presentation to the church of Reculver should stand, although he already had the church of Coleshill in the diocese of Salisbury. "To him, after God", the king writes, "I owe my life and recovery from my recent illness" and again, "I have such confidence in him

Simon died between 24 May, the date of his letters of protection and 23 August, when his successor was presented to Reculver. A papal letter allows us to go further and say that he died before 19 July, for on that date Clement V refers to the prebend of Bishop's Hampton (*Hampton Episcopi*) in the diocese of Hereford as void through the death of Simon of Faversham. That this again is our Simon is clear, not only from the proximity of the dates of death, but from the description of the holder of the prebend, when he was instituted in 1304, as Simon of Faversham, rector of Harrow. We may conclude that, as Simon's death was known at the papal court as early as 19 July, he died on his journey.

Thus, from a few stray references in a papal letter, episcopal registers, university decrees, pleadings in a law-suit and royal letters it has been possible to put Master Simon of Faversham back among his contemporaries and to rescue him, in some slight degree, from oblivion. Probably, though

that I have entrusted my body entirely to his care"(11 September, 1306). Edward died in July, 1307. Nicholas was unable to keep the king alive, but he kept the church of Reculver. In 1306 he would seem to have been in the prime of life, for nearly twenty years later we find him taking an active part in the academic politics of Oxford. In 1325 a dispute arose in Balliol College over the question of the courses of study which, according to the intention of the founder, should be permitted there. The two *magistri extrinseci domus* were asked to decide the matter; Robert of Leicester, a Franciscan theologian, was one, Nicholas of Tingewick *doctor in medicina et bachularius sacrae theologiae*, the other. In the presence of four former fellows of Balliol, all doctors in theology, they decided that only attendance in arts could be allowed (Salter, *Oxford Balliol Deeds*, no. 570, p. 285). Of the four doctors who sat with the arbitrators, at least three are well known men. One was Richard Fitzralph, the future archbishop of Armagh and opponent of the friars, another was Richard de Camsale, a third Walter de Horkestowe, a champion of the seculars in the university against the Dominicans. The fourth was a divine named Richard of Retford.

As academic reputations go, the physician was in distinguished company. He was not altogether forgotten in Oxford. There is a heavily annotated manuscript in Merton College (Merton MS. N. 3, 3,) containing the *Isagoge in artem Galeni* of Honein ben Ishak (*Iohannicius*) and eight other medical items, and among the matter on one of the end fly leaves may still be seen the *Tabula afforismorum secundum ordinem m. Nicholai de Tyngewyk*.

not certainly, he came from the little town in Kent which gave him his name[1]. As he was a regent master in theology when he was confirmed as chancellor of the university in January, 1304, and appears with Duns Scotus and others as a disputant in discussions of theological questions which can be dated 1300–1302[2], he had probably begun his studies about the year 1280 or earlier. His life as a scholar was almost contemporaneous with the reign of Edward I, and he passed the later years at Oxford, where he received the greatest honour which the university could pay. He won favour in the sight of a king, an archbishop and a bishop, and he died while he was seeking justice from a pope. He served his university as teacher and administrator, and learning as a commentator on Aristotle. This is not quite all, for in 1933, eight years after this essay first appeared, Dr. Martin Grabmann pointed out that, according to a note in a manuscript at Vienna, a series of questions on Aristotle's Posterior Analytics, attributed to Master Simon the Englishman (the usual description of our philosopher) was disputed by him at Paris. Hence we may conclude that Simon probably graduated as master of arts in Paris and lectured on Aristotle there before he settled in Oxford. Unfortunately we cannot say when precisely he was in Paris, nor which of his numerous commentaries and disputations in the various philosophical writings on Aristotle were the outcome of his teaching there.

When we know that Simon lived during the reign of Edward I, there is no further difficulty in assigning the Merton manuscript which contains his work to the early years of the fourteenth, if not to the last decade of the thirteenth century. It then becomes an important as well as an

---

[1] It is curious that a ship owner of Dublin, named Simon of Faversham, was drowned with his three sons on 1 November, 1295, while carrying the king's taxes from Ireland to Anglesey (*Cal. Patent Rolls*, 1296–1302, p. 117).

[2] Little and Pelster, pp. 232, 236.

interesting collection of philosophical texts, for the first item is seen to be a very early text of Duns Scotus on the Metaphysics, a work of exceptional significance in the history of scholasticism[1]. The work of Simon of Faversham on Aristotle would naturally belong to his earlier years as a master in arts. Apart from the *questiones* on the Physics, reported by Clothall, the most interesting item is Simon's *questiones* on the third book of the *De Anima*, for through it we are able to identify the short piece which precedes it (f. 357 b) as the lost work upon the same book of Aristotle by the famous Averroist, Siger of Brabant. The title of Simon's *questiones* runs as follows (f. 364): *"Incipiunt questiones super tertium de anima disputate a M.S. de Faversham, et precedentes sunt M. Sigeri super eundem tertium"*. *Precedentes sunt M. Sigeri*. So at last Father Mandonnet's scepticism as to the survival of any such writing by Siger of Brabant is seen to be without foundation. [2]

Siger attached much importance to this commentary, for his theory of the unity of the soul and the eternity of the world rested in the main upon the third book of Aristotle's treatise. [3] The problems raised in the famous Averroist controversy

---

[1]Merton MS. O. I. 8. f. 1. *Questiones* on the metaphysics, *secundum Otley*. The *incipit* shows that it is the work of Duns Scotus, and *Otley* seems to be a misreading. Apart from this and Simon's works, the MS. contains two of the philosophical writings of John Sackville, an Englishman who was rector of the university of Paris in 1256, and Grosseteste on the Posterior Analytics. The manuscript is a large folio and is written in different hands. The last leaf of the text (*verso*) has the inscription *Liber de philosophia. Liber aule de Merton in Oxonia.* Father Pelster described the manuscript in 1930. Simon's work on the third book of the *De Anima* has been edited by Miss D. E. Sharp in *Archives d'hist. doctrinale et littéraire du moyen âge*, ix (1934) 307-368. A Leipzig manuscript contains Simon's commentary on the whole of the *De Anima*.

[2]Mandonnet, *Siger de Brabant*, second edition, i, 313. After I had noticed this reference to Siger in the Merton manuscript, I learned that Monsignor Pelzer had already discovered and examined Siger's *Questiones*. Cf. F. van Steenberghen's essay on Pelzer's scientific work in the *Mélanges Auguste Pelzer* (Louvain, 1947), pp. 12, 13.

[3]Siger, *De eternitate mundi*, edited Mandonnet, *op. cit.*, ii, 137.

at Paris in the second half of the thirteenth century were, as is well known, keenly discussed in Oxford; and the juxtaposition of the works of Siger and Simon of Faversham in the Merton manuscript suggests that Simon took a leading part in the discussion. Other scholars, whose names do not appear in our histories, also joined in the fray. One such was Simon's contemporary, Henry de la Wyle, a fellow of Merton who became chancellor of Salisbury in 1313. His commentary on the three books of the *De Anima* exists in a manuscript of Magdalen College, Oxford.

During the greater part of the fourteenth century philosophical work in Oxford continued in the conventional form of lectures and disputations upon the text of Aristotle, just as theologians adopted the conventional form of commentaries upon the Sentences. But in the orgy of discussion many minds fell victims to the charms of dialectic or sophistical exercises for their own sake, another indirect testimony to the influence of thirteenth century Paris and of Siger of Brabant. The dialecticians of Merton college were especially conspicuous. They established a tradition upon which logic throve, or deteriorated, in Europe until the sixteenth century. The logical work of Kilmington, Swineshead, Heytesbury, even of the great Bradwardine, helped to form this tradition. Copies of it are to be found in most continental libraries. Yet there was a distinct reaction against it in the mathematical work, which in some respects was closely connected with it, in experimental science and the study of astronomy, and in the return to Augustinian theology, of which Bradwardine's *De causa Dei* was the most famous exposition. The bequest, for example, to Merton College by John Staveley, who would seem to have been a disciple of Bradwardine, was almost entirely theological and included no less than eleven volumes of St. Augustine's works. In the third quarter of the fourteenth century the life of the Church in England was enriched by a group of Mertonians who had felt the scientific and theological influence of the college. William Rede, bishop of Chichester, Simon Bredon the physician, warden of the hospital at Maidstone, the distinguished Heytesbury and several others were some of this company of friends and colleagues. We may regard Edward I's physican Nicholas of Tingewick, the successor of Simon of Faversham as incumbent of the Kentish church of Reculver, as a link between the Oxford of Duns Scotus and Faversham and the Oxford of Bredon and Bradwardine.

XIII

DANTE'S ROMEO[1]

The whole of the sixth canto in the *Paradiso* is Justinian's great song about Rome and empire and the weakness, "the last infirmity of noble mind", which may diminish the brightness and vitality of the good spirits who lead men in earthly states, but does not mar their joy in living justice. The true and good governor of man is spurred on in his task by the thought of honour and fame, but the desire for them may make him swerve so that *i raggi del vero amore in su poggin men vivi*. The rays of true love mount up with less life; but, as just spirits, their joy itself is enhanced by the sight of justice. The exact apportionment of desert by the living justice is "part of their joy". The living justice sweetens affection. Indeed, the modulations of this exact and equitable disposal and recognition of merit in themselves enrich and strengthen the music of the spheres: just as divers voices upon earth make sweet notes (*noti*), so the divers seats (*scanni*) in *our* life create harmony amongst these wheels—*rendon dolce armonia tra queste rote*. And then, as though to drive home this truth by means of an example, Justinian, passing over all emperors and kings and princes and governors, fastens on Romeo:

> Within this pearl of ours, Mercury, shineth the light of Romeo, whose great and beautiful work was so ill answered. But the Provençals who wrought against him have not the laugh. He takes a bad road who turns another's good work to his own loss. Raymond Berengar had four daughters, each a queen. Romeo, a lowly man, a pilgrim (*peregrina*) did

[1] Read on 15 February, 1944 to the Oxford Dante Society.

this for him. Squinting words, words askance, moved Raymond to demand an account of this just man, who gave him five and seven for every ten, then, poor and old, went on his way. And if the world only knew the heart of this man, begging his life by crust and crust, it would praise him more even than it does.

The spokesman of the great rulers of the world picks out a humble pilgrim, who for a time had served a count in the valley of the Rhone, to show the brightness of dominion in all its force and purity, a brightness quite unaffected by that desire for fame and honour which, if rightly used, is in itself a good quality in lordship. The wise and just pilgrim who sought nothing for himself had in his heart a treasure denied to Cæsar. Who was this Romeo, this casual pilgrim, who inspired Dante, almost incidentally, to make one of his noblest flights?

The story of Romeo was known in Italy, for it is told by the Florentine historian, Villani, Dante's contemporary. Villani tells the story *à propos* of the conquest of the kingdom of Sicily and Naples by Charles, count of Anjou and Provence, who in 1263 accepted the offer of the crown by Pope Urban IV. Charles had married Beatrice, the youngest daughter of the last count of Provence in the Aragonese line, Raymond Berengar V. Beatrice's three elder sisters were married and had had their marriage portions. One was queen of France, another queen of England, the third by 1263 was also a queen, for her husband Richard earl of Cornwall, the brother of King Henry III of England, had been elected King of the Romans, that is, of Germany, in 1257. The conquest of Sicily and Naples made Beatrice a queen in her turn. Villani, after praising Raymond Berengar, tells how, among other men who sought his court, there came a certain Romeo, who was returning from a pilgrimage to St. James at Compostella.

Romeo, who was wise and valorous, won the count's favour and trust. Raymond made him master and steward of all he had. Virtuous, religious, industrious, prudent, Romeo in a short time increased his master's revenue threefold, enabled him to be victorious in war, and arranged the marriages of his four daughters.

> And it came to pass afterwards, through envy, which destroys all good, that the barons of Provence accused the good Romeo of mismanaging the count's treasure, and they called upon him to give an account. The worthy Romeo said, "Count, I have served you a long time and raised your state from small to great, and for this, through false counsel, you have little gratitude. I came to your court a poor pilgrim, and I have lived here virtuously. Give me back my mule, my staff and my scrip. I renounce your service." The count wished him to stay, but he would not. So he departed and no one knew whence he came or whither he went. But many believed that he was a sainted soul.

Naturally enough, the later embellishments of the story belong in the main to the literature of Provence. After Dante's fine gesture, nothing more could be made of it in Italy. He had put Romeo among his immortals. Indeed, by the time that Dante's commentator, Benvenuto da Imola, came to speak of him, Romeo, who was an historical personage of much distinction, was, so to speak, on his way back to that no-man's land to which the story attached to him naturally belongs. He was, Benvenuto says, a pilgrim from Compostella who came not into Provence but to Toulouse, attracted the attention of the count and in a short time delivered the count from the money-lenders. Entrusted with full administrative powers, he wiped off the count's debts and multiplied his revenue. "Often asked his name and condition, he called himself *Romaeus*". Pilgrims to Rome were called *Romei* in Dante's time; and in Catalan and Provençal the word *romeu* means "pilgrim" and was the word normally used of those who made the pilgrimage to Compostella[1]. My friend Professor W. J. Entwistle has suggested that the original tale, later attached to a Provençal named Romeu—who, for all we know, may have made the pilgrimage—was a bit of Compostellan propaganda, and had its source in the book of Tobit, the angel in disguise who brought prosperity; and he compares it to Tolstoi's story *What men live by*, about a young man who, given refuge and a home by a shoemaker, is at last revealed as the archangel Michael, under temporary banishment from heaven.

However the legend became attached to Romeu of Villeneuve in Provence, in course of time it was accepted and fantastically played with as a theme pleasing to Provençal egotism. So before I turn to the historical Romeo, I will say something about his career in later literature. Here I am merely plagiarizing a Provençal scholar, Raoul Busquet, who put the evidence together in a discourse to the Marseilles academy of sciences, letters and fine arts (1925) and in 1930 reprinted it in a volume of studies.

For some centuries the legend of Romeo seems to have survived if at all only in oral tradition, though of course it would be known to all readers of Villani. It had no critical history. Early in the seventeenth century, Pierre Le Loyer of Angers referred to Romeo in his book, *A history of spectres and spiritual apparitions*. Romeo, in his eyes, was not a man but an angel, sent from the other world. But, from about this time, the historians, moralists and finally the romancers began to take an interest in him. This was due to Cæsar Nostrodamus, who lied for the glory of Provence. His verse, taken from

---

[1] In the *Vita Nuova* §41, Dante says that the general word *peregrini* is applied in a narrower sense to those who visited the tomb of St. James at Compostella in Galicia, while pilgrims to Rome call themselves *Romei*, though in his sonnet he calls them *peregrini*. He is of course referring to Italian usage.

Dante and Villani, with imaginative additions, was used by the Polish continuator of Baronius and by Scipio Dupleix in his *Histoire générale de France*. Next a royal historiographer, Michel Baudier, gave to Romeo the honour of independent treatment in a work of eighty-two pages. Although the title sounds well, *History of the incomparable administration of Romeo, a great statesman of Provence*, Baudier had only Villani to go upon. He rewrote Villani's chapter in his own style, based on the historical manner of Livy, and included, as historical, several speeches. The historians, in fact, had nothing to say. The Provençal archives had not yet been searched. Those who mentioned Romeo were now sceptical. They dismissed Villani's story or said nothing about Romeo. So the fame of the statesman was kept alive by a few moralists, and, in the nineteenth century, by romanticists. In 1751 the aged Fontenelle wrote an unfinished story about him, a *conte philosophique*. Raymond Berengar has conversations with Romeo in the manner of the eighteenth century. He suggests that Romeo is really a man of quality who had committed a serious fault and in penitence was wandering about the world in this wretched fashion. Romeo replies in effect that, even if this were so, he had lost nothing, for the respect of the world would be given, not to him, but to his rank. On another occasion the count begs for some account of his travels. What were the most remarkable things he had seen among Greeks, Turks and Saracens? The reply is "nothing". But other travellers have such marvels to relate. No doubt, Romeo replies, some eyes see marvels more easily than others. I have seen Greeks, Turks and Saracens, even Tartars, but I have only seen men, and I can see them in France. And so on.

Romeo gave better material to the historical romancers. M. Busquet mentions three works, two of 1824, one of 1869.

In 1824 the vicomte de Bargemon published *Lyonnel or Provence in the thirteenth century*, in five volumes, and a Piedmontese, Falletti di Barolo, a work of two volumes with the title *Peregrinazioni ed aventure del nobile Romeo di Provenza*. Both books are a curious mixture of history and imagination. The writers had studied the period and depicted Provençal society as well as an obsession with courteous love and an ignorance of the texts would allow. In the one Romeo appears as a great troubadour. When he arrived in his pilgrim garb "the fire in his eye and his noble mien revealed a genius accustomed to command." He becomes a sort of Richelieu, whose beneficent activity left the Provençal nobles free to devote themselves to the service of ladies and to discuss problems of gallantry. In the other book, Romeo is given a squire and is made to travel eastwards. He is captured and taken to Egypt. Escaping with difficulty from the unwelcome attentions of the Sultan, he returns to Italy and takes part in the wars of Charles of Anjou against Manfred and Conradino. He dies in the defence of Queen Beatrice against Neapolitan rebels. Maurice Bouquet's romance (1869) was issued in the series *Provence Amoureuse* under the title *Le sire de Chantegrillet*. The author makes Romeo bring peace and prosperity to Provence and induces the count to nerve his languid soldiery by the organization of tournaments and other strenuous exercises.

Finally a great writer turned his back on all this nonsense and brings us round again to our starting point. Mistral wrote a simple tale for simple readers without any striving after the archaic. He takes as his theme the envy and spite of the nobles who tried to alienate Romeo from Raymond Berengar. "Open your eyes," they say, "This vagabond whom you have made your minister has a little room to which nobody is allowed entrance. We have often watched him slip in secretly. There is no doubt that he hides your treasure there. There is still time, but take care that he does not use your money to advance himself." Raymond Berengar summons his first minister. "Romeo", he says "I must see your chamber where you shut yourself up so mysteriously." "Come with me, Monseigneur." Romeo opens the door of the room and what is to be seen? A pilgrim's robe hanging from a nail, a hat with cockleshells, a gourd, a staff—nothing more. Raymond Berengar bursts into tears.

Romeo of Villeneuve in Provence was a great man in his day. Romeo or Romeu was his actual name, and carried with it no further significance. Romeo, for all we know, may have made the pilgrimage to Galicia, and his name was sufficient to suggest that he had been there. So, once his legend had begun, the way to fame in travel was easy. Provence was a stage in life's pilgrimage, not his home. Moreover, as Charles of Anjou settled down in Provence and made it the starting point of his dramatic career in Italy, the contrast between the days of Raymond Berengar and the days of the hated French from the north excited every troubadour in the Midi. Nothing was too bad to be said about Charles. In such an atmosphere the memory of Raymond Berengar's greatest minister might well become legendary. I suspect that troubadours prepared the way for the legend known to Villani and Dante. Romeo had helped to negotiate the marriage between Charles and Beatrice; this is historical. After the death of his master he brought the stranger in. Raymond Berengar died in August 1245. Romeo was one of the two counsellors appointed in his will to advise his heiress. In spite of many claimants and much opposition his widow and these counsellors, with the aid of the pope, completed the arrangements for a marriage with Charles. This took place on 31 January, 1246. After Charles's arrival, with his French counsellors, Romeo, though not dismissed, lost his predominance. In 1251 he died, and in his will he refers to certain debts which he owed the new count. After his death Charles, with the consent of the executors, took possession for the time being of Villeneuve and other castles which Romeo had held. All this was according to form. Romeo's descendants continued in the male line in Provence until the nineteenth century. There was no expulsion, no disinheritance. But Romeo had not died as Charles's chief minister and Charles had claims on his estate. This would be quite enough to suggest his fall and the count's ingratitude. The next step was dramatically appropriate. Romeo, it was suggested, had arranged Beatrice's marriage as well as the earlier marriages (in which he had doubtless had an important voice) during the lifetime of Raymond Berengar and had been suspected of malversation and had withdrawn in dudgeon. So the legend could begin to grow, and to gather bits of folklore about it.

The chief source of information about Romeo is the accounts, letters, charters and other instruments which survive in departmental archives. These were explored by V. L. Bourrilly, professor at Aix, and Raoul Busquet, the archivist of les Bouches-de-Rhone, and worked up into their important *History of Provence in the Middle Ages* (1924). The details are innumerable, but the outline of Romeo's career is clear and simple. He first appeared in office about 1223. Until 1234 he was the *judex* or chief judicial officer of Provence. From 1234 until Raymond Berengar's death eleven years later he was much more than this. He was the leading man in the state, and the administrator of extensive bailiwicks in the south east. Raymond Berengar was a very active and successful ruler—a great prince in a key position. He brought peace and order out of chaos. And during the

most formative years of his rule, when he reorganized the
local administration and enacted important laws, he had
beside him a great minister. This was Romeo. Romeo was
variously described as vicar and bailiff of Provence. The
Grand Master of the Knights of St. John on one occasion
refers to him as constable. No great military operation, no
treaty, no settlement was made without him. A quittance of
25 May 1241 referring to his good administration *in tota
Provincia* is still extant. There is no doubt whatever of the
importance of Romeo. And there is no doubt that he acquired much wealth. He had the kind of success which
inevitably breeds envy and he could hardly have done all he
did without making enemies.

One problem remains, the relation between Villani and
Dante. The critical study of Villani is still in its infancy. At
first sight the conclusion that Dante read Villani is ruled out,
for does not Villani occasionally refer to Dante's poem and
under the year of his death (1321) give a most interesting
appreciation of his life and works? But this would be a very
facile and short-sighted conclusion. Chronicles were frequently circulated in early recensions. It is possible sometimes, for example, to restore from a plagiarist the first text
of passages which were afterwards altered or deleted. And
chroniclers sometimes stopped, recording their work as
ended, only to carry it on further in later years. Matthew
Paris brought his great chronicle to a close at the year 1250,
but as we have it, it ends in 1259. He took it up again later.
Now, merely as a suggestion, I hazard the guess that Villani
in the first instance carried his chronicle down to the year
1300, the year of the great jubilee in Rome at which he was
first inspired to write the history of his own city, and that
Dante knew the earlier books of Villani's chronicle which
cover the ages from the dispersion of peoples after the build-

ing of the tower of Babel to the jubilee of 1300. The parallel passages noted by Philip Wicksteed in the handy volume of selections from Villani, intended " as an aid to the study of Dante," go to confirm this view. Of course there are numerous passages in the later books which refer to persons and incidents mentioned by Dante, but these seem to be parallels only. Both of them, Villani and Dante, had personal experience. On the other hand many of Dante's references to persons and incidents described by Villani in Books i—viii §36 could hardly have been made without a knowledge of Villani. Among these the story of Romeo appears to me to be the most notable and certain.

The poet was a wanderer, an observer of men and things. He was a critic of and commentator upon history, not an historian. " In this Comedy," writes Villani himself, "he delighted to denounce and to cry out after the manner of poets, perhaps in certain places more than was fitting; but maybe his exile was the cause of this." Maybe his exile was the cause of his exaltation of Romeo, the pilgrim, the man of inscrutable thoughts and feelings too deep and too high to be known, as he begged crust after crust.

XIV

AN AMERICAN SCHOLAR :
GEORGE LINCOLN BURR[1]

To call attention to this book is for me a pious duty. Dr.
George Burr was one of my friends and showed me much
kindness. My acquaintance with him would be of interest
only to myself, if it did not impose an obligation to tell
British readers about a man whose name is known to few in
this country, but who probably did as much as any scholar
of his time to guide and stimulate the study of history in the
United States. His influence, it is true, is not obvious. He did
not, like Frederick Jackson Turner, put out a significant idea
which led to the reinterpretation of American history. He did
not, like Charles Homer Haskins at Harvard, form a great
school of post-graduate study. And, unhappily, he never
wrote the big books of which he dreamed. One of the best-
read, exact, and hard-working scholars of his age, he now
seems to many to have frittered his time away. His most
sustained piece of work is hardly remembered, although it
sets out with punctilious and scholarly care the results of
intense study on historical and cartographical problems in
the Dutch archives. It is hidden away in the four volumes of
reports made by President Cleveland's Venezuela British
Guiana Boundary Commission (Washington, 1897). Burr
had characteristically allowed himself to be drawn, in the

[1]A review in *Medium Aevum* (xiii, 1945) of *George Lincoln Burr, his life* by
Roland H. Bainton: *selections from his writings* edited by Lois Oliphant Gibbons.
Ithaca, New York. Cornell University Press; Humphrey Milford, London,1943.

interests of peace and historical truth, into an investigation quite outside the range of his own historical interests; and it was also characteristic of him that he never regretted the labour, although the credit due to the Commission was soon lost to mind after the two countries involved in this famous dispute agreed to an international commission of arbitration. The President's independent Commission was no longer required to present its elaborate report. Burr felt no sense of frustration. He read a paper before the American Historical Association in 1898 on the work done by the Commission; and after the tribunal's award, he wrote an article comparing its findings with those of the Commission. Both can be read in this book. Peace had been kept. Historical truth had been ventilated. Nothing else mattered. It was the same throughout his life. Many would regard his career as a history of frustrated effort. Such an idea could never have occurred to him. "His students and friends," writes his biographer, "have long lamented that the treasures of his mind so richly stored passed largely with him. How tragic, say they, that he never wrote a book. Never wrote a book! He wrote hundreds of them. His books are to be found wherever the sons and daughters of Cornell have gone to the ends of the earth, for he wrote not on tables of stone, but on tables of flesh—your hearts."

Burr's long life (1857-1938) was given to Cornell University, from the time when he became the literary assistant of his teacher Andrew Dickson White (afterwards President of Cornell and for some time American Ambassador to Berlin), to his years of official rather than actual retirement as emeritus professor. The story is told with authority by Mr. Bainton. To an English reader Mr. Bainton's enthusiasm may bring some discomfort. It leads him into detail which might well have been omitted. His hero-worship knows little reticence. But Burr's pupils have long desired to see justice done to a great teacher and it is not for us to quarrel with them. This book deserves to be widely known. It reveals Burr as an expert bibliographer with a flair for the discovery of books and manuscripts which seems uncanny until we realize that it was the fruit of profound study. It brings out the fact that his main life-work, the history of witchcraft, was inspired by his passion for intellectual liberty and rooted in his unusually wide knowledge of the whole range of history. And it makes us know a very good man, simple, unselfish, wise, and fearless. So much for the biography. The rest of this volume is still more important.

The editor prints twenty-five articles, including three reviews, and adds a bibliography of Burr's scattered writings. When collected, as they are here, for the first time, the articles make an impressive series. They reveal a powerful mind and a consistent purpose, not in achievement but in life. I can best describe the impression which they make on me if I say that I know of no book that I should prefer to advise a young historical scholar to read as an introduction to the work of his own life. Burr's passion for liberty, nurtured by his friendship for President White and strengthened by his own much more profound studies, sprang from a deeply spiritual nature. Something of this can be seen in two intimate addresses on the living gospel (1891) and on loyalty and liberty (1919); but the reader should turn to these later, after his respect for the speaker has been established. He should begin with Burr's view of history, expounded in the three fine addresses on history and its neighbours (1908), the Middle Ages (1912), and the freedom of history (1916). The last of these is a remarkable survey of the course of historiography, starting from the Greek word and its meaning, for "history" is not originally a word for the experience of rational man in his human relationships, as we conveniently use it, but the carefully chosen epithet for research or investigation, as something more than narration. And research implies freedom. The lectures and papers to which our reader might next turn illustrate the application of the historical mind to its subject matter, halfway between general reflection and absorption in a theme. They are the lecture on European archives (1901), a pleasant and learned talk entitled "A witch-hunter in the book shops" (1902), and a lecture, "Liberals and liberty four hundred years ago" (1932), on the real meaning of the so-called anabaptist movement in Germany and adjacent lands. Here we have a ripe and humane scholar at his best, when his sympathies, his learning and powers of exposition are fully revealed in a single masterly effort, without a trace of pedantry or strain. It makes one realize how great an historian Burr might have been, or rather might have shown that he was. The other papers in this volume deal in the main with the problem and history of witchcraft, but first two other essays should be noticed, one on the year 1000 and the antecedents of the crusades (1900) and a very remarkable study of a new fragment on Luther's death with other gleanings from the age of the reformation (1910). The former, though slighter in form and matter, reminds us of Burr's fine contribution, not reprinted here, to the second volume of the Cambridge Medieval History on "The Carlovingian revolution and Frankish intervention in Italy" (1913). The latter, based on his experience as a librarian and book collector, is as good an example as one could find of the use to which a truly good scholar can put a few casual notes on a margin or on a flyleaf.

I pass by a similar but less important note on Savonarola and his biographers (1889) and an introduction written for

a new edition of Hallam's *Middle Ages* (1899) and turn to
the papers which bear more directly on what came to be
Burr's main interest, the nature and history of witchcraft.
This was no morbid interest. Nothing would have horrified
his scrupulous and sensitive mind more than the suggestion
that he was fascinated by the perverse, the cruel, and the
macabre in the heart of man, as revealed in the past. His
friends cannot but be greatly relieved that he did not live
to be tortured in spirit by the dreadful happenings of this
present time. We have only to read his castigation of the
anthropological vagaries of Miss Margaret Murray and the
sensationalism of the Reverend Montague Summers, or his
criticism of Professor Kittredge's apologetic for the persecutors of New England to see that he was incapable of compromise with the revolting theme. His hatred of persecution,
not a lurking sympathy, lay at the root of his interest in the
history of witchcraft; and with this went his immediate reaction, shown so often in his own life at Cornell, against the
slightest tampering with the principle of liberty and the duty
to uphold it. "The old witch-mania was no mere survival of
the Middle Ages. It was born and came to its prime in centuries which saw the greatest burst of Christian civilization.
If I would have History unflinching, it is not because I think
we are better than our fathers. It is because deep in ourselves
I feel still stirring the impulses which led to their mistakes.
It is because I fear that they who begin by excusing their
ancestors may end by excusing themselves." I think that he
would have welcomed, with punctilious reservations, the
little book published in 1941 by the late Charles Williams on
the subject of witchcraft.

Burr was drawn to this unsavoury subject by four deep-
seated impulses in his nature. The first was his passion for
liberty and, it should be added, for it is the converse of the

same feeling, his sympathy with suffering. The second was his reverence for the teacher who opened his mind to what seemed to him to be ultimate truths. The best way to see how he approached his work is to read his eulogy on Andrew White (1918) and the story given in the memoir of his self-effacing but very frank relations with this scholar. Burr co-operated with White, often with some misgivings, in the book *The warfare of science with theology in Christendom* (1896).[1] He found a more congenial, though less intimate, object of reverence in Henry Charles Lea, whose posthumous *Materials toward a history of witchcraft*, arranged and edited in three volumes by Professor Arthur Howland (1939), were at first entrusted to Burr and owe much to him. Burr's introduction to Lea's book, reprinted in this collection of essays is perhaps the best exposition of his own view. The third impulse in Burr was his love of exact and meticulous research. The fourth was his instinct as a hunter of rare books and manuscripts, an instinct whose value was at once realized by White, who sent Burr to Europe to study and also to collect rarities for him. This opportunity made Burr one of the foremost bibliographers of his time. Its firstfruits were his deliberate search for and discovery at Trier of the manuscript of the book written against the delusions of the persecutors of witches by Cornelius Loos—a discovery which won him the respect of the great German scholar Jannsen. His own account, given in 1886, is printed here.

Unhappily, all that remains of Burr's elaborate and prolonged studies are a paper on the literature of witchcraft (1889), an important study, much wider in its range than the title suggests, on New England's place in the history of

---

[1] This book was needed at the time and caused much stir; but it did not possess the greatness which make a book an enduring classic. It would now "date" itself.

witchcraft (1911), the introduction to Lea's *Materials* already mentioned, and a long detailed essay on the fate of Friedrich Flade of Trier who was executed in 1589. Burr had discovered the minutes of Flade's trial in a bookseller's catalogue in 1882; the manuscript was bought for White's library and is the basis of Burr's masterly essay (1890). Like all his work this essay gives the reader much more than he might expect. It gives a picture of an age seen in the workings of the institutions, the ecclesiastical life, the personalities and passions of a German city in the sixteenth century. The rise of witchcraft and the development of the law which condemned it were two aspects of the same thing. Witchcraft is not to be confused with magic. It had its roots in social fear and in a perverted theology. Its wretched persecutors were the victims of a disease, a disease of the soul, on which envy, spite, revenge, the itch to inform, the dread of becoming a victim, pain, and all sorts of horrible things could feed.